THE GREAT DISSENT

THE GREAT
DISSENT

How Oliver Wendell Holmes Changed
His Mind—and Changed the History of
Free Speech in America

THOMAS HEALY

METROPOLITAN BOOKS
HENRY HOLT AND COMPANY   NEW YORK

Metropolitan Books
Henry Holt and Company, LLC
Publishers since 1866
175 Fifth Avenue
New York, New York 10010
www.henryholt.com

Metropolitan Books® and ▥® are registered trademarks of
Henry Holt and Company, LLC.

Library of Congress Cataloging-in-Publication Data

Healy, Thomas.
   The great dissent : how Oliver Wendell Holmes changed his mind and changed the history of
free speech in America / Thomas Healy.—First Edition.
        pages cm
   Includes bibliographical references and index.
   ISBN 978-0-8050-9456-5
   1. Abrams, J., 1886–1953—Trials, litigation, etc.   2. Holmes, Oliver Wendell, 1841–1935.
3. Trials (Anarchy)—New York (State)—New York—History—20th century.   4. Freedom of
speech—United States.   I. Title.
   KF224.A34H43 2013
   342.7308'53—dc23

                                                                                        2012047539

Henry Holt books are available for special promotions and
premiums. For details contact: Director, Special Markets.

First Edition 2013

Designed by Kelly S. Too

Printed in the United States of America
1 3 5 7 9 10 8 6 4 2

To Arlene

CONTENTS

THE GREAT DISSENT

An Unexpected Visit

On Friday, November 7, 1919, as federal agents launched a nationwide raid on the homes and meeting halls of Russian immigrants, three members of the United States Supreme Court mounted the steps of a redbrick town house in Washington, D.C., just blocks away from the White House. Unlike the agents, who had been dispatched by an ambitious young official named J. Edgar Hoover, the justices were not hunting for communists. They were there to call on their colleague Oliver Wendell Holmes Jr., Boston Brahmin, Civil War veteran, and sage of the common law. But their visit, unusual and unexpected, was linked to the larger mission being carried out that day, and, to the justices at least, it was every bit as important.

They were greeted by Holmes's wife, Fanny, and led up the steep stairs to the second floor, where Holmes had his study. In those days, the justices did not have offices at the Supreme Court; instead they researched and wrote their opinions at home, sending notes and drafts to one another by messenger. Holmes's study was spacious and bright, two high-ceilinged rooms connected by sliding double doors. In the rear room, looking out over a small garden, stood a cherrywood desk that had belonged to his grandfather, a judge on the Massachusetts Supreme Judicial Court, as well as an old-fashioned upright desk. This is where Holmes worked, alternating between the two desks and a comfortable leather chair in front of the fireplace. On the mantel were photographs of several young female friends, and high above them hung two crossed swords, one used by his great grandfather during the French and Indian War and another carried by Holmes himself during the Civil War. Through the doors was a smaller room where his secretary worked at a desk handed down by Holmes's father, the famous doctor and author. Bookshelves lined both rooms, climbing the walls and wrapping around the windows and doorways like ivy. Their shelves were packed tight with books—more than ten thousand volumes in all, mostly law, philosophy, and history, but also the occasional detective story or racy French novel.

Because the Court term was under way, Holmes was dressed in a morning coat with a stiff white shirt and high collar. He welcomed his visitors into the study and motioned to his secretary, Stanley Morrison, to stay in the adjoining room with the doors open. Like nearly all the rest of Holmes's secretaries, Morrison was a recent graduate of Harvard Law School who had been handpicked for the job by a trusted faculty member. He was also the friend of another Court secretary that year by the name of Dean Acheson, and after the visit he told Acheson what had happened. Acheson, of course, went on to achieve his own fame as secretary of state during the Cold War, and when he wrote a memoir of his early years in Washington he recounted the incident, which is how we know about it today.

After they were seated and had exchanged pleasantries, the three justices—Willis Van Devanter, Mahlon Pitney, and a third whose name Acheson could not remember—explained the reason for their visit. The day before, Holmes had circulated a dissenting opinion in a case the Court had heard two weeks earlier. It was an important case testing the government's power to punish the anarchists and agitators who had spoken out against the recent war. And for most members of the Court, it was an easy case. Of course the government could punish such troublemakers. Freedom of speech was not absolute, and if the defendants had intended to disrupt the war, they deserved to be treated as criminals.

The majority of the Court, and anyone who followed its decisions, might have expected Holmes to agree. After all, just nine months earlier he had written three opinions for the Court saying pretty much the same thing. One of those cases was an appeal by Eugene V. Debs, the leader of the Socialist Party and a frequent candidate for president, who had been sentenced to ten years in prison for a speech he had given in the summer of 1918. It was essentially a stump speech, an effort to fire up the base in advance of the fall elections, and Debs had chosen his words carefully. He said nothing that explicitly urged interference with the war, though he did praise party members who had opposed the draft. For Holmes, that had been enough. In a short and dismissive opinion, he had accepted the jury's verdict that Debs meant to illegally obstruct military recruiting and had affirmed his conviction.

So when the Court heard arguments in the anarchists' case, few people expected Holmes to side with the defendants. But something had changed. Instead of voting with the majority, Holmes said the convictions should be reversed. The defendants had no intent to undermine the fight against Germany, he explained. They were merely upset with President Wilson's decision to intervene in the Russian Revolution. Besides, he argued, their speech was protected by the First Amendment. This last point was no small matter. In spite of its seemingly clear command—"Congress shall make no law . . . abridging the freedom of speech"—the First Amendment at that time was still largely an unfulfilled promise. The Supreme Court itself had never ruled in favor of a free speech claim, and lower courts had approved all manner of speech restrictions, including the censorship of books and films, the prohibition of street corner speeches, and assorted bans on labor protests, profanity, and commercial advertising. Even criticism of government officials could be punished, the courts had ruled, if it threatened public order and morality. But now, with the country gripped by fear of the communist threat, Holmes was proposing something radical: an expansive interpretation of the First Amendment that would protect all but the most immediately dangerous speech. His opinion was passionate and powerful, especially the long concluding paragraph. This began strangely, incongruently, as though Holmes were making the case against free speech, not for it:

> Persecution for the expression of opinions seems to me perfectly logical. If you have no doubt of your premises or your power and want a certain result with all your heart you naturally express your wishes in law and sweep away all opposition. To allow opposition by speech seems to indicate that you think the speech impotent, as when a man says that he has squared the circle, or that you do not care whole heartedly for the result, or that you doubt either your power or your premises—

Then, just as the reader began to blink in confusion, wondering if something had gone wrong, if perhaps the printer had made an error, Holmes suddenly—brilliantly—changed direction:

> But when men have realized that time has upset many fighting faiths, they may come to believe even more than they believe the very foundations of their own conduct that the ultimate good desired is better reached by free trade in ideas—that the best test of truth is the power of the thought to get itself accepted in the competition of the market, and that truth is the only ground upon which their wishes safely can be carried out. That at any rate is the theory of our Constitution. It is an experiment, as all life is an experiment. Every year if not every day we have to wager our salvation upon some prophecy based upon imperfect knowledge. While that experiment is part of our system I think that we should be eternally vigilant against attempts to check the expression of opinions that we loathe and believe to be fraught with death, unless they so imminently threaten immediate interference with the lawful and pressing purposes of the law that an immediate check is required to save the country.

No one else on the Court wrote like this. Only Holmes could translate the law into such stirring, unforgettable language. Yet even by his high standards this was unusually fine, and his colleagues worried

about the effect it might have. Although the war had ended a year earlier, the country was still in a fragile state. There had been race riots
that summer, labor strikes that fall. A bomb had exploded on the
attorney general's doorstep—the opening strike, the papers warned, in
a grand Bolshevik plot. A dissent like this, from a figure as venerable as
Holmes, might weaken the country's resolve and give comfort to the
enemy. The nation's security was at stake, the justices told Holmes. As
an old soldier, he should close ranks and set aside his personal views.
They even appealed to Fanny, who nodded her head in agreement. The
tone of their plea was friendly, even affectionate, and Holmes listened
thoughtfully. He had always respected the institution of the Court and
more than once had suppressed his own beliefs for the sake of una-
nimity. But this time he felt a duty to speak his mind. He told his colleagues he regretted he could not join them, and they left without
pressing him further.

Three days later, Holmes read his dissent in *Abrams v. United States*
from the bench. As expected, it caused a sensation. Conservatives
denounced it as dangerous and extreme. Progressives hailed it as a mon-
ument to liberty. And the future of free speech was forever changed.

The justices' visit to Holmes is a remarkable piece of constitutional
history. Nowhere else in the annals of the Supreme Court has there
been such a personal appeal to one justice by a group of his colleagues.
That it took place in the privacy of Holmes's study, in the presence of
his wife—that the justices sought her help with their appeal—only
heightens the intrigue.

And yet, the visit isn't the most surprising part of the story. What is
truly remarkable is that the justices had reason to be there in the first
place. Contrary to the popular view of him today as a great civil libertarian, Holmes was not always a staunch defender of free speech. In
fact, prior to his dissent in *Abrams* he had done as much as any judge
to render the First Amendment toothless. In one of the first Court
opinions to address the topic, he had embraced the cramped English
view that freedom of speech prohibits only prepublication censorship

but places no limits on the government's power to punish speakers after the fact. In another case, he had affirmed the conviction of a small-time anarchist for inciting . . . nude sunbathing. His earlier opinions as a judge on the Massachusetts Supreme Court were no different. When a policeman complained that he had been fired for expressing his political views, Holmes had famously responded, "The petitioner may have a constitutional right to talk politics, but he has no constitutional right to be a policeman."

It wasn't that Holmes had a particular dislike of free speech. He disdained all constitutional rights. His most well-known opinions (dissents, all) had come in a long line of cases involving progressive labor laws. The conservative majority of the Court had repeatedly invalidated these laws, arguing that minimum-wage and maximum-hour regulations deprived businessmen and workers of their "liberty"—the ability to sell or buy labor on whatever terms they wished—and thus violated the Fourteenth Amendment. Of course, the laissez-faire conservatives cared little about the "right" of employees to work fourteen-hour days at rock-bottom wages; they were really protecting the ability of employers to get cheap labor. But while Holmes's dissents in these cases made him a hero to progressives, he was not motivated by any sympathy for the common workers, the "thick-fingered clowns," as he once called them. What irked him about those decisions was the focus on individual rights in general, implying that there are limits on what a democratic majority can do. Holmes would have none of it. "Every society rests on the death of men," he liked to say. If a nation needs soldiers, it seizes young men and marches them off to war at the point of a bayonet. If an epidemic breaks out, it forces the public to get vaccinated. The same is true, Holmes thought, even when there is no emergency. If the majority, acting through its elected lawmakers, wants to limit the workday of bakers to ten hours, it should be permitted to do so, regardless of whether that decision is misguided or conflicts with some ideal of freedom. And he, as a judge, had no business standing in the way. "If my fellow citizens want to go to Hell I will help them," was another favorite saying. "It's my job."

In short, Holmes was in many ways the justice least likely to stick his neck out for the right of free speech—and for the Court's role in enforcing that right. So why did he do it? Why did a man who sneered at liberal sentimentality his whole life write one of the canonical statements of American liberalism, a document that has been compared to the speeches of Lincoln and the essays of Milton? Was his opinion somehow consistent with everything he had said and done throughout his life? Or did Holmes undergo a conversion of sorts? And if so, what triggered his sudden change of mind? Was it something he read? Something he witnessed? Something he remembered from his past?

These are not mere idle psychological questions. Holmes's dissent in *Abrams* marked not just a personal transformation but the start of a national transformation as well. The power of his words and the force of his personality gave his opinion an authority far beyond the normal judicial dissent. Civil libertarians immediately embraced it as an article of faith, and Holmes's tribute to the "free trade in ideas," along with his concept of "clear and present danger," became not only cultural catchphrases but, in time, the law of the land. Indeed, it is no exaggeration to say that Holmes's dissent—the most important minority opinion in American legal history—gave birth to the modern era of the First Amendment, in which the freedom to express oneself is our preeminent constitutional value and a defining national trait. Nor can it be disputed that, nearly a century later, his dissent continues to influence our thinking about free speech more than any other single document.

Unraveling the mystery behind Holmes's transformation will therefore tell us not only much about him; it will tell us much about ourselves, too. But how is the mystery to be solved? Holmes has been dead for more than seventy-five years, and even if we could travel back in time to ask him, it is far from certain that he would—or could—provide an explanation. He was an extremely private man who took great pains to protect his public image. He destroyed most of the letters he received and instructed his many correspondents to do the same (fortunately, almost none of them complied). One might also doubt his powers of self-examination. Although generally self-aware, Holmes had blind spots like anyone else. He was defensive, sensitive to criticism, and reluctant to give credit for his ideas to others. Would he be capable of the honest introspection necessary to crack such a case? The truth is he would likely scoff at the entire inquiry. "The trouble with all explanations of historic causes," he told a friend, "is the absence of quantification: you never can say *how much* of the given cause was necessary to provide how much effect, or how much of the cause there was. I regard this as the source of the most subtle fallacies."

Objection noted. But the subjects of history should never be permitted the final word, for that deprives us of the opportunity to make our own sense of the past. Besides, even Holmes admitted that such speculations "always are amusing and tickling if new."

Our only option, then, is to plunge headlong into the past, to immerse ourselves in that distant time and place, to sort through the remains of Holmes's life and reconstruct the story behind those famous words. As it turns out, that story is as fascinating as the events that took place in his study on that strange November day. It is a story of intellectual exploration and emotional growth, of chance encounters, wartime hysteria, and terrorist plots. It is a story about an intense behind-the-scenes effort to change the mind of a legal icon. It is a story about the unlikely friendships between an old soldier and the "young lads" who rescued him from loneliness and despair, urging him on to the crowning achievement of his career. Finally, it is a story about the power of free and vigorous debate to change the course of history. In that sense, it is a vivid affirmation of the very principle Holmes so eloquently defended.

1

Train Fever

A story like this—retracing a man's journey toward enlightenment—could begin at any number of moments. It could begin in 1902, when Holmes fulfilled his lifelong ambition and was appointed to the United States Supreme Court. It could begin twenty years earlier, when he abruptly left his job as a professor at Harvard Law School to take a seat on the Massachusetts Supreme Court. It could begin even farther back, in 1864, say, when he reluctantly began his legal studies after quitting the army; in 1861, when he was commissioned an officer in the Massachusetts Twentieth Regiment fresh out of Harvard College; or even, if we were determined not to leave a single stone unturned, in 1841, when he became the firstborn child of Amelia Lee and Dr. Oliver Wendell Holmes Sr. But this story begins in June 1918, at the start of the Court's long summer recess, as Holmes and Fanny prepare to travel to their vacation home on Boston's North Shore. We choose this moment—and it is a choice, to be sure—because of the extraordinary chain of events that will unfold over the next seventeen months and because, over the course of those months, there will be ample opportunity to reflect on the experiences in Holmes's past that made him the man he was.

When the Court adjourned that June, Holmes was seventy-seven years old and had just finished his sixteenth term on the Court. All told, he had been a judge nearly half his life. It was the only job he ever really liked. War was "an organized bore," he said, and his career as a lawyer had been mostly a disappointment. Though he was sharp on his feet and won his share of cases (fourteen of thirty-two in the state's highest court), he disliked the business side of legal practice and relied on his partners to bring in clients. He found greater satisfaction in the scholarly work he did on the side, writing articles for the *American Law Review* on arcane topics such as privity and common carriers and producing his dense masterpiece *The Common Law*. But whereas the practice of law was too close to the sordid and petty affairs of the world, scholarship was too far removed. In the one year he spent as a professor at Harvard, he "began to grow sober with an inarticulate sense of limitation." Ultimately, he concluded that "academic life is but half life—it is a withdrawal from the fight in order to utter smart things that cost you nothing except the thinking them from a cloister."

Being a judge was the perfect middle ground. It made him feel that he was still in the fight yet allowed him to keep his hands clean and indulge his taste for abstraction. And he was good at it. Probing and incisive, he could spot the wrinkle in a case quickly and iron it out nearly as fast. He worked hard, churning out opinions at twice the rate of some of his colleagues and taking on extra cases when he finished his own. The other justices sometimes grumbled that Holmes was able to produce so much only because his opinions were so short. But they appreciated his eagerness to help out, his genial, conciliatory manner, and his obvious concern for the reputation of the Court.

His own reputation in 1918 was mixed. When he had been appointed to the Court by Theodore Roosevelt, some observers were skeptical, describing him as a "literary feller" with a "strong tendency to be brilliant rather than sound." In certain quarters, that assessment still held. He relied too heavily on clever aphorisms, critics said. He glossed over counterarguments, was often obscure, and provided insufficient guidance to lower courts. These criticisms wounded Holmes, and for a long time he feared he would never receive the recognition he desired, which was nothing less than greatest jurist in the world. But in the past few years, his stature had grown considerably. A circle of young progressives, attracted by his willingness to uphold social reforms, had begun to praise him as a paragon of judicial virtue. The circle included such rising stars as the legal scholar Felix Frankfurter, the political theorist Harold Laski, and the journalist Walter Lippmann. To these and other idealistic young men, Holmes was more than just a great judge; he was an inspiring, romantic figure, a sort of philosopher-poet whose intellectual curiosity, dazzling style, and contrarian impulses seemed like a breath of fresh air in the musty world of government and law. They published tributes to him, feted him with parties and dinners, and passed around his opinions like sacred texts. And though Holmes was not yet the national celebrity he would later become—the wise prophet whose Rushmore-like head graced the cover of *Time* in 1926, the Magnificent Yankee who was immortalized on Broadway and the silver screen—he was beginning to feel as though his life's work had been worthwhile.

His personal life was also in good order. Apart from some toothaches and a cough that bothered him at night, he was healthy and vigorous, walking the two miles home from Court each day and occasionally breaking into a jog to cross the road or catch a streetcar. He carried his tall frame erect, with the bearing of a soldier, and if he was not as lean as he had once been, the extra bulk only added to his grandeur. Always handsome, his features had also grown more impressive with age. He had thick snowy hair, piercing blue eyes, and that famous white mustache fanning out past the edges of his face, ridiculous and glorious at the same time. His marriage to Fanny, forty-six years and counting, was as comfortable as the old alpaca coat he sometimes wore to keep warm in his study. They had dropped out of society long ago, but the young men who worshiped at his feet brought laughter and cheer to their home, making up for the lack of children. It was, Holmes reminisced later, one of the happiest periods of his life.

Not that there weren't occasional moments of gloom. As the years piled up, more and more of his old friends were dying off. Just this past term, Henry Adams had passed away, his long, fruitless education finally at an end. Two years before, it had been Harry James, known to his readers as Henry. And the year before that, John Chipman Gray, the Harvard law professor who had long ago vied with Holmes and James for the attentions of a free-spirited and ill-fated young woman (known to James's readers as Daisy Miller). When he was a line commander in the Union army, Holmes had watched helplessly as, one by one, his young friends were cut down on the battlefield. Now the same thing was happening in old age, and he once again felt like the lone, accidental survivor.

The current war was also a source of strain. Holmes had no qualms about the United States' entry into the European conflict. "Damn a man who ain't for his country right or wrong" summed up his views on the matter. But the war brought hardships, even for a Supreme Court justice. There had been a shortage of coal the previous winter, which, combined with the coldest weather in twenty years, had made life miserable for the poor and uncomfortable for the rich. Fanny closed off the upper floors of the house and canceled their Monday afternoon teas. They ate their meals quietly at home and rarely went out. Even the arrival of spring was darkened by news from the front. In late March, the Germans mounted a last desperate drive across France, pulling within a few days' march of Paris. One night, as shells rained down on the City of Lights and the kaiser predicted imminent victory, Holmes lay awake in bed with heartburn and the beginning of a violent cold.

For the most part, however, he did his best to ignore events across the ocean. He avoided the newspapers—as he always did—and tried not to talk or write about the war. Instead he renewed his boyhood passion for art, spending Saturday afternoons at a gallery across from the British embassy, where he chatted with the curator and browsed through prints of the old Dutch masters. He even bought a few small engravings that he tucked into the corners of his study—two van Dycks, a Rembrandt, and a Whistler he passed off as a Christmas gift for Fanny. The total came to several hundred dollars, and some of his friends reproached him for spending money that could have gone to war bonds. Holmes defended himself, arguing that if philosophy and art were given up the war would become "a fight of swine for swill."

But he also sought reassurance, asking one young woman whose son had been drafted, "Do I seem too detached in giving any time to such things?"

More than anything, he threw himself into his work. As usual, he wrote more opinions than anyone else that term. Most of these were small change, barely of greater significance than the disputes he had resolved as a state court judge. There was the case of the six-year-old boy who lost his leg while trying to retrieve a marble from beneath a railroad car. (Holmes dismissed the boy's suit under a New Jersey law that barred recovery for those injured while playing on railroad tracks.) There were property and contract disputes, an admiralty case, a bankruptcy proceeding, and various questions of statutory interpretation. But two dissents near the end of the term stood out, illustrating what made Holmes so popular among progressives. In the first case, the Court struck down the federal government's effort to eliminate the growing scourge of child labor. The majority ruled that the law exceeded Congress's power to regulate interstate commerce. Holmes, adhering to his belief that judges should not thwart the public's will, disagreed. If Congress could shut down the interstate market in lottery tickets, prostitution, and contaminated eggs—all of which the Court had approved—then why, he asked, could it not also regulate child labor?

The second case was an appeal from a Toledo newspaper that had been convicted of contempt by a federal judge for questioning his handling of a pending case. A majority of the justices rejected the claim that the conviction violated freedom of the press, reasoning that the paper had tried to improperly influence the judge's conduct, and Holmes was initially inclined to go along. But his close friend on the Court Louis Brandeis privately urged him to dissent, and when the majority opinion was circulated in late May, Holmes agreed to do just that. He dashed off a few paragraphs and read them to Brandeis that afternoon, then sent his colleagues a revised version the next day. His argument was modest. He did not mention the First Amendment or freedom of the press. He did not even claim that the conviction was unjustified. He merely wrote that federal law required the judge to submit the matter to a jury—rather than render the verdict himself—because the newspaper posed no immediate threat to the administration of justice. This was a technical point, the kind of objection one seizes upon when not willing to tackle the main issue in a case; it hardly qualified as a ringing defense of free speech. And yet, for anyone worried about the creeping pall of censorship, for anyone unsettled by the growing persecution of socialists and pacifists, Holmes's dissent offered a glimmer of hope. His emphasis on the lack of immediate danger and his assertion that a federal judge should have the fortitude to withstand public scrutiny suggested that here, at least, was a man who could be counted on to resist the hysteria sweeping the country. Or so one might have thought.

That dissent was handed down on Monday, June 10, the last day of the term. Now it was Friday, and Holmes was visibly drained. While the Court was in session and he was working furiously to finish his opinions, he could keep going through a combination of adrenaline and willpower. But once the work stopped, he was hit with a sense of emptiness and collapse, as if the bottom had dropped out. "It was sad to see him," Brandeis wrote to his wife, Alice. "With the work of the term over he relaxed and grew old over night. A disillusionment like seeing the prima donna the next day in bright daylight with curlpins en dishabille."

Holmes put on a gray suit and soft-collared shirt—his regular attire for "the undress season"—and fidgeted uselessly about the house. In two days he and Fanny would depart for their summer home in Beverly Farms, Massachusetts, stopping in New York and Boston along the way. He had always been an anxious traveler, fearful of missing the train, forgetting his tickets, or leaving luggage behind. He called his condition "train fever," and he felt it coming on now as Fanny and the servants packed their trunks and made last-minute preparations for the trip.

He went into his study and took out a sheet of paper. "Dear Pollock," he wrote, beginning a note to Sir Frederick Pollock, the English barrister and legal historian whom he had known for half a century. The two men exchanged letters roughly twice a month, and Holmes hated to fall behind, preferring to shift the obligation of a response onto his friend. He got no further than a few lines, however, when Fanny came in to remind him that the messenger needed their tickets today and that their trunks would go to the station tomorrow. He felt his pulse quicken. "Such things make one twitter," he wrote. "No, not *one* but *me*." He tried to calm his nerves, describing his two dissents at the end of the term, which he assumed the majority "thought as ill-timed and regrettable as I thought the decisions." But it was no use. He was interrupted again, this time with instructions to go to the Express Office to pick up an order of whiskey from Baltimore. Congress had banned alcohol in the capital, he explained to Pollock, but the law was easy to get around by signing an affidavit before a notary public. "The Notary Public," he added, "like the domestic dog is found everywhere."

That was it, he could write no more. He sent his love to Lady Pollock, scratched his initials across the bottom of the page, and departed in haste, his fever rising.

On Sunday, Holmes and Fanny arrived at the station early. He had never missed a train and wasn't about to start now. "Fanny did once," he confided to his secretary, "and she never forgot it." Union Station was packed that summer. Hordes of visitors poured in and out of Washington—soldiers, diplomats, civil administrators, temporary government workers—and nearly all of them passed through the white granite concourse at the edge of town. The crowds, and the shortage of coal, made it difficult to get tickets, and trains were often delayed, sometimes taking as long as twelve hours to reach New York. The government raised fares to discourage travel and pleaded with the public to stay home, but neither step had much effect. To make matters worse, the railroads had eliminated many of the old luxuries. There were few dining or sleeper cars anymore, and it was sometimes hard to find even a simple club car.

The journey to New York was also marked by reminders of the ongoing war. As the train rattled north, passengers could glimpse the massive shipbuilding plants that had sprouted up along the Delaware River.

On Hog Island, just outside Philadelphia, thirty-five ships were under construction, while across the water two dozen torpedo boats were nearing completion. And as the train cut through the lowlands of New Jersey on its approach to Manhattan, dozens of munitions storehouses appeared on the horizon.

Holmes and Fanny disembarked at Pennsylvania Station while their servants went ahead with the trunks. When they had first moved to Washington, Holmes sometimes traveled alone to New York on weekends to shop, attend the theater, and flirt with a few young women he knew there. But those excursions had ended years ago, and now when he and Fanny passed through the city their schedule was less diverting. They called on a few acquaintances, strolled down Fifth Avenue, and browsed through the local bookstores, always on the hunt for a good summer read.

After three uneventful nights, they were back on the train headed for Boston. They had made this trip countless times before, always without incident, and there was no reason to think that anything unusual would occur this time. There was certainly no reason to think that the future of free speech might be altered by what transpired over the next five hours. And yet that is exactly what happened. For at some point between Grand Central Terminal and Boston's South Station, Holmes got up from his seat and wandered away from Fanny. Perhaps he went to the bathroom or to get a drink of water. Perhaps he simply needed to stretch his long legs. Whatever the reason, while making his way through the crowded train he spotted a short, stocky man with a square head, thick black eyebrows, and the sad, entreating face of a pug. The face smiled, Holmes smiled back, and the wheels of history began to turn.

The face belonged to Learned Hand, a federal judge in New York who was on his way to join his wife and children at their summer home in Cornish, New Hampshire. At forty-six, Hand was one of the most respected young judges in the country. He had been on the bench for nine years and had recently been considered for promotion to the federal appeals court. He was also friends with many of the young lawyers and journalists who clustered around Holmes, and the two men had crossed paths from time to time. But Hand was never completely at ease around Holmes. He worshiped the justice more than any other man except his late father. And just as he had often been nervous around Hand senior, so he was also nervous in the presence of Holmes.

In truth, Hand was on edge his whole life. Born into a strict, religious family in Albany, he was an anxious and fearful child who frequently woke up screaming from nightmares and spent most days alone in his room, reading Greek myths and organizing his stamp collection. He rarely went outdoors, too shy and self-conscious about his clumsiness to play with the other boys. And he was sensitive about his name—Billings Peck Learned Hand. He worried it sounded pretentious or, even worse, sissy; it didn't help that his sister and mother called him Bunny. As he got older, he dropped the Peck, shortened the Billings to B and encouraged his classmates to call him Buck. Eventually, he identified himself simply as Learned Hand.

The main reason for Hand's insecurity was the shadow cast by his father, a successful lawyer active in state politics. The family regarded Samuel Hand as a genius, a true intellectual destined for the national stage. And for a while, at least, he seemed to be on his way. He sat briefly on New York's highest court and served as an adviser to then governor Grover Cleveland. But just as he reached the peak of his influence, he was diagnosed with cancer. Learned Hand was only fourteen when his father died, and the loss devastated him. Although their relationship was distant and formal, he accepted the family's idealized portrait of his father and became convinced he would never live up to him. Even in old age, when he was the most famous judge in America not on the Supreme Court, he continued to insist that Samuel Hand had been a greater man than himself.

With his father's legacy to live up to, Hand pushed himself hard at school and won admission to Harvard, which should have erased any self-doubts he had. But as an awkward grind from the unfashionable town of Albany, he felt as if he would never fit in. He was excluded from most of the clubs that mattered and failed to make the football team. The one area in which he excelled was academics. He started out in classics, as his father had always urged him to do, but switched to philosophy in his sophomore year. The change transformed him. Instead of the rote learning of Greek and Latin—gymnastics for the brain, his father called them—he learned to ask difficult questions and distrust easy answers. He graduated summa cum laude and was admitted to Harvard Law School, where he fell under the influence of James Bradley Thayer, one of the earliest advocates of judicial restraint—the idea that judges should defer to the judgment of elected officials. This was a view shared by Holmes, of course, and one that would become central to the debate over free speech.

Although Hand continued to doubt his abilities after law school, he gradually hit his stride, moving to New York and becoming active in public affairs. He campaigned against the corruption of Tammany Hall, joined several reform groups, and published an article in the *Harvard Law Review* condemning the Supreme Court's interference with progressive legislation in much the same spirit as Holmes. He also befriended some of the city's leading lawyers and power brokers, including Henry Taft, brother of the president. And when, in 1909, Congress allotted money for a new seat on the federal court, Hand's connections helped him secure the spot.

His appointment to the bench finally alleviated many of his insecurities. He thrived in the job and was soon one of the country's leading judges, known for his erudition and careful reasoning. He emerged, too, as a central player in the progressive movement, advising Teddy Roosevelt on his independent run for the presidency in 1912 and allowing his own name to appear on the Bull Moose ticket as a candidate for New York's highest court. He lost the election but quickly found another outlet for his reformist zeal when his friend Herbert Croly founded a political magazine called the *New Republic*. Hand was deeply involved in the new venture, helping to recruit the staff, sitting in on board meetings, and contributing essays on legal topics. It was through this work that he came into contact with Holmes, one of the *New Republic*'s early supporters. Holmes was just the kind of man Hand had always wanted to be, or at least be accepted by—an aristocrat, a sophisticate, a descendant of the oldest families in New England,

and a member of the most exclusive clubs at Harvard. Holmes was actually remarkably free of airs, as perhaps only a true aristocrat can be. But that only made him more imposing in the eyes of Hand.

So when the two men sat down for a tête-à-tête as the train rumbled north toward Boston that day, Hand was naturally filled with a sense of awe and humility. Which makes what he did next all the more out of character. Instead of simply making polite conversation with Holmes—perhaps encouraging the justice to repeat some of his favorite anecdotes—Hand steered the discussion toward a heated and contentious issue. And instead of deferring to the older man's views on that issue, Hand picked a fight with him.

The reason was clear. The previous year, Hand had presided over a trial involving the newly enacted Espionage Act. Passed in June 1917, shortly after Congress declared war on Germany, the law punished any form of spying against the United States, from surveillance of military facilities to code breaking to the stealing of classified documents. The law didn't stop there, however. Washington was worried not just about cloak-and-dagger threats but also about a more subtle and pernicious danger to the country's safety. It was worried about dissidents, people who for one reason or another opposed the war and wanted it to end short of victory. So the law also punished anyone who willfully obstructed the draft or caused insubordination in the military, as well as anyone who published false reports intended to interfere with the war. And because the most likely way to accomplish any of these things was to circulate pamphlets and periodicals through the mail, the law gave the postmaster general the power to block any publication he thought illegal. In other words, the law created a censor.

The postmaster at the time was perhaps the worst person that power could have been given to. He was Albert Burleson, a reactionary racist from Texas who despised labor unions and the people who supported them. As soon as the new law went into effect, Burleson began a campaign to root out magazines and newspapers that promoted socialist or radical causes. One of the publications he targeted was the *Masses*, a leftist journal edited by the poet and political activist Max Eastman. Eastman hated the war, especially the draft, and in the summer of 1917 he ran a series of poems and cartoons expressing that hatred. (One of the cartoons showed a naked boy strapped to the mouth of a cannon; another showed a cabal of rich bankers plotting the war behind Congress's back.) Burleson believed that these items would cause insubordination among soldiers and draftees, and he informed Eastman that all future issues of the *Masses* would be excluded from the mail. Eastman, in turn, filed a lawsuit against Burleson, arguing that the items in question did not violate the Espionage Act and that, in any case, they were protected by the First Amendment.

The suit came before Hand just a month after passage of the law, making him the first judge in the country to rule on its validity. He was already familiar with Eastman and the *Masses*. In fact, a year earlier he had written a letter on the magazine's behalf after a distributor refused to carry it on New York newsstands. Hand didn't agree with the magazine's views, he made clear in the letter, but he did think it should be free to express them. He felt the same way now and was inclined to rule in Eastman's favor. The problem was that striking down the law would conflict with the principle of judicial restraint he had learned from Thayer and Holmes. So Hand did something that had the appearance of restraint but was in fact quite *un*restrained. He changed the meaning of the law by construing its words narrowly. Congress could not have meant to forbid mere criticism of the war or the draft, he explained, for that would "contradict the normal assumption of democratic government that the suppression of hostile criticism does not turn upon the justice of its substance or the decency and propriety of its temper." Instead, Congress must have intended to ban only explicit incitement to break the law. And no matter how offensive one found the items in the *Masses*, he concluded, they did not qualify as incitement.

It was a courageous decision, particularly for someone as self-doubting and anxious as Hand. And he knew well the risk he was taking. Shortly before writing it, he told his wife that he was probably throwing away any chance he had at the seat that was then open on the appeals court. If the case didn't settle, he explained, he would have to decide against the government, "and then whoop-la your little man is in the mud." Hand was right: President Wilson appointed one of Hand's junior colleagues to the appeals court instead. Even more discouraging, Hand's decision met a quick demise. It was reversed three months later by the same court he had just been denied promotion to, and the *Masses* was never published again.

That ended the matter as far as the courts were concerned, but Hand was still upset about the case a year later. He was convinced he had been right, not only about his interpretation of the Espionage Act but also about the larger issue of free speech. Yes, the times were dangerous. And yes, Congress had the power to punish those who encouraged law breaking. But "to assimilate agitation, legitimate as such, with direct incitement to violent resistance," he thought, "is to disregard the tolerance of all methods of political agitation which in normal times is a safeguard of free government."

And that was the subject he wanted to discuss with Holmes: tolerance. Hand felt that everyone had been against him since his *Masses* decision: the appeals court, his fellow judges, even his cousin Augustus Hand (also a federal judge), who called the decision an example of Hand's "natural perversity." Hand was looking for someone who would sympathize with him, someone who would agree that the country had lost its head and needed a strong dose of perspective. So he turned to the person he respected most—a man who rarely followed the crowd, who cherished debate and admired independent thinking. Surely Holmes would agree with him. Surely someone who so often found himself in the minority would see the folly of persecuting those who dared to dissent.

Hand was mistaken. Holmes had little interest in the kind of tolerance Hand was advocating. As a believer in society's right to impose its will on the individual, he thought persecution of dissenters made perfect sense. And as a former soldier who had taken up arms against his fellow countrymen, he was not afraid to follow that principle to what he thought was its logical, if shocking, conclusion. "You strike at the sacred right to kill the other fellow when he disagrees," he told Hand in his typically blunt and provocative fashion.

This was not the response Hand had expected or hoped for, and he didn't know what to say. He had wanted Holmes's support more than anyone else's, and now he was struck dumb—maddeningly, frustratingly dumb. Then, before he could collect his thoughts and offer a rebuttal, Holmes was on his way. Worried about rejoining Fanny, he said a hurried good-bye and ran off to gather his things before the train pulled into Boston.

One can imagine how Hand must have kicked himself after Holmes slipped away, how he must have brooded over his silence and thought of all the things he should have said. One can imagine the arguments that must have played out in his head as the train continued north through the mill towns of the Merrimack Valley, then veered west past the clear deep waters of Sunapee Lake on its way to Cornish. One can imagine all this but one doesn't have to, because Hand wrote it down. Three days after arriving at his summer home, he sent the following letter to Holmes, arguing that "incredulity"—that is, skepticism and doubt—should lead to a policy of forbearance:

June 22, 1918

Dear Mr. Justice:

   I gave up rather more easily than I now feel disposed about Tolerance on Wednesday. Here I take my stand. Opinions are at best provisional hypotheses, incompletely tested. The more they are tested, after the tests are well scrutinized, the more assurance we may assume, but they are never absolutes. So we must be tolerant of opposite opinions or varying opinions by the very fact of our incredulity of our own.

   You say that I strike at the sacred right to kill the other fellow when he disagrees. The horrible possibility silenced me when you said it. Now, I say, "Not at all, kill him for the love of Christ and in the name of God, but always realize that he may be the saint and you the devil. Go your way with a strong right arm and a swift shining sword, in full consciousness that what you kill for, and what you may die for, some smart chap like Laski may write

a book and prove is all nonsense." I agree that in practical
application there may arise some difficulty, but I am a philosopher and if Man is so poor a creature as not to endure the truth,
it is no concern of mine. I didn't make him; let the Galled Jade
wince, speaking reverently of course.

I sat under the Bo Tree and these truths were revealed unto me.
Tolerance is the twin of Incredulity, but there is no inconsistency
in cutting off the heads of as many as you please; that is a natural
right. Only, and here we may differ, I do say that you may not cut
off heads, (except for limited periods and then only when you
want to very much indeed), because the victims insist upon
saying things which look against Provisional Hypothesis Number
Twenty-Six, the verification of which to date may be found in its
proper place in the card catalogue. Generally, I insist, you must
allow the possibility that if the heads are spared, other cards may
be added under that sub-title which will have, perhaps, an
important modification.

All this seems to me so perfectly self-evident, self-explanatory
and rigidly applicable to the most complicated situations that
I hesitate to linger upon it, lest I should seem tolerant of any
different [sic] of opinion concerning it.

I greatly enjoyed my good fortune in meeting you on the
train.

Faithfully yours,
Learned Hand

This is what he had wanted to say on the train. This is what he had
wanted to say in his *Masses* decision and in his conversations with his
cousin Gus and his fellow judges. Here, in his letter to Holmes, Hand
had finally clarified what he meant by tolerance. He didn't mean aban-
doning one's convictions or refusing to fight for one's beliefs. Though
not a veteran like Holmes, Hand accepted society's right to defend
itself from existential threats, whether internal (as in the Civil War) or
external (as in the current war). That is why he had been silenced by

Holmes's remark on the train and agreed that limiting that right was a "horrible possibility." But there was a difference between killing those who threaten your survival and killing those who question some current dogma. With respect to the latter, Hand thought, we should be tolerant—and not because they have an inalienable right to express themselves. As Hand knew, Holmes would have scoffed at an appeal to some lofty notion of natural rights. So instead Hand offered a pragmatic argument. We should be tolerant of those who disagree with us because there is a chance we are wrong and they are right. And if they are right and we suppress their views ("cut off heads," in Hand's words), then we will lose the benefits of their wisdom.

With its Buddhist allusions ("I sat under the Bo Tree") and Shakespearean references ("let the Galled Jade wince"), Hand's letter displayed both his deep learning and his desperate desire to impress. But what would Holmes think? Would he dismiss it all with a casual, clever remark as he had done on the train? Or would he also find Hand's reasoning to be "perfectly self-evident"? Hand did not have to wait long to find out. As soon as Holmes received the letter in Beverly Farms, he sent back an enthusiastic reply:

June 24, 1918

Dear Hand,

Rarely does a letter hit me so exactly where I live as yours, and unless you are spoiling for a fight I agree with it throughout. My only qualification, if any, would be that free speech stands no differently than freedom from vaccination. The occasions would be rarer when you cared enough to stop it but if for any reason you did care enough you wouldn't care a damn for the suggestion that you were acting on a provisional hypothesis and might be wrong. That is the condition of every act.

You tempt me to repeat an apologue that I got off to my wife in front of the statue of Garrison on Commonwealth Avenue, Boston, many years ago. I said—if I were an official person I should say nothing shall induce me to do honor to a man who broke the fundamental condition of social life by bidding the very structure of society perish rather than he not have his way—expressed in terms of morals, to be sure, but still, his way. If I were a son of Garrison I should reply—Fool, not to see that every great reform has seemed to threaten the structure of society, but that society has not perished, because man is a social animal, and with every turn falls into a new pattern like the Kaleidoscope. If I were a philosopher I should say—Fools both, not to see that you are the two blades (conservative and radical) of the shears that cut out the future. But if I were the ironical man in the back of the philosopher's head I should conclude—Greatest fool of all, Thou—not to see that man's destiny is to fight. Therefore take thy place on the one side or the other, if with the added grace of knowing that the Enemy is as good a man as thou, so much the better, but kill him if thou Canst. All of which seems in accord with you.

If I may repeat another chestnut of ancient date and printed in later years—When I say a thing is true I mean that I can't help believing it—and nothing more. But as I observe that the Cosmos is not always limited by my Cant Helps I don't bother about absolute truth or even inquire whether there is such a thing, but define the Truth as the system of my limitations. I may add that as other men are subject to a certain number, not all, of my Cant Helps, intercourse is possible. When I was young I used to define the truth as the majority vote of that nation that can lick all others. So we may define the present war as an inquiry concerning truth. Of course you won't suspect me of thinking with levity on that subject because of my levitical speech. I enjoyed our meeting as much as you possibly could have and should have tried to prolong it to Boston but that I feared my wife would worry.

Sincerely Yours
O.W. Holmes

When this letter arrived in Cornish, Hand must have been elated. Holmes had taken his argument seriously and was apparently won over. "I agree with it throughout," he had written. And yet . . . if Hand read the letter carefully, he had to wonder whether Holmes really did agree. Hand had argued that because opinions are nothing more than provisional hypotheses, we must be tolerant of conflicting views. Holmes did not deny the provisional nature of opinions: he was as skeptical of the notion of objective truth as anyone. To Holmes, however, that lack of certainty did not necessitate tolerance. "If for any reason you did care enough [to stop freedom of speech]," he had written, "you wouldn't care a damn for the suggestion that you were acting on a provisional hypothesis and might be wrong. That is the condition of every act." *That is the condition of every act.* We are always acting upon a provisional hypothesis, was Holmes's point. We can never be sure we're right. But that shouldn't stop us from acting.

His apologue in front of Garrison's statue drove the point home. William Lloyd Garrison was a fervent abolitionist who had opposed all compromise over the issue of slavery in the years leading up to the Civil War. Holmes had been an abolitionist himself before the war; he even served as a bodyguard at an antislavery rally in Boston. After the war, however, he grew to detest the abolitionists, as well as all other ideologues, on the left and the right. He had seen the horrors ideology could produce: the blood spilled, the dreams ruined, the lives lost. Yet strangely, he didn't lose his taste for battle. He didn't become the philosopher who thinks both sides are foolish for fighting because neither can know the truth. Instead, he became the ironical man in the back of the philosopher's head, the man who thinks there's no choice but to pick a side and fight, even if one might be wrong, even if one might be killed as a result. So Hand's doubts and insecurities—his incredulity— meant little to Holmes when it came to tolerance. If we feel strongly enough about our beliefs, Holmes thought, we should not hesitate to act upon them, whether that means marching to war, passing laws to stamp out child labor, or suppressing the speech of those who stand in our way.

Holmes did not agree with Hand after all. If Hand realized this, he must have been devastated. He had put forth his strongest case, had said all that he wanted to say, and yet still he had been unable to make Holmes see the light. The skirmish was lost.

But the campaign had just begun.

2

A Smart Chap

Beverly Farms was a world away from Washington. Forty-five minutes by train from Boston, it lay at the heart of the North Shore, a twisting ribbon of rock and sand that stretches for a hundred miles along the Massachusetts Bay. Once a desolate and windswept coastline where farmers herded cattle and fishermen cast their nets, the North Shore had been transformed during the nineteenth century into a summer playground for Boston's social elite. Grand hotels and mansions sprang up among the dunes, yachts skimmed across the surf, and the literati of Beacon Hill held court amid the breeze. Eventually, as the railroads extended their tentacles northward, much of the shore was overrun by the working class, with skating rinks and amusement parks taking the place of tennis courts and sailing clubs. But Beverly Farms and its neighbors, Manchester and Magnolia, remained aloof and exclusive, the destination of choice for barons, presidents, and poets. "Find the Yankee word for Sorrento and you have Beverly," wrote James Russell Lowell. "It is the Bay of Naples translated into the New England dialect."

Holmes had seen the town once as a young boy and said the granite rocks pushing up through the soil were his "first recollections of country." He returned as a grown man when his father rented a cottage near the train station. ("Beverly-by-the-Depot," the doctor called it, a jab at friends who pretentiously signed their cards "Manchester-by-the-Sea.") The family later moved to a larger house near the water, and when his father died Holmes took over the lease and then bought the place outright. It was a rambling brown Victorian with a covered porch wrapping around the front, a shingled roof, four chimneys, and eight bedrooms. Perched on a slight rise next to a stand of pines, it was only a few hundred yards from the crescent of white sand known as West Beach. From his study on the second floor, Holmes could glimpse the waves breaking just off the shore and, a half mile beyond them, the hazy outline of the Misery Islands, two barren and jagged shipwreckers bobbing in Salem Sound. The acre of grass and shrubs that surrounded the house was lush and well tended. Honeysuckle and woodbine shaded the porch, roses and geraniums ran riot in the garden, and tall spikes of purple delphiniums clustered by the split-rail fence. The most striking feature was a massive boulder rising twenty-five feet out of the earth and laced with nasturtium vines. A wooden bench was wedged into a crevice on its face, and Holmes liked to sit there on pleasant days and read.

It was not just the salt air and ocean views that made Beverly Farms feel so removed. It was the pace. In Washington, Holmes worked seven days a week, hearing arguments, sitting in conference, writing opinions, and reviewing petitions for appeal. He had little time or energy for the serious books he longed to read—"Day of Judgment" books, he called them, since one might be asked about them on that big final exam in the sky. At Beverly Farms, however, time was abundant. Once he had recovered from the strain of the trip and sorted out his bank accounts, he could lounge for days on end, debauching on German historicism, Greek drama, French philosophy, and English literature. If he tired of reading, he could walk with Fanny to the village or take a bouquet of roses to one of the pretty young socialites who vacationed in the neighborhood, Mrs. Codman perhaps or Mrs. Curtis, with whom he had carried on a long Victorian flirtation.

This summer he would also have another playmate, though one not quite as attractive as Ellen Curtis. Harold Laski—the "smart chap"

Hand had referred to in his letter—was renting a cottage with his wife and daughter in Rockport, a short drive up the coast. Just twenty-four years old (to Holmes's seventy-seven) and recently arrived from England, Laski was an instructor in history at Harvard and a contributor to the *New Republic*. He was brilliant, prolific, charming, effusive, irrepressible, and a notorious self-promoter. And of all the young men who had wriggled their way into the justice's heart, he was Holmes's favorite.

They had met two years earlier, in 1916, through Felix Frankfurter, an up-and-coming professor at the law school who had become a friend of Holmes while working in Washington for the Taft administration. Laski pleaded with his colleague for an introduction, and Frankfurter willingly obliged, inviting Laski to join him on a weekend visit to Beverly Farms. It was love at first sight—or rather intellectual infatuation at first hearing, since the bond between Holmes and Laski was Platonic in its truest sense. They talked late into the evening about law, history, economics, and philosophy. When Laski "inadvertently" left behind a hairbrush, he seized the opportunity to continue the conversation by letter. From there, the relationship ripened quickly. The two men wrote each other seventeen letters in the first two months alone, Laski invited himself back to Beverly Farms a month later, and by the end of the year Laski was signing his letters "Yours Always," while Holmes was addressing his to "My Dear Lad."

They were an odd couple, to say the least. Begin with their physical appearances. Standing at least six feet two with a straight back and fine lines, Holmes was the image of a retired cavalry officer. He was "possessed of a grandeur and beauty rarely met among men," wrote Dean Acheson. "His presence entered a room with him as a pervading force, and left with him, too, like a strong light put out." Laski, by contrast, resembled an underfed schoolboy. Five foot eight in shoes and 120 pounds when wet, he had pale knobby legs and a big throbbing brain. Edmund Wilson described him as "elfishly small," while others called him "a mousy little man," "a pint-sized colossus," and "an unassuming little Titan." The most vivid description, however, comes from Ayn Rand, who used Laski as the physical and intellectual model for her socialist villain in *The Fountainhead*. "At a first glance," Rand wrote,

one wished to offer him a heavy, well-padded overcoat—so frail and unprotected did his thin little body appear, like that of a chicken just emerging from the egg, in all the sorry fragility of unhardened bones. At a second glance, one wished to be sure that the overcoat should be an exceedingly good one—so exquisite were the garments covering that body. The lines of the dark suit followed frankly the shape within it, apologizing for nothing: they sank with the concavity of the narrow chest, they slid down from the long, thin neck with the sharp slope of the shoulders. A great forehead dominated the body. The wedge-shaped face descended from the broad temples to a small, pointed chin. The hair was black, lacquered, divided into equal halves by a thin white line. This made the skull look tight and trim, but left too much emphasis to the ears that flared out in solitary nakedness, like the handles of a bouillon cup. The nose was long and thin, prolonged by the small dab of a black moustache. The eyes were dark and startling. They held such a wealth of intellect and of twinkling gaiety that his glasses seemed to be worn not to protect his eyes but to protect other men from their excessive brilliance.

The contrast in appearance between the two men was not just superficial; it was the physical manifestation of a stark difference in pedigree, one that would have been obvious to anyone who saw them walking arm in arm down the street. Holmes was New England blue blood through and through. Each of his three names—Oliver, Wendell, and Holmes—represented a family line that could trace its roots back to the earliest settlers. The Olivers arrived in the New World in 1632, the Wendells ten years later, and the Holmes clan ten years after that. Laski had arrived in 1914 from Manchester, England. His own father was a successful cotton merchant, but that's as far back as the family's accomplishments went. Before that the Laskis were struggling Jewish immigrants from Poland, working as jewelers in the grimy, sodden towns of the industrial north.

Perhaps most incongruent were their political views. Holmes was a lifelong Republican, which in those days was the only respectable choice for a New England WASP. He believed loosely in free markets, thrifty habits, big business, and the prerogatives of the ruling class, but mainly he believed that strong ideological commitments were both foolish and dangerous. And he had no taste for political involvement. When, in his forties, a group of influential Bostonians suggested he give up his seat on the Massachusetts Supreme Court to run for governor, he laughed at the idea. "4 years on the bench was worth a lifetime in the Presidency," he later wrote. Laski, on the other hand, lived and breathed politics. As an undergraduate at Oxford, he was one of the most vocal members of the student union, the training ground for England's political leaders. His views were just to the right of Marx—he was a militant suffragist and a revolutionary syndicalist—and he broadcast them openly, debating conservative classmates, berating eminent speakers, and generally making a nuisance of himself. Once, during the annual race week between Oxford and Cambridge, he chartered a boat and motored up and down the Thames shouting "votes for women" through a megaphone (he barely escaped a beating at the hands of angry spectators). Another time he hijacked a London conference on nonviolent resistance and persuaded the audience to cross the street and attempt a raid on the House of Commons. His most daring and dubious stunt, however, was strictly undercover. With the help of a friend, he planted a homemade bomb in the men's lavatory of the Oxted railway station. The bomb detonated but did little damage because the fuse failed to ignite the gas. Afterward Laski fled the scene, hiding under a rug in the backseat of a car to Dover, then catching a ferry to France, where he made money giving tours to clueless Americans. He returned to England four days later and was never identified as the culprit.

By the time Laski met Holmes he had tempered his militancy. He gave up violent protests in favor of the lecturer's podium and remade himself into a scholar and public intellectual. He was also cautious about what he said to Holmes, reading the older man's cues and tailoring his responses accordingly. He would often praise some writer or thinker only to backpedal when Holmes offered a contrary assessment. "Your comment on Boswell is as true a thing as I know," began one retraction. "I was on the whole content with your sentence on Proudhon," began another. But he never retreated from his overall philosophy. In his first letter to Holmes he enclosed a copy of *Reflections on Violence*, the syndicalist tract written by Georges Sorel. And he made no secret of his desire for a guild takeover of industry, though he added tentatively, "I wonder how you feel about this anarchical doctrine."

So what drew them together? How did two men born a half century apart, on different continents, of different faiths, and with diametrically opposed political views become such intimate friends? From Laski's perspective, the answer is fairly obvious. He was an ambitious young outsider attempting to break into the closed, hidebound world of New England society. Friendship with Holmes was like being on the guest list for the most exclusive party in town: it guaranteed him instant access and credibility. But although part of his attraction to Holmes was surely opportunistic, Laski also genuinely admired and cared for the older man. He had read many of Holmes's opinions and scholarly writing even before they met and considered him one of the greatest legal thinkers alive. There was also an openness and freshness about Holmes that appealed to Laski and other young intellectuals. Unlike most men of his background and stature, he never talked down to them or laughed at their idealism, even though he rarely shared it himself. Instead, he let them know that he understood exactly how they felt and sympathized with their ambitions. In the words of one journalist at the time, he received "their ideas with the courtesy, admiration and speculative curiosity accorded to honored guests."

For Holmes, the attraction to Laski was more complex. Part of the explanation certainly lies in Laski's astounding erudition. If there was one thing Holmes valued more than any other, it was intellectual firepower, and Laski's arsenal was loaded. In a letter to Pollock shortly after meeting his young friend, Holmes described him as "one of the most learned men I've ever met of any age." On another occasion he described him as "diabolically clever and omniscient." Laski also had a way of ingratiating himself with the rich and powerful, dispensing flattery and praise with the deftness of a courtesan. When he was just seventeen, he befriended the eighty-eight-year-old scientist and founder of eugenics, Francis Galton. And throughout his long public career in England—a career that saw him become the most recognizable socialist in the English-speaking world and that culminated in his appointment as chair of the Labour Party in 1945—he used his remarkable facility at making friends to earn the confidence of such disparate leaders as Franklin Roosevelt, Winston Churchill, and Jawaharlal Nehru.

In spite of their political differences, the two men held a number of views in common. Both were attracted to eugenics in the years before the war (though Laski, unlike Holmes, never embraced its more draconian implications). Both were also heavily influenced by Darwin and the scientific method. And both were nonbelievers who thought religion was responsible for much of the superstition and irrationality that afflicted the modern world.

But Holmes's affection for Laski was founded on more than intellectual admiration or a few shared beliefs. In a very real sense, Laski was the son he never had. Though the reason for Fanny's and his lack of children remains a mystery—one relative claimed that Holmes was impotent, while most biographers simply assume he did not want to be distracted from his work—it is clear that by the end of his life the issue was painful to him. Asked once if he was sorry not to have been a father, he became emotional, as though filled with regret. Another time he replied sharply, "This is not the kind of world I want to bring anyone else into."

Holmes also had a strained and awkward relationship with his own father. A diminutive man with an outsized personality, the elder Holmes began his career as a doctor and medical professor but made his name as a public speaker and author, turning out thousands of lines of verse, three novels, and a regular column for the *Atlantic Monthly*, the magazine he christened and helped to found. By the time of his death, in 1894, Dr. Holmes was one of the most popular writers in America, beloved for his easy, conversational style and pleasing blend of humor and sentimentality. To his son, he was a dilettante and gadfly whose indiscreet chattering was riddled with bad puns and thoughtless barbs. (When Holmes was recuperating from a gunshot to his foot during the Civil War, his father, noticing that a doctor had used a slice of carrot as a poultice for the wound, pinched Holmes's heel and asked what vegetable he had turned the carrot into. "Why a Pa's Nip!" he exclaimed, as his son groaned in exasperation.) Holmes also resented the way the elder Holmes picked at him, telling him his neck was too thin and his singing voice off key. And he never forgave his father for using his experiences during the war as fodder for his own journalistic dispatches.

For Holmes, then, there was emptiness at both ends of the filial tree. And Laski was the perfect person to fill the void. Raised in an Orthodox household, he became estranged from his family at the age of eighteen when he eloped with Frida Kerry, a Gentile masseuse eight years his senior. His parents forced the young couple to separate while Laski attended Oxford, then withheld financial support when the two moved in together a few years later. It was largely to escape his family's disapproval that Laski and Frida relocated to North America, settling first in Montreal, where Laski taught at McGill University, before moving to Harvard with their newborn daughter, Diana, in 1916.

So Laski needed a father, Holmes needed a son, and Holmes needed to ease the pain of the relationship with his own father, which he could do by giving Laski the unconditional support he felt he had never received at home. It was a complicated kind of transference, but it seems to have worked. Holmes's attitude toward the late doctor softened as he grew older, while his relationship with Laski became increasingly paternal. Diana took to calling Holmes "Grandpa," Holmes referred to Laski as "my son," and when the young man returned from England years later to celebrate Holmes's ninetieth birthday, the justice excitedly told his maid, "My boy will be here Saturday."

He was equally excited to see his boy in the summer of 1918. Within a few days of arriving at Beverly Farms, he sent a note to Laski at

Rockport: "Here we are at last—and I hope before long to see you." When Laski proposed a visit the following week, Holmes responded with the giddiness of a teenager. "Tuesday ten it is," he wrote. "I am dying to talk with you." Then, along the margin, he scrawled, "When we meet we will make schemes—I doubt not—without difficulty."

One of the things Holmes was dying to talk about was his encounter on the train with Hand. He had mentioned it briefly in his note—"I had a good talk with Judge Hand (Learned) coming on which led to a characteristic and mighty good letter carrying on the talk"—but was eager to recount the full story. Laski knew Hand through the *New Republic* and would surely be intrigued by the judge's views. Besides, the young lad was always eager for a good debate. So when he arrived at the house Tuesday morning, Holmes wasted no time sharing Hand's letter with him and soliciting his reaction.

Even at this early point in his career, Laski's position on free speech was already well formed. His main scholarly agenda since arriving at Harvard was to promote his theory of pluralism—the idea that the state is not preeminent but merely one of many entities that shape society's progress. Laski believed that voluntary associations, such as trade unions, clubs, and churches, were just as important in the lives of most people as the organs of government. Moreover, he denied that the state had any special claim to the public's allegiance. If the state wanted loyalty and obedience from its citizens, he argued, it had to earn them in a Darwinian competition with other groups. This frankly anarchistic theory was primarily designed to advance the cause of labor by insisting that the state must not serve the interests of capital alone. But it also had implications for civil liberties. If people were free to pledge their loyalties to whatever institutions best promoted the public good, they must necessarily be free to debate the virtues and vices of those institutions. Laski made this clear in his 1917 book, *Studies in the Problem of Sovereignty*. "Progress is born from disagreement and discussion," he wrote. "The price of liberty is exactly divergence of opinion on fundamental questions."

It was entirely clear, therefore, where Laski stood in the debate between Hand and Holmes. But Laski was a smart chap, as Hand had said. He rarely disagreed with Holmes explicitly, instead couching any difference in their views as trivial and incidental to their agreement on some larger issue. He took the same tack now. Hand's thesis reached the correct result, he told Holmes in a letter a few days later, but for the wrong reasons and without considering all the difficulties involved. His own belief in toleration was grounded in the faith that even false or dangerous ideas would eventually be rejected. "I mean that there are all kinds of theories, e.g. Christian science, which seem to me stupid and wrongheaded, but looking at the natural history of such theories I don't think either their stupidity or wrongheadedness has a sufficient chance of survival to penalise the ideas themselves." The one exception, he added, is when a tyrant comes along who thinks toleration is nonsense and wants to slay all who think differently. If such a tyrant and Hand were the last two people on earth, "how could Hand secure the survival of toleration except by killing him? All of which surely means that there *is* something in Carlyle's ultimate question, Can I kill thee or can'st thou kill me?"

It was classic Laski, glossing over his agreement with Hand while suggesting that Holmes was right on the ultimate question. His quotation of the Scottish satirist Thomas Carlyle ("Can I kill thee or can'st thou kill me?") even echoed Holmes's letter to Hand ("but kill him if thou Canst").

Holmes was smart too, however. He saw through Laski's disingenuousness and pointed it out to him the following day:

July 7, 1918

Dear Laski

Just a line to say that I don't see where your quarrel with Hand is. It rather should be with me if either—but I don't see any quarrel. My thesis would be (1) if you are cocksure, and (2) if you want it very much, and (3) if you have no doubt of your power— you will do what you believe efficient to bring about what you want—by legislation or otherwise.

In most matters of belief we are not cocksure, we don't care very much, and we are not certain of our power. But in the opposite case we should deal with the act of speech as we deal with any other overt act that we don't like.

> To be continued on Friday.
>
> Affly—
>
> O.W.H.

This was essentially what Holmes had said to Hand, only sharper and more concise. When we believe in something strongly enough, we fight for it, free speech and tolerance be damned. If Laski was guilty of equivocation, however, so was Holmes. *I don't see any quarrel*, he had written, in spite of the obvious disagreement between the two men. Was this a sign that he was beginning to budge, that he really did think he and Laski were in accord? More likely, it was simply the gesture of a gentleman. "I agree that the logical result of a fundamental difference is for one side to kill the other—and that persecution has much to be said for it," he wrote to the diplomat Lewis Einstein the same week, repeating what he had told Hand on the train. "But in private life we think it more comfortable for disagreement to end in discussion or silence."

Laski was not a brooder or self-doubter like Hand. When Holmes disagreed with him, he didn't take it personally; he took it as a challenge. Holmes might be fifty years older and a justice on the Supreme Court, but Laski backed down from no one when it came to intellectual combat. Besides, he had a weapon Hand lacked: an encyclopedic knowledge of books. At a moment's notice, he could call up some obscure title on ancient usury practices or medieval church architecture to prove a point or smash a thesis. This was partly the result of writing book reviews for the *New Republic* to supplement his meager teaching income. It also helped that he had a photographic memory and could read up to two hundred pages an hour.

So the next time Laski called at Beverly Farms, he came prepared. It was a Friday night, ten days after his last visit. He and Frida took the train down for dinner. The weather was horrid. Heavy winds whipped in from the sea, a thunderstorm blackened the sky, and hailstones raked the ground, splitting tomatoes and grapes from their vines. The two couples watched the storm through the shutters, and Holmes teasingly blamed Fanny for not serving up clear skies. But the conversation was lively, as always. Laski wondered who had been the greatest man of the nineteenth century. Was it Shelley? Beethoven? Marx? Holmes thought the question too subjective and impossible to answer. "It depends on your interests—where you will put the emphasis," he reflected. "If greatest means the greatest number of human foot-pounds, probably the greatest was some cuss we never heard of."

When talk turned to free speech, Laski produced a fat leather-bound volume he had brought with him. Its title was *The Theory of Toleration under the Later Stuarts*, its author a Cambridge fellow named A. A. Seaton. Laski had discovered the book as part of his research on pluralism and thought the justice might find its perspective illuminating. Holmes eyed the volume warily. He hated borrowing books for fear he would damage or lose them and could never relax until they were returned safely to their owners. Nevertheless, he graciously accepted Laski's offering and began reading it almost as soon as his guests had departed.

Seaton's book was not actually about freedom of speech. It was about the struggle for religious freedom in late seventeenth-century England. Still, many of his conclusions applied to both subjects. He argued, for instance, that forced conformity of religious beliefs had largely failed, producing resentment and hypocrisy instead of genuine unity. He also argued that the natural appeal of persecution had diminished over time, as the Enlightenment ushered in an attitude of inquiry and skepticism. But unlike Hand, Seaton believed that skepticism alone was an insufficient basis for toleration. Even if we cast doubt on long-accepted beliefs, those who seek to impose them on us may feel strongly enough to take the chance of being wrong. The case for toleration must therefore have a positive aspect, appealing to the dignity of man and the quest for truth. For when "it is grasped that we have not the total sum of truth as a treasure to be guarded with fire and sword, but an infinitesimal portion of it to be increased, if possible, by zealous and humble search, the question assumes a different aspect," he wrote. "There can hardly be a nobler motive to toleration than the conception of the multitudinous religions of mankind contributing each its quota—infinitesimal it may be, but precious . . . to some vast synthesis of religious thought, aspiration, and experience at present beyond the limits of our narrow intellectual range."

Holmes was not religious himself. (Asked once why she and Holmes had joined the Unitarian Church, Fanny replied, "In Boston in those days one had to be something, and Unitarian was the least one could be.") He could best be described as agnostic since he disclaimed any knowledge one way or the other. But he was not insensitive to the cause of religious freedom. As an undergraduate at Harvard, he had joined a liberal, nonsectarian club called the Christian Union—not because he shared its members' faith but because he wanted to take a stand against a more orthodox group known as the Christian Brethren. In his sophomore year he contributed an essay to the campus literary magazine in which he railed against sectarian dogma: "A hundred years ago we burnt men's bodies for not agreeing with our religious tenets; we still burn their souls." And when he thought he was dying after being shot for the first time, at Ball's Bluff in 1861, "the reflection that the majority vote of the civilized world declared that with my opinions I was en route for Hell came up with painful distinctness." So Seaton's call for toleration—his appeal to "the dignity and prerogatives of the intellect"—resonated with Holmes, even if he was not fully persuaded. "I have read it with profit and pleasure," he told Laski when he returned the book at the end of the week. Although Seaton was somewhat tiresome "in his effort to secure precision at every step," the notion that even the humblest ideas can contribute to the search for truth "always is amusing."

Over the next month, Laski continued to feed Holmes a steady diet of progressive literature. There was *The Town Laborer* by J. L. and Barbara Hammond ("Sounds as if it might be a bore," Holmes wrote. "Is it?"), a biography of Isaac Causabon by the Reverend Mark Pattison ("An interesting picture of a poor, real scholar"), *The Nature of Peace* by Thorstein Veblen ("He is remarkable and stimulating, but I incline that you . . . over-rate him"), and *The History of Freedom and Other Essays* by Lord Acton ("I was instructed without delight"). Holmes diligently read each book, then noted it down in a black ledger he had kept for more than forty years. Finally, by mid-August he had had enough.

The book that pushed him over the edge was volume 2 of *Science et technique en droit privé positif* by the French scholar François Gény. Written in French and more than four hundred pages long, it summarized various theories of law advanced by jurists from Rudolf Stammler to Léon Duguit. Its primary emphasis, however, was on natural law—the theory that there are certain overarching principles that can be derived from reason and are true for all people at all times. Natural law—and the theory of natural individual rights it supports—had deep roots in Anglo-American jurisprudence. It provided the framework for the Declaration of Independence ("We hold these truths to be *self-evident . . .*") and served as the basis for the Supreme Court's rejection of progressive labor laws in the early twentieth century. Holmes, who had dissented from those decisions, thought it was drool. There are no absolute and universal laws, he believed, at least not that we can identify. There are only the decisions of courts. He had made this point most memorably in his celebrated essay "The Path of the Law," published in 1897. "If you want to know the law and nothing else," he had written, "you must look at it as a bad man, who cares only for the material consequences which such knowledge enables him to predict, not as a good one, who finds his reasons for conduct, whether inside the law or outside of it, in the vaguer sanctions of conscience."

That statement, with its insistence that law and morality are separate domains and that the former can be ascertained only by asking how the courts will rule, summed up Holmes's entire jurisprudential outlook. It was also the foundation upon which his reputation as a modern, visionary jurist rested. But in spite of the brilliance of his insight, the myth of natural law still exerted a powerful force, as Gény's book demonstrated. It was enough to spoil a pleasant day by the sea, and Holmes did not attempt to hide his irritation. "A lot of learned second raters they seem to me," he complained to Laski, "and I am tempted to write a short piece on the demand of man for the superlative and his foolish unwillingness not to believe that he is in on the ground floor with God. But I expect it will be only a companion of my walks and not get on to paper."

In fact, it did get on to paper. Shortly after dispatching his note to Laski, Holmes sat down at his desk "in a kind of rage" and drafted a response to Gény. It was not long, only a few pages, but it was forceful and passionate. And it weaved together many of the views he had expressed in letters and conversations for decades—a sort of greatest hits of Holmesian chestnuts. He was pleased with the result, not only for its substance but for its style, and when he and Fanny traveled to Rockport a few days later to dine at the Laskis' bungalow, he took the essay with him. The weather obliged this time: the sky was clear, the air mild. They sat on a terrace looking north across the harbor. To their left was the old T wharf, straining under the weight of the new cold-storage plant. Straight ahead lay Bearskin Neck, a hook-shaped sliver of earth lined with artists' studios and colorful fishing shacks. And to their right bulked the headlands, a rocky outcrop climbing up above the sea. As the sloops and schooners drifted past and a foghorn wailed in the distance, Holmes took out a thin sheaf of paper and began reading aloud to his host:

> It is not enough for the knight of romance that you agree that his lady
> is a very nice girl—if you do not admit that she is the best that God
> ever made or will make, you must fight. There is in all men a demand
> for the superlative, so much so that the poor devil who has no other
> way of reaching it attains it by getting drunk. It seems to me that this
> demand is at the bottom of the philosopher's effort to prove that truth
> is absolute and of the jurist's search for criteria of universal validity,
> which he collects under the head of natural law.

For ten minutes he continued in this vein, deriding the natural law's quest for absolutes and mocking its illusion of truth. "Certitude is not the test of certainty," he declared. "We have been cocksure of many things that were not so." "Deep-seated preferences cannot be argued about," he proclaimed. "You cannot argue a man into liking a glass of beer." "Men to a great extent believe what they want to," he avowed, "although I see in that no basis for a philosophy that tells us what we should want to want." But his attack was not limited to natural law. Widening his scope, he took aim at the entire field of moral absolutism. "Now when we come to our attitude toward the universe," he went on, "I do not see any rational ground for demanding the superlative—for being dissatisfied unless we are assured that our truth is cosmic truth, if there is such a thing—that the ultimates of a little creature on this little earth are the last word of the unimaginable whole. . . . Why should we employ the energy that is furnished to us by the cosmos to defy it and shake our fist at the sky? It seems to me silly."

When he finished, he folded the pages and put them away, slightly embarrassed at the length and vehemence of his monologue. He looked at Laski, waiting for a reaction. It was hard to know what his young friend would think. Certainly he would appreciate the attitude of skepticism and the combative, irreverent tone. But Laski had also shown a weakness for some of the very habits of thinking the essay skewered. Just eight months earlier, he had embraced Duguit's claim that the state is bound by legal principles superior to itself. "The truth is that we are witnessing a revival of 'natural' law," he had written to Holmes, "and 'natural' is the purely inductive statement of certain minimum conditions we can't do without if life is to be decent." Would he repeat the same rubbish now, insisting, as he had before, that there was more to Duguit and the rest of the second-raters than Holmes had allowed?

Of course not. Laski had an instinct about these things—he knew when to push and when to ease up. And now, relaxing on the terrace, breaking bread with his guests, a postcard view spread out before them, was not the time to push. Besides, he needed articles for the *Harvard Law Review*, which he was helping to edit while the students were away at war. "I do not mind the extent of your reflections, but I want that piece for the *Law Review*," he wrote to Holmes the next day. "I know a good thing when I see it. There are only two things of yours that, at first sight, have moved me so much. One is *The Soldier's Faith*; the other the 1913 address to the *Law Review* Association. And it is on a level with them both. Behind this, there is the full knowledge of how absurd it is for me to estimate what you write. However, judgment is inevitable when one loves deeply."

He could hardly have pleased the old man more. "Your letter moved me much," Holmes responded two days later. "As to my little piece I have copied it in the attempt to secure legibility for a cold world in which chirography seems to be an almost forgotten art. I shall keep it a day or two to see if minute tinkerments occur to me. . . . But I am settled in my wish to put the little titman into your hands."

The rest of the summer slipped pleasantly by. Holmes continued his regimen of reading, though he was done with "all the improving works on social themes that I mean to bother with." Instead he returned to the classics, reading a study of Virgil ("a good wallow among the flowers"), three books of the *Odyssey* ("with more pleasure than formerly"), *Othello* ("a rotten and repulsive play"), and *Hamlet* ("a bill filler"). He and Laski toured the old Garrison House in Pigeon Cove, which had sheltered woodcutters and fishermen from Indian raids during King Philip's War. And he received a visit from Frankfurter, who was back in Washington handling labor issues for President Wilson.

On September 17, he celebrated the anniversary of Antietam, where he had been wounded fifty-six years before. The injury was the second of three he sustained during the war and in some ways the one that brought him nearest to death. He was hit by a musket ball in the back of the neck while retreating from an ambush. It missed artery and spine by a fraction of an inch and passed straight through his throat, rendering him briefly unconscious. When he came to, the battle had moved on and the field was abandoned. He staggered to a farmhouse where the wounded had gathered. His friend and classmate Penrose Hallowell was there, his left arm badly shot up. As the two friends lay on the floor waiting for help, a Confederate soldier put his head through the window and tossed them a canteen of water. Fifteen minutes later the same soldier returned, on the run and out of breath. "Hurry up there!" he shouted. "Hand me my canteen! I am on the double-quick myself now!"

The first doctor who saw Holmes said the wound was not fatal, but later, when he had been moved to a hospital tent in Keedysville, the surgeon just shook his head. His job was to attend to those who had a chance, he told an officer, and Holmes had none. The officer, recognizing Holmes as the son of the famous writer, asked if there was anything *he* could do, to which the surgeon replied, "Wash off the blood, plug up the wound with lint, and give him this pill of opium." The treatment was successful. A few days later, Holmes was on his feet, a bandage around his throat, walking listlessly through the streets of Hagerstown. A kind family took him in, dressed his wounds, and kept him company until he was strong enough to catch the train to Harrisburg, where he was met by his father. "How are you, Boy," the father asked. "Boy, nothing," the son replied.

Holmes never forgot these events. He spoke and wrote about them often. When dignitaries came to Washington, he escorted them out to Maryland to see the battlefield. And each year, when September 17 appeared on the calendar, he commemorated the day with a toast to old comrades, living and dead. This year he hoped to mark the occasion with his newest comrade. But Laski was engaged, so Holmes and Fanny traveled down the coast to visit the old burial ground that overhangs Marblehead. They climbed to the top of the steep hill, its green slopes erupting with boulders. Above them loomed two sun-bleached obelisks, monuments to the heroes and casualties of the past. At their feet lay the graves of six hundred Revolutionary soldiers, many of them untended and unmarked. The headstones that survived were faded and falling over, as if being washed away by a slowly receding tide. But the view was inspiring. Above the maples and pines, they could see the sailboats moored in Dolliber Cove, their bare masts paying tribute to the dead. And as they strolled across the uneven ground, stepping carefully to avoid giving offense, Holmes thought again about his own escape from death and was filled with emotion.

Then the summer was over—"just as it seemed beginning," he

lamented to a friend. Why does time pass more quickly for the old, he wondered. Is it because old age is filled with thoughts, whereas youth is filled with events? Probably it is because the journey speeds up when the scenery is familiar. "Going out over a new road seems much longer than the return," he explained. "The terms of the Court did the same before I was accustomed to the work."

The servants closed down the house, and Fanny booked their return trip to Washington. They would travel straight through to the capital this time, not stopping in New York. On their last morning in Beverly Farms, a letter arrived from Laski. Holmes read it eagerly, then went into the study and penned a quick reply. "Your letter comes as we are departing, so this is but a word of adieu," he wrote. "You have added more than anyone to my pleasure this summer. I wish that we might have had more talks together, and am glad that I have begun to know your wife. . . . And so—goodbye for the present."

3

The Habit of Intolerance

When Holmes returned to Washington at the beginning of October, he was worried about the same thing as everyone else in America, and it wasn't the war. It was the flu. The virus that had passed through the country relatively unnoticed the previous spring had returned with a vengeance. It struck first in late August on the docks of Boston Harbor, where thousands of sailors slept each night on their way to and from distant ports of call. Within a few days it migrated to the city's civilian population and then to Camp Devens, an overcrowded army base thirty miles to the west, where it spread rapidly, infecting more than twelve thousand soldiers in two weeks. From there it blazed down the coast to the Mid-Atlantic region, then followed the railroad lines and rivers across the country—to the Midwest, the Gulf Coast, the Rocky Mountain states, and finally California and the Pacific Northwest. Aggressive and merciless, it came upon its victims suddenly, often in an hour or two, and knocked them off their feet. The lucky ones recovered after a week of severe aches, chills, and fever. But many people were not lucky. Fluid filled their lungs, blood leaked from their ears, and they died gasping for air. It was the worst pandemic in history, claiming three times as many lives as the war that was just winding down in Europe. In the United States, the death toll was more than five hundred thousand; worldwide, it was between fifty and one hundred million.

As an urban hub with a large wartime population and several military bases nearby, Washington was hit hard. At the peak of the crisis in mid-October, more than a thousand new cases were being reported each day—so many that doctors ran out of the index cards on which they were supposed to record them. An emergency hospital was built next to the National Mall, volunteer nurses treated the sick and dying in their homes, and a division of city workers did nothing but dig graves. One of the biggest problems was a shortage of coffins. Washington officials, responding to reports of price gouging, commandeered the city's supply and pressured local factories to build more. They also engaged in opportunistic behavior of their own, intercepting two railroad cars of coffins that were bound for Pittsburgh.

Holmes followed the situation closely. He had heard reports of the epidemic before leaving Beverly Farms and worried it might disrupt his trip back to the capital. He was also scared of catching the bug himself, a fear that quickened when his throat turned ticklish and his nose began to run at the end of September. He was lucky, though; it turned out to be just a cold, and not even a bad one at that. After a few days of rest and sparing his voice, he was back to his usual vigorous self.

In reality, he was never seriously at risk. One of the oddities of the 1918 virus was that, unlike most other strains, which fall hardest upon the young and old, this one was most deadly for those between the ages of twenty and forty. But Holmes took no chances when it came to his health. He had cut back on champagne and cigars years before and made sure to sleep at least eight hours a night. He also avoided going out in bad weather whenever possible. (Each time the presidential inauguration rolled around, he complained bitterly about having to sit "on the windswept platform where the old are killed every year by pneumonia.") He was equally concerned about the health of his young friends. He nagged Laski and Frankfurter to eat well, get plenty of rest, and not "run the machine too hard." And when a new secretary arrived from Cambridge each fall, he explained that his philosophy was "divided into two parts, each equally important: the first—keep your bowels open; and the second—well, the second is somewhat more complex and a part of your duties is to hear it during the next nine months."

His secretary for the 1918–19 term was Lloyd Landau, a Wisconsin native who had graduated first in his class from Harvard and was president of the *Law Review*. He had been selected by Frankfurter, who took over the job of hiring a new man each year after the death of Holmes's old friend John Chipman Gray. Unlike modern Supreme Court clerks, Holmes's secretaries had little responsibility. They looked up citations, summarized petitions for appeal, balanced Holmes's checkbook, and accompanied the justice on afternoon walks. Occasionally Holmes would read a decision aloud and ask whether his reasoning was clear. But the secretaries had almost no input into the substance or style of his opinions. Their main job was to keep the old man company and listen to his reflections on life and the law. It was for this reason that Holmes insisted they be single and childless. "If baby has the megrims," he told Frankfurter, "Papa won't have the freedom of mind and spirit that I like to find."

The first month of Landau's term was especially quiet. In response to the epidemic, the Court postponed oral arguments until the first Monday in November. There was still work to do—petitions to be reviewed, motions to be decided—but the pace was slower than usual, and Holmes took advantage of the lull. He organized his study, caught up on his correspondence, and reviewed the proofs for his essay on natural law. He noticed that one phrase echoed a line of Ruskin and winced at the thought of "dropping into some ready-made expression—it shows that one is not living through the sentence." Then he recalled the old superstition that an officer who survives several battles without so much as a nick is likely to be killed outright in the next one, and he decided to leave the phrase in "as a safeguard against greater miseries." Near the end of the month, a friend sent him a biography of Lincoln, which he read dutifully but reluctantly. "It seems to me artistically done," he told Pollock, "but I hate to read of those times." Far more pleasurable was a visit to the print rooms at the Library of Congress. The library was closed on account of the flu, but Holmes was given permission to browse through the collection. A pretty young lady waited on him—a granddaughter or niece of the Civil War general George Meade, he thought. She fetched the portfolios he requested, then sat with him as he turned over their contents. He resisted the urge to add to his collection that fall, having already invested more than he cared to on the Fourth Liberty Bond. But as he told Laski, it was heavenly to "wallow in potentialities."

The two friends did not see each other for several months, though they kept in touch by letter. As insurance against the flu, Laski had received one of the new vaccines being given to those most at risk. The inoculation was painful, and he was laid up in bed for nearly two weeks. Holmes fretted over his condition until Laski assured him that everything was fine. He was resting comfortably, he said, reading sentimental novels and frivolous magazines.

When the worst of the epidemic was over, the Court finally opened for business. The docket was backlogged, and the justices scrambled to catch up, hearing more than fifty cases in the first three weeks of November. There was a suit by the Associated Press against a rival for stealing its stories. (The Court sided with the AP over the dissents of Holmes, Brandeis, and Justice Joseph McKenna.) There was a case involving the Seamen's Act, which outlawed the practice of peonage. (The Court held that the law did not apply outside the United States, Holmes, Brandeis, and McKenna again dissenting, joined this time by John Hessin Clarke.) And there was a complicated antitrust suit that had taken five months to try in the lower court. The chief justice asked Holmes to write the opinion, which daunted him at first "and then, as five hundred times before, gradually shrank to the dimensions of a poodle, no longer diabolic except for the long windedness and confused argument of counsel."

There were also several cases on the docket concerning the Espionage Act. Although the lower courts had been struggling with questions about the law's validity for more than a year, the Supreme Court had not yet weighed in on the matter. If these cases caught Holmes's eye, he didn't mention them. But Laski did. Still convalescing in early November, he sent Holmes a short but suggestive note. "I see that you have some 'free speech' cases to listen to," he wrote, "so that the next few weeks won't be without excitement."

Laski was not the only one thinking about the Court's upcoming speech cases. Two hundred miles to the south, in an elegant Manhattan town house, the editors of the *New Republic* also had the subject on their minds. Founded just four years earlier, in 1914, the magazine had quickly become an influential voice in American politics. Its contributors included many of the leading writers and intellectuals of the day— John Dewey, George Santayana, Theodore Dreiser, H. G. Wells—and its thirty thousand readers were heavily concentrated in the halls of power in Washington and New York. Its point of view was progressive—it supported labor unions, higher taxes, women's suffrage, and the regulation of trusts—but its editors had a larger agenda as well. Unlike many reformers of the time, they did not believe in shrinking government and returning to a small-scale, Jeffersonian-style democracy. Instead they wanted to give the federal government *more* power to cope with the challenges of the Industrial Revolution and to ensure a fairer distribution of wealth. Their goals were essentially socialistic, but they preferred to be called nationalists because they wanted change to be driven by an enlightened middle class rather than by factory workers. And they were pragmatists, which meant they rejected the dogma of Marxism and the inevitability of violent revolution. In today's vernacular, they would be called liberal Democrats.

The leader of the magazine, Herbert Croly, was a shy, bespectacled man of forty-nine. The son of two journalists, he had studied at Harvard on and off for thirteen years without receiving a degree, then worked as an editor for an obscure architectural magazine. As he neared forty, however, he took a leave from his job to write down a few of the ideas he had been quietly forming over the past two decades. The result, published in 1909, was *The Promise of American Life*, a sprawling, ambitious work that claimed the "American experiment" had failed and that offered a detailed prescription for getting it back on track. Croly believed the nation's history was a struggle between the forces of agrarian individualism and economic centralization, represented by Thomas Jefferson and Alexander Hamilton, respectively. Unfortunately, according to Croly, the Jeffersonian forces had prevailed and fashioned a democracy of narrow self-interest. Croly wanted to reverse that victory. Instead of simply enforcing the negative rights of property and capital, he argued, government should actively promote the economic welfare of its citizens.

The Promise of American Life was a huge and unexpected success. Overnight, Croly transformed himself from an unknown architectural editor into one of the leading political theorists of his generation, embraced by such influential figures as Theodore Roosevelt and Willard Straight, a diplomat and businessman who had made his name brokering deals in China. It was Straight and his wife, Dorothy, heiress to the massive Whitney fortune, who suggested that Croly start a magazine to promote his ideas and then agreed to fund the venture themselves. They bought adjoining town houses on West Twenty-first Street and converted them into a magazine office, complete with a dining room where a French couple served exquisite lunches. Croly, meanwhile, sketched out the magazine's format, gave it a name, and assembled a staff. The first two editors he hired were Walter Weyl and Walter Lippmann, two rising young journalists who had also recently published important books (Weyl's *New Democracy* came out in 1912, Lippmann's *Preface to Politics* in 1913).

The plan was for the magazine to focus primarily on domestic issues, since that's where the editors' interests and experience lay. But that plan was soon thwarted. A few months before the first issue was published, war broke out in Europe and the editors were forced to turn their attention to international affairs. Consistent with their pragmatist philosophy, they resisted the extremes of dogmatic pacifism and knee-jerk militarism. Instead they endorsed Wilson's call for neutrality, while at the same time rejecting the lure of isolationism. When the sinking of the *Lusitania* made strict neutrality implausible, they argued for a policy of "benevolent neutrality" that favored the Allies yet still sought to keep the United States out of the conflict. But when Germany went back on its pledge to discontinue attacks on merchant

ships and Congress declared war on April 6, 1917, the magazine supported the decision wholeheartedly.

Like much of the rest of the press, the *New Republic* was initially
preoccupied with the details of raising an army and mobilizing a
nation. So when Congress passed the Espionage Act in early June, the
editors did not object. Conceding that some censorship was necessary,
they urged only that it be applied with wisdom and discretion. And
over the next few months, as the draft went into effect and federal
prosecutors began arresting the radicals and pacifists who spoke out
against it, the magazine continued to send mixed signals. Indeed,
based on a prominent article by Dewey, one might almost have thought
it supported the government's actions. Dewey voiced frustration with
those who continued to protest the war, arguing that they were out of
touch with reality and were forfeiting the opportunity to shape the
postwar world. He did not endorse the suppression of their views, of
course. But he expressed far less concern for their right of free speech
than for the damage they were inflicting on the progressive cause.

As the war stretched on, however, the persecution of dissenters
became more and more difficult to ignore. In the fall of 1917, the government launched a campaign against the Industrial Workers of the
World, a radical union better known as the Wobblies. Agents raided
forty-eight of its meeting halls across the country and arrested scores
of its members on charges of obstructing the draft. Encouraged by the
government's example, private vigilante groups carried out their own
crusade of harassment, spying on suspicious neighbors, tampering
with the mail, and searching homes without warrants. In some towns,
German sympathizers were tarred and feathered, and in Butte, Montana, a union organizer was dragged through the streets behind a car
and lynched. To make matters worse, in the spring of 1918 Congress
passed the Sedition Act, an amendment to the Espionage Act that made
it a crime to say anything "disloyal" or "scurrilous" about the country's
form of government, as well as anything intended to encourage resistance to the war against Germany, curtail the production of arms, or
obstruct the sale of bonds. Nearly two thousand indictments were
ultimately brought under the two laws, many based on the thinnest of

reeds. One person was convicted for forwarding a chain letter that advocated an immediate peace, another for making a movie that depicted British soldiers killing Americans during the Revolutionary War, and still another because she claimed that capitalists were profiting from the war. The punishments were often severe. At least two dozen people were sentenced to prison for twenty years, while many others received terms of five, ten, and fifteen years. Magazines and newspapers were targeted too. In addition to shutting down the *Masses*, the postmaster general censored more than fifteen other publications, including the *Nation*, the *Milwaukee Leader*, and the *New York Call*. He even threatened to block an issue of the *New Republic*.

The editors observed all this with increasing alarm but with some ambivalence about what to do. In the two years since Wilson's reelection, the magazine had become closely allied with his administration. Croly and Lippmann met weekly with Colonel Edward House, the president's foreign policy adviser, and both Lippmann and Weyl spent time working for the War Department (precursor to the Department of Defense). An editorial attacking the government's actions would not only draw the attention of the censors but also strain the magazine's relationship with the White House. Croly appealed to Wilson privately, telling him in a letter that the wave of suppression was dividing the country and making it hard for liberals to support his administration. But although Wilson reassured him that he too cared about civil liberties, he did little to rein in the excesses of his subordinates. Finally, after the arrest of the socialist leader Eugene Debs in June 1918, the staff of the magazine demanded that it take a firmer stand against censorship. Relenting, Croly agreed to solicit an article analyzing the situation from an expert on free speech.

The question was who that expert would be. In 1918 the First Amendment was still a relatively uncharted area of the law. Drafted by James Madison as part of the Bill of Rights, it had generated almost no public debate when ratified in 1791. Not until seven years later, when Congress passed the Sedition Act of 1798, banning "false, scandalous, and malicious" statements about the government, did the first interpretations of its meaning appear, and those interpretations differed wildly. The Federalists, who had introduced the Sedition Act as a way to silence their political opponents, argued that the First Amendment simply codified the common law of England. And because the common law encompassed the similar crime of seditious libel, they reasoned, the Sedition Act was perfectly constitutional. Madison, among others, disagreed. Defending a Virginia resolution that declared the act unconstitutional, he argued that the First Amendment was designed to check governmental abuses of power. Therefore, any law that insulated the government from criticism was necessarily invalid. The Federalists prevailed in the courts, as several judges upheld indictments under the act. But they were trounced in the election of 1800, losing the presidency and both houses of Congress. And when Thomas Jefferson took over the White House, he allowed the Sedition Act to expire and pardoned those who had been convicted under it.

For the next half century, the issue of free speech largely receded from view. Part of the reason was an 1833 Supreme Court ruling that the Bill of Rights applied only to the federal government, not to the states. This meant that if a state infringed on free speech, individuals could not challenge that action under the First Amendment. Federal restrictions on speech could still be challenged, of course, but the federal government at that time was far smaller than today, so laws conflicting with the First Amendment were actually quite rare. Even during the Civil War, federal officials largely refrained from curtailing speech. Although some of Lincoln's generals attempted to impose censorship in areas under their control, the president himself adopted a policy of restraint. Believing that the persecution of dissenters created more problems than it solved, he instructed his commanders not to arrest speakers "unless the necessity" for doing so was "manifest and urgent." When one general defied this order and arrested a newspaper editor in St. Louis, Lincoln wearily responded, "Please spare me the trouble this is likely to bring."

After the war, debates over free speech flared up sporadically. In the 1870s, controversy raged over the Comstock Act, a federal law that prohibited the interstate mailing of obscene material. Named after Anthony Comstock, a religious crusader turned postal inspector, the law was enforced against a wide range of material that Comstock found offensive, from birth control ads to anatomy textbooks to the plays of George Bernard Shaw. Critics mocked Comstock as a Victorian prude, but the courts overwhelmingly sided with him, ruling that the First Amendment did not protect speech harmful to the public morals. Three decades later, the battle for free speech moved to the streets. In a series of confrontations known as the free speech fights, cities across the country banned labor unions such as the Wobblies from spreading their message on sidewalks and street corners. A few public officials expressed sympathy for the plight of the Wobblies, including New York police commissioner Arthur Woods, who argued that all people were entitled to speak on the public streets. The courts took a different view, ruling that the preservation of order outweighed the Wobblies' interest in airing their views.

Perhaps most devastating to the cause of free speech was a 1907 Supreme Court case by the name of *Patterson v. Colorado*. An appeal from a Denver newspaper that had been fined for criticizing the Colorado Supreme Court, the case was fiercely contested. The newspaper claimed that its criticism was honest and fair, while the government argued that the paper had tried to pressure the state court into reversing a recent decision. The Court sidestepped these competing claims, ruling that they were questions of local law not within its jurisdiction. The only issue before the justices was whether the fine violated the First Amendment. And to that question, the Court offered a simple answer. Even if the rights of free speech and freedom of the press applied to the states (a doubtful proposition in light of the Court's 1833 ruling to the contrary), their main purpose was "to prevent all such *previous restraints* upon publications as had been practiced by other governments, and they do not prevent the subsequent punishment of such as may be deemed contrary to the public welfare."

With that statement, *Patterson* enshrined into law what was known as the Blackstonian view of free speech. According to William Blackstone, the preeminent English jurist of the eighteenth century and a major influence on colonial legal thinking, free speech "consists in laying no previous restraints on publications, and not in freedom from censure for criminal matter when published." In other words, individuals are not required to obtain government approval before speaking, but once they open their mouths (or take up their pens), all bets are off; they can be fined or jailed for the most innocuous comments. Blackstone's view was actually a significant breakthrough for civil liberties in England. For much of the seventeenth century, Parliament had operated a licensing system that banned any publication not approved by an official censor—a system that inspired Milton's famous plea for free speech in *Areopagitica*. To early twentieth-century progressives, however, the Blackstonian position seemed pinched and formalistic. What was the point of free speech if you could still be punished for anything you said? The government might as well appoint a censor, since at least then you would know ahead of time whether your words could land you in jail.

Thus, by the time Croly went looking for his expert, free speech in the United States was hardly more than a slogan, with little practical force. And its status among legal scholars reflected that reality. Most law schools did not offer courses on the First Amendment, and textbooks on constitutional law touched on it only briefly. A few civil libertarians had explored the subject more deeply, men like Theodore Schroeder, who helped establish the Free Speech League in the early 1900s. But Schroeder was a lightning rod who subscribed to a nearly absolutist view of the First Amendment, and the pragmatists at the *New Republic* did not believe in absolutes. They wanted a more credible author, someone who would approach the subject from a scholarly, detached perspective.

Their quandary was solved by Laski. Among the many people he had met and charmed at Harvard was a young law professor named Zechariah Chafee Jr. At first glance, Chafee was an unlikely spokesman for the cause of free expression. The scion of a wealthy Rhode Island family, he had helped manage his father's iron foundry for several years after law school before being hired to teach at Harvard. His specialty was business law, which consisted of dry, practical courses such as Insurance and Bills and Notes. However, he also taught a class called Equity, which examined the power of courts to go beyond the usual monetary remedies of the law and order a losing party to take, or refrain from taking, specific action. One of the questions the course posed was whether a judge could block the publication of a libelous statement—a question that turned, in part, on an understanding of free speech. Chafee knew almost nothing about the First Amendment at the time, so he studied the few cases he could lay his hands on. Then, as the war drew his attention away from business and toward the pressing issues raised by the Espionage Act, he began to read the decisions being handed down by federal courts across the country. One ruling in particular caught his attention. Written by a judge named Learned Hand, it argued that the new law should be interpreted narrowly so as not to chill political discussion. Chafee had never been an ardent defender of free speech himself. In law school he had signed a petition to boycott a Boston newspaper because of its political views, and in Providence he had lobbied to shut down a play about a young woman who leaves her department store job to become a rich man's mistress. (Chafee thought the play might "persuade real salesgirls to follow the heroine's example.") But the instinct to fight tyranny was in his blood: he was descended from the great Rhode Islander Roger Williams, who had dedicated his life to the cause of religious freedom. And Chafee had a patrician's sense of right and justice. "My sympathies and all my associations are with the men who save, who manage and produce," he once said. "But I want my side to fight fair."

Inspired by Hand's *Masses* opinion, Chafee decided to write an article for the *Harvard Law Review* challenging the government's suppression of speech. Laski, of course, was one of the *Review*'s editors, and when he heard about Chafee's plans he suggested that Croly ask him to write a shorter piece for the *New Republic*. Croly agreed and offered the young professor fifty dollars for an article on the constitutionality of the government's actions. The article should be written for the lay reader, he explained in a letter to Chafee, "although still dealing with the matter from the point of view of a professional lawyer."

When Chafee received Croly's letter, he was ecstatic. His real ambition in life was to be a writer, not a lawyer, and this was the first time someone had offered him money to write. He accepted the offer at once and spent the next month working diligently on the article. It was accepted with only minor revisions and appeared on November 16, 1918, under the straightforward title "Freedom of Speech."

The article began by attempting to show that the First Amendment did not adopt Blackstone's understanding of free speech but instead limited government's power to punish dissent both before and after the fact. This was no easy task. In addition to the Supreme Court's decision in *Patterson*, many state courts had embraced Blackstone in interpreting their own constitutional guarantees of free speech. But Chafee ignored these precedents and went straight to the constitutional source, arguing that the framers never meant to codify Blackstone's views. They had seen the way the British crown silenced its critics, he argued, and intended to make such suppression impossible in this country. And when the Federalist Party disregarded that intent, passing the Sedition Act of 1798, two of the most influential founding fathers, Jefferson and Madison, were quick to cry foul. Of course, there was a flip side to this argument. If the founding generation rejected the Blackstonian view, why did the Congress of 1798 pass the Sedition Act in the first place? Chafee did not consider this question, perhaps assuming that even the framers sometimes failed to follow their own principles. As far as he was concerned, he had routed Blackstone from the field.

That was only part of his goal. He also wanted to elucidate the purpose of free speech and show how the Espionage and Sedition Acts had undermined that purpose. His argument on this point was not especially novel, having been cribbed largely from Milton and the British philosopher John Stuart Mill, but he made it forcefully nonetheless. The purpose of free speech, he wrote, is the discovery and spread of truth, which "is possible only through absolutely unlimited discussion, for . . . once force is thrown into the argument, it becomes a matter of chance whether it is thrown on the false side or the true, and truth loses all its natural advantages." This didn't mean that speech could never be punished. Being a good pragmatist, Chafee acknowledged that "there are other purposes of government, such as order, the training of the young, protection against external aggression." Freedom of speech sometimes conflicts with these interests, he noted, and when it does the competing interests must be balanced against one another. But he made clear that "freedom of speech ought to weigh very heavily in the scale."

Did the Espionage and Sedition Acts get the balance right? Chafee argued that the 1917 Espionage Act, which prohibited obstructing the draft and causing insubordination, reached an acceptable balance because it was closely linked to military operations. As long as the law was applied only to speakers who *expressly* advocated unlawful conduct, as Hand had argued, it was within constitutional bounds. But the 1918 Sedition Act did not get the balance right. That act made it a crime to say almost anything against the war or even to make the case for peace. This was a grievous mistake, Chafee argued. "The pacifists and Socialists are wrong now, but they may be right the next time," he wrote. "The only way to find out whether a war is unjust is to let people say so."

Chafee ended his essay by invoking the tradition of free speech in England and America—a tradition that was not nearly as long and deep as he suggested. He noted that the Sedition Act of 1798 led to the ruin of the Federalist Party, that Lincoln resisted calls to punish disloyal newspapers during the Civil War, and that England fought both the Crimean and Boer Wars without persecuting those who opposed them. "We have made a mistake under the pressure of a great crisis," he concluded. "We should admit it frankly before intolerance becomes a habit in our law."

4

Catspawned

Although Chafee did not say so in his article, the justice who had written the Blackstonian view into Supreme Court case law in *Patterson v. Colorado* was none other than Holmes. He had been a justice only four years when that case came to the Court and had based his opinion on a ruling by the eminent jurist Isaac Parker, one of his predecessors on the Massachusetts Supreme Court. But while those circumstances might have given him cover to retreat from *Patterson*, he had never renounced the views he expressed in that case. Even the previous June, when he had objected to the conviction of a Toledo newspaper for maligning a federal judge, he relied on a federal statute, not the First Amendment.

So Chafee's article was in large part an attack on Holmes's views. And it appeared in one of the few publications he actually read. In fact, Holmes was an enthusiastic supporter of the *New Republic* and the men who edited it. He had read Croly's second book, *The Progressive Democracy*, when it was published in 1913 and wrote him a long letter filled with praise. He regarded Lippmann as "a monstrous clever lad," and Francis Hackett, the magazine's literary editor, as a genius. He also paid regular visits to the town house in Washington where many of the magazine's contributors lived and socialized. It was nicknamed the House of Truth, and Holmes often stopped in to join the men for dinner or a game of cards on his way home from court. He delighted in their youthful enthusiasm, their vitality, and their earnest intellectual pursuits. So what did he think when these same men published an article assailing his views on free speech?

No one knows. If the article bothered Holmes, he didn't say so, not in his letters to Laski, to Frankfurter, or to anyone else. His main concern in the weeks following its publication was how busy he was at work. But whatever he thought of the article, its argument soon became highly relevant. For at the very moment Chafee's piece was being mailed to subscribers, the justices were considering the first of the Espionage Act cases to reach the Supreme Court.

It was a peculiar case for the Court to begin with. The defendants were a group of twenty-seven socialists from a small farming community in South Dakota. Some were from Russia and some were born in the United States, but all were of German descent and modest means, and only a few spoke English. Like many other socialists, they were opposed to American involvement in the war, viewing it as a capitalist conspiracy against the working class. But they had a more specific complaint as well. When the draft quotas for each county were announced in the summer of 1917, the number for their county was higher than for neighboring counties. The reason for this was simple: more young men in those counties had voluntarily enlisted, which meant that fewer had to be forced into service. But the farmers thought they were being targeted for their political beliefs and German heritage. So they composed a petition and sent it to the governor, who was in charge of administering the draft. Brief and clumsily written, the petition demanded that the quota for each county be fixed without regard to the number of volunteers. It also demanded that the governor call a referendum on the draft and that he oppose the use of bonds to fund the war. Failure to meet these demands, the petition declared, "will spell sure defeat for you and your party and your little nation J. P. Morgan at the next election."

One might have thought the government had more important matters to attend to than a barely literate petition signed by a group of South Dakota farmers. After all, only the governor and two of his aides had seen the petition; it hardly posed a threat to the nation's war effort. But in August of 1917 one of the administration's biggest concerns was enforcing the recently enacted draft, which was about to be put to use for the first time. And it happened that the farmers lived in the same county as a large group of Mennonites who opposed the war on religious grounds. The Mennonites had already met with the governor to express their opposition to military service, and as the first draft call approached they made clear that their members would not cooperate. So quelling antidraft sentiment in the region had become a high political priority. And the farmers, who had signed their names to the petition, were an easy target. A few weeks after mailing their complaint to the governor, they were rounded up at their homes and charged with obstructing the draft. A jury wasted no time convicting them, and a federal judge sentenced them to one to five years in prison. Their only hope was an appeal to the Supreme Court, which at that time could take several years to run its course. But the attorney general, anxious to get the justices' approval of the Espionage Act, requested an expedited hearing, which is how *Emanual Baltzer et al. v. United States* became the first wartime speech case to reach the Court.

The hearing took place on Wednesday, November 6, 1918, just five days before the armistice. The Court did not yet have its own building so arguments were heard in the Old Senate Chamber of the Capitol, where Daniel Webster and John Calhoun had once clashed over nullification and where the abolitionist Charles Sumner had been beaten with a cane by an enraged Southern congressman. Modeled after the amphitheaters of antiquity, the chamber was semicircular, with a half-domed ceiling, pale gray walls, and a row of green marble columns supporting a second-story gallery. In front of the columns, on a raised dais, stood a long wooden bench and nine black chairs. Behind the center chair hung a red curtain, and on top of the curtain, clutching three arrows in its talons, perched a large gilded eagle. The lawyers sat at heavy wooden desks facing the bench, while the spectators assembled on leather pews that curved around the sides of the room. For notorious and high-profile cases, the court might be packed with members of the bar, congressmen, and a sprinkling of socialites. For a small-time criminal case like this, however, attendance was usually sparse.

A few minutes before noon, the Capitol police roped off the corridor outside the chamber and the justices emerged from a robing room across the hall. "Christ, what dignity!" Holmes once heard a tourist exclaim as they filed solemnly past in their long black robes. They entered a door to the right of the bench and took their seats as the marshal cried "Oyez, Oyez, Oyez. All persons having business before the Honorable, the Supreme Court of the United States, are admonished to draw near and give their attention, for the Court is now sitting. God save the United States and this Honorable Court!" Third in seniority, Holmes was seated to the immediate left of the chief justice, Edward Douglass White, a former lieutenant in the Confederate army and the only other member of the Court to have fought in the Civil War. A large bearish man with heavy jowls and tired eyes, White was the son of the former governor of Louisiana and had himself served in the U.S. Senate before his appointment to the bench. Though once enemies on the battlefield, he and Holmes were now good friends, united by their shared memories of the war. They walked home from court together most days, and on the anniversaries of each of Holmes's three combat injuries, White brought him a red rose to mark the occasion.

There were two other arguments on the calendar that day, and it was not until midafternoon that the chief justice called case number 320, *Baltzer v. United States*. Joe Kirby, the attorney for the defendants, rose first. A tall, thin man with a Lincolnesque beard, he was no stranger to the Supreme Court. Nineteen years earlier, he had appeared before the justices in this same chamber—not as a lawyer but as a defendant. Convicted of receiving stolen postage stamps from two of his clients, he appealed all the way to the high court, where he won a reversal on technical grounds. Since then he had returned to the Court three times, twice representing business clients and once on behalf of a man charged with sending obscenity through the mail. Originally from Iowa but now living in Sioux Falls, Kirby was one of the most successful and powerful lawyers in the state. He was self-educated, hardworking (the only time he took off was for Sunday morning mass), and always ready for a good fight. He once broke down a courtroom door after being locked out of a hearing, and when the power company planted a utility pole in front of his house, he grabbed an axe and chopped it down.

His strategy in *Baltzer* was what lawyers call the kitchen sink approach: throw in every claim possible and hope that one of them succeeds. He argued that the selection of the trial jury was flawed, that the judge excluded key evidence, and that the prosecutor made prejudicial comments about his clients. But his only plausible claim was that their convictions violated the First Amendment. His point here was surprisingly subtle. He did not rely solely on the amendment's guarantee of free speech; instead he also cited a less familiar but equally important provision: "the right of the people peaceably to assemble, and to petition the government for a redress of grievances." It was a shrewd tactic since most jurists agreed that the right to petition was broader than the right of free speech, and Kirby milked it for all it was worth. "No matter how poor in spelling, no matter how ill the penmanship, no matter how deficient in grammatical construction, or weak in thought," he told the justices, "if it is in truth and in fact a petition for redress of a grievance, real or imaginary, its authors who gathered together for the formation of the same are not amenable to the law."

Though clever, Kirby's argument was long and rambling, laden with extended quotes from ancient cases and yellowing treatises. A small clock above the bench showed the minutes ticking by—fifteen, thirty, forty-five, sixty—but in those days the Court was not so efficient and it was common for lawyers to speak for two, or even three, hours at a time instead of the thirty minutes allotted now. The justices sometimes interrupted to ask questions; mostly they just sat and listened. Some corrected proofs or wrote letters, some whispered to their colleagues, and some paced back and forth behind the bench.

Holmes was the only one who took detailed notes during oral argument. Leaning over a black copybook, he jotted down facts and citations to the record so that he could write the opinion quickly if the case was assigned to him. When he was satisfied he had everything he needed, he would lean back in his chair, close his eyes, and doze off until one of his colleagues nudged him awake.

Kirby was still talking when the court adjourned at 4:30, but was permitted to finish his presentation the next day. He was followed by the government's attorney, John Lord O'Brian, special assistant to the attorney general for war work. A graduate of Harvard College and Buffalo Law School, O'Brian had served as U.S. attorney for the Western District of New York for nine years before his current appointment. Although a Republican, he was active in progressive causes and believed strongly in free speech. However, he also had a job to do, part of which included enforcing the Espionage Act. So in spite of some misgivings about the law, he argued that it did not violate the First Amendment. To support this claim, he cited *Patterson v. Colorado*, the decision in which Holmes had adopted the Blackstonian view of free speech. If free speech was a guarantee only against prior restraints, O'Brian told the justices, the defendants had no case since they were punished *after* sending their petition to the governor. But even if the First Amendment went beyond Blackstone's understanding, the convictions should still be upheld. Freedom of speech was not a license to say anything one wished, O'Brian explained. The Constitution authorized Congress to raise troops and declare war, and if the defendants interfered with the exercise of those powers they could not avoid punishment by invoking the First Amendment. Nor did it matter that their interference took the form of a letter to the governor. What they were forbidden to do through actions or spoken words, they were equally forbidden to do through a formal petition.

When O'Brian and Kirby were finished, the chief justice thanked them for their time and submitted the case for decision. The justices did not cast their votes at once, however. In keeping with tradition, they waited until the Saturday conference at which they discussed all the cases that had been argued during the previous week. It was held in a small, windowless room on the ground floor of the Capitol, just down the hall from the Senate barber shop. The justices arrived at 10:00 a.m., shook hands with one another (also a tradition), and took their seats around a large table. In earlier years a group of pages sat on a nearby leather sofa, ready to fetch water and cigars or run errands for the justices. But after reports of a leak in 1909, the pages were banned from the room, and the only people allowed inside now were the nine members of the Court.

For Holmes, the conferences were the most tedious part of the job. He enjoyed the challenge of working through the issues in a case, but he disliked the bickering and grandstanding that many of the justices engaged in. Much of this was the fault of White. Though generally an effective chief justice, he set a poor example at conference, sometimes speaking for an hour straight and roaring loudly across the table to stress a point. By 4:00 p.m., when they adjourned, everyone was tired and tense. "We waste two thirds of the day in solemnly spouting our views and our differences," Holmes complained to a friend. "But it is usage and not without a touch of pompous impressiveness."

When the Court debated *Baltzer* that Saturday, the outcome quickly became clear: in spite of some reservations on the part of Brandeis, a majority agreed with the government and voted to uphold the convictions. The justices noted the result in their docket books, then moved on to a complicated railroad dispute between the state of Georgia and the Cincinnati Southern. Later that night, White drew up the writing assignments and sent them around by messenger. He assigned the opinion in *Baltzer* to Joseph McKenna, a California centrist. Holmes got the railroad case.

Over the next month the Court continued to dig itself out from under a crippling backlog, and *Baltzer* faded into the background. Holmes issued his railroad opinion (he sided with the Cincinnati Southern), and the Court took a two-week recess so the other justices could finish their decisions. But when McKenna circulated his draft opinion to the Court in early December, Brandeis was troubled. He wanted the Court to delay a ruling in *Baltzer* until it heard the remainder of the Espionage Act cases in January. And if that wasn't going to happen, he wanted to make sure there would be a powerful dissent to cast doubt on the majority's view. So he did what he often did in such circumstances: he called on his good friend Holmes.

They had known each other for forty years, ever since Brandeis graduated from Harvard Law School and formed a partnership with Samuel Warren, a young associate from the firm of Shattuck, Holmes, and Munroe. Holmes drank champagne and beer with the two men on the night Brandeis was admitted to the bar, and Brandeis helped to raise money for the professorship that Holmes briefly occupied at Harvard. After that, their careers diverged. While Holmes toiled away on the Massachusetts bench, riding circuit to backwoods courthouses and churning out hundreds of mostly insignificant opinions, Brandeis built a successful commercial practice, representing paper companies, real estate developers, manufacturers, and banks. With his mastery of detail and his insistence on serving not just as a hired gun but as a counselor to his clients, he developed a reputation as one of the ablest lawyers in the country. He also got rich, earning his first million by the age of fifty and taking his seat among the Boston aristocracy. Then, when his fortune was secure, he threw himself into progressive causes on behalf of labor and the poor. In his abhorrence of trusts, his support for unions, and his pursuit of the public good, Brandeis had much in common with the reformers at the *New Republic*. But whereas they wanted to combat economic inequality by expanding the size of the federal government, Brandeis opposed largeness of any kind, whether in the private or the public sphere. He thought it sapped the democratic spirit and undermined individual freedom. He also believed that most large institutions, instead of becoming more efficient, simply became tired and unwieldy—a view reflected in his 1934 book, *The Curse of Bigness.*

If Brandeis wanted others to scale back their endeavors, however, he was unwilling to limit his own. As a reformer, he was bold and ambitious, seeking not just to root out corruption but to bring about systemic change. He was also tireless, sending letters to newspapers, giving speeches, meeting with potential allies and foes, and commanding a host of lieutenants in the field. He did most of this work for free, explaining that just as corporations have attorneys to represent their interests so also the people should have someone to represent them. For this reason, he became known as the People's Attorney, a Robin Hood of the law, and progressives around the country embraced him. But not everyone viewed his efforts in such heroic terms. To the Boston establishment, the Back Bay gentry and State Street bankers, Brandeis was an unscrupulous zealot, a man who had weaseled his way into their parlors and boardrooms only to turn against them once he had made his name.

As that name grew, Brandeis became increasingly active in politics. Raised a Republican, he abandoned the party of Lincoln in the 1880s when it fell under the control of big business. Not yet prepared to join the Democratic Party, he allied himself instead with the Mugwumps, a reform-minded movement that opposed the spoils system and promoted honest, efficient government. He supported Roosevelt and Taft in the first decade of the twentieth century, but after meeting with Woodrow Wilson in the summer of 1912 he officially became a Democrat. Brandeis played a key role in Wilson's victory, drafting his antitrust policy, writing magazine articles, and giving stump speeches on his behalf. By the time Wilson took up residence in the White House, Brandeis was one of his most trusted advisers, making the short list for both attorney general and secretary of commerce. Still, it surprised everyone when Wilson nominated him to the Supreme Court in 1916, the first Jew ever to achieve that distinction.

For Holmes, Brandeis's arrival in the capital was a godsend. Although he was friendly with the chief justice, he felt little connection with the other members of the Court. They seemed rigid and uninspired to him, oblivious to the deeper currents of thought coursing through the law. Brandeis was different. A brilliant student, he had graduated first in his class at Harvard with a record that was not surpassed for eighty years. His mind was powerful and expansive, crammed with all variety of useful data and information. And though they differed in outlook—Brandeis was an idealist, Holmes a skeptic—both believed that law should keep pace with changes in society and that judges should not impede this evolution. It was natural, then, that they would become allies on the bench and friends off it. Indeed, Brandeis quickly became Holmes's closest companion on the Court, conferring with him on cases and dropping by during adjournments to check up on him. He also began to influence Holmes's decisions, nudging him gently to the left on a range of issues. Not surprisingly, Holmes's Brahmin friends back in Boston resented this and wondered whether he was still "thoroughly Anglo-Saxon." Even Fanny snubbed Brandeis, rarely inviting him to the house and making no effort to befriend his wife. But Brandeis was undeterred. He respected Holmes too much to write him off as one of the ossified members of the Court. He also needed Holmes to help confer legitimacy on his untraditional views. And so whenever he wanted to challenge a ruling but worried that his own voice would not be authoritative enough, he paid a visit to Holmes, as he had done in the Toledo newspaper case the previous June.

And as he did now with *Baltzer.* It was Tuesday, December 3, the second week of the recess. Holmes was at home with Fanny, looking forward to a rare day of leisure after a spasm of work and repeated trips to the dentist. He slept late, enjoyed a simple lunch, and began a letter to Laski. Suddenly the calm was shattered. One of Fanny's cousins arrived, with sister, babies, and servants in tow. The phone began to ring. And then, in the middle of the confusion, Brandeis appeared, hat in hand, hoping to have a word about *Baltzer.* Holmes invited him up to the study, and they talked alone for half an hour. When they were finished, Brandeis bowed good-bye to the ladies and Holmes went back to his letter.

"A whirlwind struck me in the middle of the last sentence," he explained to Laski. "It has taken the wind out of me, esp. as when I can get calm I am catspawned by Brandeis to do another dissent on burning themes—and half an hour ago I was at peace!"

In spite of his later reputation as the Great Dissenter, Holmes did not generally relish the prospect of dissenting. He would often return an opinion to its author with a note that he disagreed but would "shut up" rather than make his disagreement public. In part this reflected a concern for the credibility of the Court that all its members shared: if the justices could not agree among themselves, why should the public accept their decisions as correct? But Holmes's reluctance to dissent also stemmed from a personal dislike of friction, as well as a tendency to view cases as mere abstract puzzles in which the specific outcome mattered less to him than the larger questions of legal theory involved.

Still, he was not scared to dissent when the spirit moved him, and for one reason or another he felt moved today. Perhaps it was because Brandeis had stated his case with such clarity and vigor, as he was known to do. Or perhaps the arguments of Laski and Hand in support of tolerance were beginning to sink in. Whatever the cause, Holmes yielded to Brandeis's plea and dashed off a dissent in a few hours. As usual, it was short and to the point. The evidence against the defendants was thin, he said. They had done nothing more than sign a petition to the governor seeking a change in the law. Their action was not an obstruction of the draft; it was merely "the foolish exercise of a right." "From beginning to end the changes advocated are changes by law, not in resistance to it, the only threat being that which every citizen may utter, that if his wishes are not followed his vote will be lost." As Holmes wrote, his argument became more forceful, his words more impassioned, and he concluded with a grand, sweeping flourish:

Real obstructions of the law, giving real aid and comfort to the enemy, I should have been glad to see punished more summarily and severely than they sometimes were. But I think that our intention to put out all our powers in aid of success in war should not hurry us into intolerance of opinions and speech that could not be imagined to do harm, although opposed to our own. It is better for those who have unquestioned and almost unlimited power in their hands to err on the side of freedom. We have enjoyed so much freedom for so long that perhaps we are in danger of forgetting that the bill of rights which cost so much blood to establish still is worth fighting for, and

that no tittle of it should be abridged. I agree that freedom of speech
is not abridged unconstitutionally in those cases of subsequent
punishment with which this court has had to deal from time to
time. But the emergency would have to be very great before I could
be persuaded that an appeal for political action through legal chan-
nels, addressed to those supposed to have power to take such action
was an act that the Constitution did not protect as well after as
before.

This was different from the tone he had taken with Laski and Hand
that summer. Gone was talk of killing those who disagree with us or
treating speech like any other act we dislike. Holmes now put his eloquence to work on behalf of tolerance, invoking spilled blood and
arguing for not a tittle of abridgment. So stirring was the performance
that one might have been tempted to read it as an about-face, a renun-
ciation of all that he had said before. Except that it wasn't. Buried there
in the second-to-last sentence was a key stipulation, which made clear
that however far Holmes had come in his thinking about the First
Amendment, he still had a long way to go. "I agree that freedom of
speech is not abridged unconstitutionally in those cases of subsequent
punishment with which this court has had to deal from time to time,"
he wrote. *Those* cases? As in *Patterson v. Colorado*, the case in which
Holmes had embraced the Blackstonian view of the First Amendment
and relegated freedom of speech to a meaningless formality? If he was
not admitting that *Patterson* was wrong, exactly what freedom was he
defending? Apparently the freedom to write letters to the governor.
"The emergency would have to be very great," Holmes allowed, before
that could be made a crime.

When he finished writing, Holmes sent his pages to the Court's
printer, then circulated a clean copy to his colleagues and waited anxiously for their response. Justice Pitney was not persuaded. "I submit
with great respect that this reads as if it proceeded from the heart
rather than from the head," he wrote back. "P.S. Not a bad fault, but a
fault nonetheless." Brandeis, naturally, was on board. "I gladly join
you," he wrote that Thursday, two days after his visit. And at least one

other member of the Court also agreed with Holmes. "Please state me as joining," scrawled the chief justice in a hurried hand.

What occurred next is one of the strangest episodes in Supreme Court history. Less than a week after Holmes circulated his dissent to the other justices (and before the Court announced its decision), the government unexpectedly confessed error in the case and asked that it be sent back to the lower court for a new trial. This was a stunning development. For the government to confess error after a conviction is unusual enough; for it to do so after a case has been briefed and argued before the Supreme Court is so rare as to demand some explanation. Yet the government offered none, at least not publicly. It said only that the confession was based on technical errors at trial and not on any rights guaranteed under the First Amendment.

So what happened? In a private memo explaining the decision, Solicitor General Alexander King wrote that "upon examination" his office had determined that the evidence against the defendants was insufficient and that the trial was marred by errors. Had his office not requested a dismissal, he added, the Court likely would have reversed the convictions and issued an opinion "that might prove embarrassing in other cases." But that explanation doesn't quite add up. Not once since the defendants were found guilty had the government indicated the slightest doubt about the sufficiency of the evidence or the integrity of the trial. Indeed, the errors alleged by Kirby were transparently baseless, and the government had rightly brushed them aside in its brief. It also seems unlikely that O'Brian heard something at oral argument that made him nervous about the government's chances of winning, since a majority of the Court initially voted in its favor. Instead, the government must have been rattled by something that happened after the argument. More precisely, it must have been rattled by some*one*—someone who knew that Holmes had written a dissent, joined by Brandeis and the chief justice, and who suggested, improbably, that enough justices might change their votes before the decision was announced to turn the dissent into a majority opinion.

Who would have done that? With the new security measures adopted at the weekly conference, the only people who could have known about Holmes's dissent were the justices' secretaries, the messengers who carried their notes back and forth, and the employees at the private company that printed the Court's opinions. And according to a 1919 *New York Tribune* article on alleged leaks at the Court, all of these individuals were completely trustworthy. The secretaries, it reported, "are men who have been carefully chosen, and are supposed to be beyond corruption," while the messengers, many of whom had served the justices for decades, "are considered as much above reproach as the court itself." As for the Court's printing firm, it had handled more than fifteen thousand cases over a period of sixty-five years without a whiff of controversy. "No responsible attaché of the house would any more think of willingly violating the court's confidence or of failing to take every precaution to protect it than he would think of committing the unpardonable sin against the Holy Ghost," the *Tribune* confidently announced.

Even if one were less sanguine about human nature than the *Tribune*, it does seem unlikely that any of these men could have been the government's source. As every detective knows, a culprit needs more than opportunity; he also needs means and motive. And it is hard to see what motive a secretary, messenger, or printer would have had for tipping off the government that Holmes was writing a dissent in an obscure criminal appeal from South Dakota. In fact the only person who would appear to meet all three criteria is the one who started the entire chain of events in motion: Brandeis. He knew about Holmes's dissent, so he had the opportunity. And he was unhappy with the Court's vote in *Baltzer*, so he had a motive. As for means, no one on the Court had greater access to the Wilson administration than Brandeis. Even after his appointment to the bench, he stayed in regular contact with many high-ranking officials—Treasury Secretary William Gibbs McAdoo, War Secretary Newton D. Baker, Food Administrator Herbert Hoover—and was consulted by Wilson on a range of matters. Just that summer, the president had asked him to review the country's policy toward Turkey and Bulgaria, an assignment that many critics thought inappropriate for a Supreme Court justice. Perhaps most incriminating, Brandeis had strong connections to the Department of Justice, the very agency that was overseeing the *Baltzer* case. He was a good friend of Attorney General Thomas Watts Gregory, with whom he frequently met to discuss departmental business. In fact, the two men had dined together the night before Brandeis "catspawned" Holmes into writing his dissent. Brandeis was also close with John W. Davis, who had stepped down as solicitor general only weeks before to become ambassador to England. And Davis visited Brandeis at his house the very day that Brandeis called on Holmes. Finally, Brandeis was a mentor to another lawyer in the solicitor general's office, a young man named Robert Szold, who was active in the Zionist Organization of America, of which Brandeis was the de facto leader. Not only did Szold work for the solicitor general but according to internal government memos he was one of two lawyers who had written the government's brief in *Baltzer*. Brandeis and Szold had already communicated that year about Zionist activities, so it would have been easy for Brandeis to casually mention Holmes's dissent and to suggest that the government voluntarily dismiss the case.

If Brandeis did intervene, it would not have been the first (or last) time he pushed the bounds of judicial propriety. Shortly after his confirmation to the Court, he had recruited Frankfurter to work as his paid lieutenant in Washington, promoting various liberal initiatives and helping place friends and allies in important government posts. He also ruled on several measures about which he had previously advised Wilson, including the government's takeover of the railroads. And years later, he used the threat of judicial review to influence the course of important New Deal legislation, discouraging Roosevelt from adopting policies that conflicted with his own economic views.

Whatever the story behind the government's confession of error in *Baltzer*, the outcome is undisputed. A week later, the Court issued a one-line order reversing the defendants' convictions and remanding the case to the lower court for a new trial. The Justice Department then instructed the U.S. attorney for South Dakota, Robert P. Stewart, to dismiss the charges, and the case disappeared as if it had never happened.

Holmes was satisfied with how things turned out, even if he was ignorant of what had gone on behind the scenes. When he put together a bound volume of the year's opinions for his personal library, he included a copy of the *Baltzer* dissent, along with the following note: "After opinion written by McK but before delivery Gov't asked to restore to docket and on Dec. 16, 1918 confessed error." Both his dissent and that note remained hidden in his papers for the next seventy years. And they might never have been discovered had the story ended there.

5

The Old Ewe and the Half-Bakes

As 1918 came to a close, life in Washington slowly returned to normal. The fighting ended, the epidemic receded, and the deep gloom that had hung over the city for two years finally lifted. The capital would never again be the intimate, leisurely place it had been before the war. Many of the young men and women who had come to town for temporary jobs decided to stay permanently. New apartment buildings rose above the tree line, old neighborhoods were plowed under, and speculators poured money into the fast-growing business district. The city was also on the verge of one of the worst periods of social unrest in its history. In the year to come, it would be racked by racial violence, labor disputes, terrorist attacks, red-baiting, fearmongering, and a bitter struggle over the nation's role in the postwar world. But for now at least, the overriding emotion was one of relief, even for someone as detached from events as Holmes. "The horrible nightmare that has ridden us so long seems driven off," he told Laski, who finally recovered from his inoculation and came to visit shortly before Christmas. "Though in dealing with the Germans eternal distrust seems necessary—at least distrust until they are tied so tight they can't wiggle."

The Court adjourned for the holidays, and Holmes, having completed his opinions, used the break to catch up on books. He plowed through *Eminent Victorians* by Lytton Strachey ("off my beat"), *Other People's Money and How the Bankers Use It* by Brandeis ("impressive"), and *The Ideals of the East* by Okakura Kakuzo ("a big, little book"). A female acquaintance tried to persuade him of the superiority of the Oriental mind, but Holmes was unconvinced. "I said, Produce the documents," he reported to a friend. "I can show you a hundred, I dare say many hundred Western books that seem to me to touch life and the world at more points and in a profounder way than anything I know of the East." He also found time to visit his favorite print shop across the street from the British embassy. He was joined there by Admiral Charles "Shaky" Davis, brother-in-law to Senator Henry Cabot Lodge. They called themselves The Club—"a club of two with Miss Biddle often looking in and sitting between us." No longer obligated to invest in war bonds, Holmes splurged on a print by Adriaen van Ostade he had been eyeing for two years. It depicted a peasant family saying grace over a bowl of porridge and was so poignant it made him want to cry. "It has the line of piety that Millet got in his Angelus—but so simple, so unconscious, so immediately sympathetic. I mean you don't feel that Ostade was seeing himself sympathize."

The break was short-lived. In the January issue of the *Illinois Law Review*, a legal scholar named John M. Zane lashed out at Holmes in an article entitled "A Legal Heresy." Zane took as his starting point a decision Holmes had authored twelve years earlier in a property dispute involving the territory of Hawaii. Explaining why an individual could not sue the government to recover land, Holmes had written that "there can be no legal right as against the authority that makes the law on which the right depends." That statement was part of Holmes's broader philosophy that natural rights do not exist and that law is the creation of the sovereign, not vice versa. To Zane it was heretical, the kind of thinking that paved the way for tyranny and had led to the recent slaughter in Europe. "If that is the point which we have reached," he wrote, "we may as well apologize at once to Germany for daring to question the divine right of government to override every law, contritely confess *nostram culpam, nostram maximum culpam*, and start anew on a truly Hegelian basis; for the divine right of government is simply the divine right of kings writ large."

The article was not just an attack on Holmes's philosophy, which Zane declared "indefensible." It was also an attack on Holmes. "To comprehend why it is that Holmes should have made his remarkable statement it is necessary to study him as a human document," Zane wrote. And what did that study reveal? "He is a master of epigrammatic expression, of vivid and illuminating thought"; "a man of letters" and of "unvarying and genial courtesy"; "a new kind of judge" who quotes Ruskin and refers to Velásquez, Whistler, Goya, and Rembrandt. "But epigrams," Zane added, "are either half-truths or not truths at all." And in spite of Holmes's peerless style and undeniable cultivation, there was something facile and careless about his work. "He does not think through a difficult matter to the end, nor does he always examine his authorities with scrupulous care." Even his landmark book *The Common Law* was filled with "hasty and ill-founded" generalizations. In short, Zane concluded, Holmes was a study in potential unfulfilled, expectations unmet. "Is it not a pity," he asked, "that Justice Holmes with all his great learning and splendid gifts just falls short of what as a judge he might have been?"

Reading those words in January, Holmes was deeply stung. Here was another critic who sought to deny him a seat in the pantheon, who failed to recognize the depth and originality of his thought. Hurt turned to anger and boiled over in letters to his friends. "John M. Zane has been walking into me for believing that the lawmaker is not bound by his own laws," he wrote. "I suspect he means a different thing than I do by the law and that the fight is more about words than he thinks. But there is a real difference expressed by him in a tone of dogmatism which I should not venture, although I think I could smash him if he would say what he thought and not only what he didn't believe."

Perhaps most galling was Zane's swipe at *The Common Law*, Holmes's one sustained contribution to legal scholarship and the work he was most proud of. Published in 1881, *The Common Law* was unlike any other legal book that had appeared on this side of the Atlantic.

Most American legal treatises were either haphazard collections of cases or pseudoscientific efforts to prove that the rules laid down by courts flowed logically from accepted postulates. Holmes rejected both approaches and instead set out to trace the historical roots of various common law subjects, such as torts, contracts, property, and criminal law. His reason was twofold. First he wanted to show that, in each of these areas, the law had progressed from a concern with moral fault (did the defendant have a bad heart?) to a focus on objective standards (did the defendant exercise the care of a reasonable person?). He also wanted to make a larger point about the nature and development of law. In his research on early legal systems, Holmes had noticed that many ancient rules survive even after the original justification for them disappears—"just as the clavicle in the cat tells only of the existence of some earlier creature to which a collarbone was useful." When this happens, he explained, judges often look for a new rationale suited to the times and then adapt the old rule to fit the new justification. But this process is largely unconscious and unseen, which is why efforts to make sense of the law from a purely logical perspective will always end in confusion. In order to truly know the law, he argued, we must study the interplay between history and the evolving needs of society. "The life of the law has not been logic; it has been experience," he announced in the book's famous opening paragraph. "The felt necessities of the time, the prevalent moral and political theories, intuitions of public policy, avowed or unconscious, even the prejudices which judges share with their fellow men, have had a good deal more to do than the syllogism in determining the rules by which men should be governed."

Holmes had worked out many of these ideas in a series of essays in the *American Law Review* in the late 1870s. But it was not until he was invited to deliver the prestigious Lowell Lectures in Boston, in 1880, that he decided to expand the essays into a book. He slaved over the effort for more than a year, ignoring his legal practice, neglecting his wife, and risking his health to complete the job before he turned forty. He had a superstition that if a man has not made his mark by that age, he never will. Holmes beat the deadline, barely. He received the book from the printer on March 3, 1881, just five days before his fortieth birthday. He and Fanny celebrated with a bottle of champagne, then waited for the reviews to come in. They were not quite what he had hoped for. A few American journals mentioned the book favorably, including the *American Law Review*, which devoted seven pages to the work of its former editor. But the *Nation* faulted its "tediously discursive and aimless air," and even the *Law Review* complained that "the reasoning in some cases is so very elliptical that it becomes almost obscure." Only the British notices fully satisfied Holmes. The *Spectator* described his book as "the most original work of legal speculation which has appeared in English since the publication of Sir Henry Maine's *Ancient Law*." And a young Pollock, writing in the *Saturday Review*, predicted that it would become "a most valuable—we should almost say a most indispensable—companion to the scientific study of legal history." Pollock's praise earned him a friend for life, and his prediction was borne out over the next few decades as the book attained the status of a classic. Yet there were still detractors and nitpickers, people like Zane who overlooked the book's larger contribution in an effort to show that it was riddled with flaws.

"I don't know whether it has serious ones or how many," Holmes griped to Laski, "but I think the material thing to be that I gathered the flax, made the thread, spun the cloth, and cut the garment—and started all the inquiries that since have gone over many matters therein. Every original book has the seeds of its own death in it, by provoking further investigation and clearer restatement, but it remains the original and I think it already is forgotten how far that is true of the C.L."

When Laski read Zane's article, he was furious. "It is not merely that the man is ignorant, he is also insolently ignorant," he wrote to Holmes. He had discussed the matter with Roscoe Pound, the dean of Harvard Law School, and both men agreed that something should be done. If Holmes did not object, he said, Pound was eager to publish a response to Zane in the *Harvard Law Review*. "I think I shall tilt at him in the *Yale Law Journal* and see that he gets properly pulverised," Laski added. "As Cicero might have written to Atticus—what a stinker!"

Laski and Pound never did follow through on their plan. Possibly they were dissuaded by Holmes, who suggested that Zane be handled with wit, not wrath. "A man who calls everyone a damn fool is like a man who damns the weather," he explained. "He only shows that he is not adapted to his environment, not that the environment is wrong."

In any event, Holmes had more pressing business to attend to. When the Court returned from its holiday recess, it once again faced a barrage of difficult cases. There was a challenge to a federal law that banned the transportation of liquor through dry states, a long-running dispute over mining claims in Montana, and a suit arising out of a traffic accident in the Panama Canal Zone. There were also four more appeals testing the validity of the Espionage Act. In their broad outlines, the four cases were nearly indistinguishable: the defendants in each were socialists who had spoken out against the war and been charged with inciting disloyalty in the military or obstructing the draft. But each case had its own history and context, and each arrived at the Court as a separate matter requiring its own resolution.

First on the docket was *Schenck v. United States*, an appeal from Charles Schenck and Elizabeth Baer, two fervent and starry-eyed officers of the Socialist Party of Philadelphia. Schenck, a small, nervous man of forty-five, was general secretary, while Baer, a gray-haired spinster and practicing physician, served on the executive committee. Neither had been arrested before, and neither had a reputation for espousing violent or seditious ideas. (In her failed run for Congress in 1916, Baer's most radical proposal was the creation of community kitchens to relieve the drudgery of housework.) But both opposed the draft and had overseen the publication of a leaflet attacking its constitutionality. Printed on cheap paper in heavy black ink, the leaflet was titled "Long Live the Constitution of the United States" on one side and "Assert Your Rights" on the other. It quoted the Thirteenth Amendment's ban on slavery, compared conscripts to convicts, and encouraged readers to write to their congressmen requesting repeal of the draft. It also advised those who were against the war to register as conscientious objectors, urging them not to be intimidated by flag-waving politicians or the capitalist press. "If you do not assert and support your rights," the document stated, "you are helping to deny or disparage rights which it is the solemn duty of all citizens and residents of the United States to retain." Some of the flyers were sent to draftees, and when the postal inspector spotted them in the mail he led a raid on the party's downtown bookstore. There, in a cluttered back office, he found several thousand copies of the leaflet, tied up with string and stacked on tables and chairs. He also found a black notebook implicating both Schenck and Baer in the mailings. They were charged with conspiracy to cause insubordination and obstruct recruiting, convicted by a jury, and sentenced to six and three months in jail, respectively.

Next up was Abraham Sugarman, a sickly twenty-two-year-old from Minneapolis with a pockmarked face, bulging eyes, and a missing right hand. The son of Russian immigrants, Sugarman was a clerk by day and an organizer for the Socialist Party by night. His conviction rested on a speech he gave in Kelso, Minnesota, during the summer of 1917 when the first wave of men was being called up for the draft. A group of farmers, worried that their sons might be shipped off to France, had telephoned the party requesting a speaker, and the party, in turn, had sent a telegram to Sugarman with instructions to make the sixty-mile drive down to Kelso. Word of the visit spread quickly through the small town, and by the time Sugarman arrived, shortly before 11:00 p.m., a crowd of five hundred had gathered in a field behind the town hall. Standing in an open automobile under the glare of an outdoor lamp, the young organizer launched into his standard recruiting pitch, extolling the value of collective ownership and invoking the natural rights of the working man. Soon he turned to the war, telling his audience that it was being fought for the benefit of the rich, that Wilson was pals with Rockefeller and J. P. Morgan, and that the people had never been given a say in the matter. He also took aim at the draft, suggesting vaguely that it was unconstitutional and would surely be overturned by the Supreme Court. In the meantime, he urged the crowd to sign a petition to Congress demanding its repeal. When one of his listeners asked what they should do if called up for duty, Sugarman was initially evasive, saying only that if they refused to serve, "you know what will happen to you, but, at any rate you won't be shot in France." When pressed further, he said that if the community stuck together, "the chances are that the government will not molest you and you will go right along running your farm and raising your pigs just as you are doing today." Then, sensing that he might have crossed a line, he added, "Now for the benefit of any federal officer there in the crowd, I want you to understand that I am not now advising these people one way or the other." It was too late. A federal officer *was* in the crowd; in fact, it was his brother who had asked the questions. And as soon as the officer filed his report back in Washington, Sugarman was arrested and charged with attempting to cause insubordination in the military. He was tried that fall, found guilty by a jury, and sentenced to three years in prison.

The third appeal was filed by Jacob Frohwerk, the editor of a German-language weekly called the *Missouri Staats-Zeitung.* Born in Prussia in the mid-1860s, Frohwerk moved to the United States at the age of eighteen and settled in Kansas City with his wife and brother. There he landed a job at the *Staats-Zeitung*, which paid him ten dollars a week to edit copy, write editorials, and solicit advertisements. The *Zeitung* was a small newspaper with a circulation of just a few thousand, but one of its subscribers was the Department of Justice, which was keeping tabs on German papers for evidence of espionage. Officials read the paper during the summer and fall of 1917 as the draft went into effect and the first casualty lists came back from Europe. They even visited the office to interview Frohwerk and the paper's owner, Carl Gleeser. But it was not until the following spring, when the department was under pressure to crack down on radicals, that they brought indictments against the two men. The charges were based on a dozen articles published between June and December 1917, with each article serving as the basis for a separate count. For the most part, and compared with much of the antiwar rhetoric, the articles were tame. Several of them criticized England, claiming it had instigated the conflict to shore up its empire and had manipulated the United States into joining the cause. A few repeated the stock socialist line that the country had gone to war to appease the bankers on Wall Street. One simply reported that Russia had signed a treaty with Germany, which would make it harder for the Allies to secure an honorable peace. The only article that came close to inciting insubordination was an editorial in August on the draft riots breaking out around the country. Although the paper agreed that the conscription law should be obeyed until struck down by the courts, it expressed sympathy for the young men who had been called upon to leave their homes and families to fight a war they knew little about in a land they had never seen. "We ask who then will arise and pronounce a verdict of guilty over such a man if he stops reasoning and follows the first impulse of nature: Self-preservation?" Like Sugarman, the paper disclaimed any intent to encourage draft resisters, stating that it did "not endorse their action in any manner." But as in Sugarman's case, the stipulation had little effect. After just three minutes of deliberation, a jury convicted Frohwerk of violating the Espionage Act, and a judge sentenced him to ten years in prison. (Gleeser, who pleaded guilty and testified against his former employee, was sentenced to five years.)

Finally, there was Eugene Victor Debs, the leader of the national Socialist Party, a battle-scarred veteran of the country's labor wars, a charismatic, divisive figure who was a prophet and hero to the working class and a charlatan and traitor to the ruling class. Born in Terre Haute, Indiana, to French immigrants, Debs dropped out of high school at the age of fourteen to work as a painter in the rail yards. He rose quickly up the union ranks, was elected to the Indiana General Assembly at the age of twenty-nine, and led a successful strike against the Great Northern Railway in 1894. But when the employees of the Pullman Company decided to walk off the job a month later, he suffered his first major defeat. The company sent in thousands of replacement workers, violent clashes erupted, and federal soldiers marched in to break the strike, killing thirteen union members in the process. Debs was vilified for his role in the conflict and spent six months in jail for ignoring a court order to halt the strike. If his enemies thought that experience would chasten him, they were mistaken. He read Marx for the first time while in jail and came out even more radical than he went in, a convert to the cause of socialism, a believer in the faith of human brotherhood. Over the next few decades he dedicated his life to spreading the word, founding the Socialist Party of America and touring the country in his Red Special railcar to speak at union halls, college campuses, political conventions, and public lyceums. Tall and gaunt with a shaved head and a preacher's mien, Debs was a fiery, flamboyant orator, and the vision he painted of a classless utopia stirred his followers to a frenzy. They nominated him as the party's candidate for president in four straight elections: 1900, 1904, 1908, and 1912. And though he never had a prayer of winning (his best showing, in 1912, was 6 percent of the popular vote), he was not some fringe political figure the major parties could afford to ignore. He was known, admired, feared, and talked about across the country.

When the fighting broke out in Europe in 1914, Debs campaigned vigorously against American involvement. The war was a struggle among capitalist rivals, he told his audiences, and there was no reason for the workers to spill their blood for the sake of capitalism. He felt the same way three years later when Congress declared war on Germany. Though not present when the Socialist Party met in St. Louis to draft its antiwar proclamation, he applauded its call for active opposition to the war. He also urged his comrades to stand firm as the government began its crusade of persecution against socialists, pacifists, anarchists, and other suspected German sympathizers.

For much of the conflict, however, Debs himself was lying down. Exhausted and on the verge of physical collapse, he had been warned by his doctor that he would not last long unless he suspended his busy travel schedule and got some rest. So in the summer of 1917, as his party faced its biggest battle yet, Debs retreated from the field, heading first to a friend's cottage by a Minnesota lake and then to a sanatorium in Boulder, Colorado. There he passed the time picking flowers, fishing for bass, and writing long, romantic letters to another man's wife back in Terre Haute. He continued to turn out columns for the socialist press, denouncing the suppression of dissent and soliciting money for the defense of his jailed colleagues. But much of what he wrote never made it past the postmaster, who was already blocking publications under the Espionage Act. And though Debs returned home from his vacation that fall, he was still too weak to do much more than visit with a few close friends.

By the summer of 1918, Debs had regained enough strength to hit the road again on behalf of the Socialist Party. He traveled first through Indiana, stumping in Fort Wayne and a dozen other blue-collar towns in advance of the midterm elections. His speeches were passionate as usual, filled with fury and outrage, but Debs was careful to stay within the law, saying nothing that could be construed as a violation of the Espionage and Sedition Acts. Even when he arrived in Canton, Ohio, for the state party's annual picnic, he initially seemed cautious and tentative. "I must be exceedingly careful, prudent, as to what I say, and even more careful and prudent as to how I say it," he told the crowd of a thousand that had gathered in Nimisilla Park on the afternoon of June 16. "I may not be able to say all I think, but I am not going to say anything that I do not think." He then delivered one of the most important speeches of his life.

He began by pointing to a workhouse at the edge of the park where three members of the party were serving time for their opposition to the draft. They were martyrs for the cause, Debs declared, their voices temporarily silenced, their courage an example to the world. And they were not the only ones. Throughout the country, friends of the working class had been harassed, slandered, beaten, and locked up for daring to speak the truth. Friends like Scott Nearing, an economist at the University of Pennsylvania who had been blacklisted for teaching the principles of Marx. Friends like Tom Mooney, a California labor leader who had been sentenced to death on trumped-up charges of murder. And friends like Kate Richards O'Hare, the editor of the *National Rip Saw*, who had been sent to prison for ten years under the Espionage Act for suggesting that American mothers were being used as breeding sows for the army. "Oh, just think of sentencing a woman to the penitentiary for talking," Debs lamented. All of these people—the entire Socialist Party, for that matter—had been branded as disloyal and traitorous. But socialists had been fighting German militarism since the party was born, he explained. It was the capitalists who had lain with the enemy—Teddy Roosevelt who had dined with the kaiser on his tour through Europe, the Fifth Avenue gentry who had licked the boots of Prince Henry of Prussia when he visited America. These were the real traitors, Debs announced, they and the rest of their kind: the plutocrats, the autocrats, the aristocrats, the capitalist captains, the industrial masters, the red-handed robbers, the Wall Street junkers, the tyrants, the parasites, the exploiters of the world. After groveling at the feet of the German leaders, they now demanded that the kaiser be stopped. And who did they want to stop him? Why, the workers, of course. That is the way it had always been: the master class declares the wars, and the subject class fights them. "They have always taught you that it is your patriotic duty to go to war and to have yourselves slaughtered at a command," Debs roared. "But in all of the history of the world you the people never had a voice in declaring war. You have never yet had!"

There was a point to all this, and it wasn't just to stir up trouble. It was to stir up votes, to gain converts, to bring sheep to the fold. For in contrast to the plutocrats and robber barons were the workers, "those class-conscious proletarians, those horny-fisted children of honest toil" who would soon triumph over the forces of greed and venality. "They are pressing forward, here, there, and everywhere, in all of the zones that girdle this globe," Debs told his audience. "Everywhere wiping out the boundary lines; everywhere facing the larger and nobler patriotism; everywhere proclaiming the glad tidings of the coming emancipation; everywhere having their hearts attuned to the most sacred cause that ever challenged men and women to action in all the history of the world. Everywhere marching toward Democracy; everywhere marching toward the sunrise, their faces aglow with the light of the coming day."

As he spoke, Debs leaned over the railing of the bandstand, stretching his long arms out toward the crowd, embracing it, drawing it close to him. He loved these people, they were his inspiration, his source of strength. When a man from the audience offered him a glass of water, Debs interrupted his speech to savor the moment. "How good the touch of the hand of a comrade is, and a sip of water furnished by a comrade;

as refreshing as if it were out on the desert of life." And the people loved him back. Though the heat was stifling and their feet ached, they stood in rapt attention during the two-hour speech. When he finished, with a final appeal to the brotherhood of all mankind, the crowd of a thousand broke into a prolonged and thunderous applause.

The speech was covered by the local press, and beforehand a reporter asked Debs if he had renounced the St. Louis proclamation, as some newspapers had reported. No, replied Debs, he stood behind its substance, though he did favor some revisions. That statement, along with an account of the speech, appeared the next morning in papers across the country. To his enemies, this was too much, a brazen act of insolence and treachery. Pundits accused him of treason, politicians called for his arrest. The federal prosecutor in Cleveland, Edwin S. Wertz, was eager to oblige. He mailed a transcript of the speech to Washington, where it landed on the desk of John Lord O'Brian, the attorney in charge of war work. True to his civil libertarian instincts, O'Brian sent back a discouraging reply. Most of what Debs had said was lawful, he explained to Wertz. And though some of his statements (such as the claim that the working class was being "slaughtered at a command") may have come close to the line, the case was "by no means a clear one." "All in all," O'Brian wrote, "the Department does not feel strongly convinced that a prosecution is advisable." Wertz did feel strongly, however. He had made his name going after radicals during the war and wasn't about to cut loose the biggest catch of all. He convened a grand jury, obtained an indictment, and ordered federal marshals to arrest Debs on the way to his next speech in Ohio.

The trial took place two months later in Cleveland before a hostile jury and an unsympathetic judge. Wertz called several witnesses to the stand to recount Debs's speech and to confirm that draft-age men had been in the crowd. He also called the reporter who had questioned Debs about the St. Louis proclamation. To Wertz, Debs's continued endorsement of the proclamation was crucial, since it helped to show Debs's intent to obstruct the draft—intent being a necessary element of a conviction under the Espionage Act. The defense attorneys countered that Debs had offered only qualified support for the St. Louis platform and had played no role in its drafting. But they held out little hope of winning an acquittal; mainly they were building a record for appeal.

The most dramatic part of the trial came after the evidence was in and the judge called for closing arguments. Instead of relying on his attorneys to defend him, Debs took the floor himself. Standing before a packed courtroom with an afternoon storm rumbling overhead, the old warrior spoke for two hours without notes or pause. He denied nothing that had been said about him during the trial. It was all true, he admitted, including his opposition to the war. "Gentlemen, I abhor war," he told the jurors. "When I think of a cold, glittering steel bayonet being plunged in the white, quivering flesh of a human being, I recoil with horror." But he was not on trial for his opposition to war, he explained. He was on trial because he had dared to question the established order, had dared to see a future that was different from the past. That was why socialists around the country had been persecuted and why they would one day be acquitted by history. "Washington, Adams, Paine—these were the rebels of their day. They were denounced, they were condemned. But they had the moral courage to stand erect and defy all the storms of detraction; and that is why they are in history, and that is why the great respectable majority of their day sleep in forgotten graves." It was a masterful performance, magnanimous and self-serving at the same time. Debs was even gracious to the judge and jury, assuring them that he bore no grudges and understood they were simply doing their duty. "My fate is in your hands," he said, as even some of the jurors wiped tears from their eyes. "I am prepared for the verdict."

Wertz looked small and amateurish by comparison. His address, delivered with a casual, folksy air, was disjointed and unfocused. He moved from one point to the other with little transition or explanation, merely inserting the word "now" to indicate a change of direction ("Now, with regard to some of the things he has said to you . . ." "Now, in accordance with the declaration of war . . ."). He relied heavily on the St. Louis proclamation, insisting that it shed light on Debs's intent and asserting (incorrectly) that Debs had voted for it. He read long excerpts from the Canton speech, attempting to tie it to the party's antiwar platform but often simply tying himself in knots. And he heaped derision and scorn on the socialist movement, describing Debs as "an old ewe" and his followers as "the half-bakes, the non compos mentis, and those who don't realize all the country means." His finest moment came when he explained the limits of free speech by noting that "a man in a crowded auditorium, or any theatre, who yells 'fire' and there is no fire, and a panic ensues and someone is trampled to death, may be rightfully indicted and charged with murder." But aside from that clever example—which would soon find its way into Supreme Court precedent—his argument seemed petty and vindictive. He even suggested that if he had his way men like Debs would be shot. The entire courtroom was mortified, including the judge, the bailiff, and Wertz's assistant, who squirmed in his seat with embarrassment. When the prosecutor sat down, not even Debs could muster the goodwill to compliment him on a job well done.

It didn't matter. After six hours of deliberation, the jury convicted Debs of attempting to incite disloyalty in the military and obstruct the draft (along with a third count that was later withdrawn). His lawyers managed to get him released on bail and quickly filed an appeal with the Supreme Court. The Justice Department, aware that the Court had three other Espionage Act cases on its docket, asked for expedited review, which the justices granted. A hearing date was set and briefs were submitted.

Then Debs, along with the rest of the country, waited to find out his fate.

6

"He Shoots So Quickly"

The four cases were scheduled to be heard together on the first day after the holiday recess in January 1919, but complications soon arose. First, the parties in Frohwerk's case could not agree on a bill of exceptions—the document that would explain to the Court exactly what evidence had been presented against him and what objections had been raised. Then Frohwerk's attorney, a socialist named Joseph D. Shewalter, filed a brief that read more like the manifesto of an insane person than a legal argument. Over three hundred pages long, with numerous digressions and extensive use of italics and capital letters, the brief was a barely coherent attack on nearly every aspect of the war—from the initial declaration of hostilities to the enactment of the draft to the seizure of the railroads. The summary alone was fourteen pages, and there was even a section entitled "The Length of This Brief." The only issue not fully addressed was the legality of Frohwerk's conviction. It was all quite bizarre and puzzling, and it didn't help Frohwerk in the least. He was forced to hire a new lawyer, who requested an extension of time to file a proper brief—a request the government graciously agreed to. As a result, the Court split the four cases into two groups and moved the arguments in *Frohwerk* and *Debs* to the end of the month.

That wasn't the only delay. On the morning of January 6, Attorney General Thomas Gregory walked into Court and announced that Theodore Roosevelt had died overnight at his home in Oyster Bay, Long Island. The news shook the capital, and the justices agreed to adjourn for two days out of respect for the former president. For Holmes, the announcement brought mixed emotions. It was Roosevelt who had appointed him to the Court almost seventeen years earlier and then welcomed Fanny and him into the social life of the capital. Indeed, for the first several years of their stay, the Holmeses were great favorites of the president, dining frequently at the White House and often joining the first couple out for nights at the theater. Roosevelt admired Holmes's military service and was amused by Fanny's wry observations. ("Washington is full of famous men and the women they married when they were young," she remarked the first time they met.) But the relationship cooled after Holmes voted to dismiss the administration's antitrust suit against the Northern Securities Company, a railroad trust led by J. P. Morgan and James Hill. Roosevelt viewed the vote as a betrayal of loyalty and never again showed Holmes the warmth and hospitality of those early years. Holmes, whose vote was based on his reading of the Sherman Anti-Trust Act, thought the episode reflected poorly on the Rough Rider, revealing his lack of respect for the law and his inability to forgive anyone who stood in his way. But he continued to regard Roosevelt as a great man who was likeable, decisive, and shrewd. And his death was yet another reminder that the world Holmes had known was quickly fading into the past.

So it was not until the second Thursday of January that the Court finally heard arguments in *Schenck* and *Sugarman* and not until two and a half weeks later that it listened to the appeals in *Frohwerk* and *Debs*. Unlike the farmers in *Baltzer*, the defendants in these cases could not rely on the right to petition the government (since they had addressed their arguments to the public, not to elected officials). Instead, their lawyers focused on the meaning and scope of free speech, making many of the same claims that Chafee had made in the *New Republic*. They argued that the founding generation had rejected the Blackstonian view, that the right to criticize the government was essential to democracy and the pursuit of truth, and that the Sedition Act of 1798 had been condemned by Jefferson and Madison and repudiated by history. The lawyers argued capably and with conviction, leading some observers to hold out hope for a victory. The only awkward moment came when Shewalter appeared and requested permission to speak for thirty minutes and to file an additional brief on Frohwerk's behalf—requests that the Court inexplicably granted.

The government was once again represented by John Lord O'Brian, who put aside his earlier doubts about the *Debs* case to argue in support of the conviction. In contrast to the defense attorneys, he spent most of his time rehashing the arguments from *Baltzer*. Whether the defendants invoked the right to petition or the right of free speech was irrelevant, he said. The Constitution gave Congress the power to raise an army, and those who interfered with that power could not hide behind the First Amendment. But there was one important difference between his argument now and two months earlier. In *Baltzer*, O'Brian had relied on the Blackstonian understanding of free speech, emphasizing Holmes's endorsement of it in *Patterson v. Colorado*. Now, after further research and reflection, he seemed willing to concede that the First Amendment might limit the government's power to punish speech after as well as before the fact. In his brief in the *Debs* case, he cited a leading treatise on constitutional law that rejected the Blackstonian view. He also quoted from an article by Roscoe Pound challenging the distinction between prior restraints and subsequent punishments. Even so, O'Brian argued, free speech was not absolute and did not protect seditious language or incitement to violate the law. He also disputed the defendants' claim that the Sedition Act of 1798 was unconstitutional, pointing out that it had been upheld by several lower courts at the time.

When all four cases had been submitted—and Shewalter had filed his supplemental brief (a surprisingly modest fourteen pages)—the justices gathered in the basement conference room to cast their votes. Sugarman's appeal was the easiest to dispose of. His attorneys had chosen not to appear before the Court and had mentioned the issue of free speech only casually in their brief. Moreover, of the thirty-one objections they raised during his trial, only two implicated the Constitution, and neither of those had a shred of merit. As a result, the justices decided they lacked jurisdiction to hear the case because it raised no genuine issues of constitutional law. The opinion would be simple to write, and Chief Justice White assigned it to Brandeis, the second-most junior member of the Court. The other three appeals were more complicated. The defendants in those cases had expressly argued the issue of free speech, which meant the Court would have to tackle those arguments head on. After a lengthy discussion, the outcome became clear: a majority of the justices, including Holmes, sided with the government; the convictions would be affirmed. But who would write the opinions? The assignment of cases was the chief justice's most important responsibility, and White thought carefully about his options. He could give the assignment to Justice McKenna, who had written the majority decision in *Baltzer* and was caught up with his work. But McKenna was a poor writer who had a history of failing to hold together a majority, and White didn't want to risk another fractured Court, as in *Baltzer*. He therefore assigned the opinions to the one person with enough authority to keep the Court intact: Holmes.

Holmes had already been given four cases from the January calendar, all of which he had finished by the end of the month. So when White sent him the new assignments, in early February, he was able to devote his full attention to the task. He prepared, as always, by reviewing the notes he had taken during oral argument and looking back over the briefs and the trial records. He settled on a line of reasoning, sketched out the opinions in his head, and then, when he was ready to write, got up from his chair and moved to the old upright desk in the corner of his study. ("Nothing conduces to brevity like a caving in of the knees," he liked to say.) He picked up his steel-nibbed pen, dipped the rusted tip into his father's inkwell, and added yet another chapter to the long history of the law.

He began with *Schenck*, which, because it had been argued first, would become the case in which the Court laid out the legal principles governing all decisions under the Espionage and Sedition Acts. "This is an indictment in three counts," he wrote, diving into a description of the charges against Schenck and Baer before turning to their first claim: that there was insufficient evidence to tie them to publication of the leaflets. Holmes dismissed this argument out of hand, citing the notebook found at the Socialist Party bookstore and chastising the defendants for raising an issue that "only impairs the seriousness of the real defence." He was equally dismissive of their claim that introducing the notebook as evidence violated their Fifth Amendment right against self-incrimination. The notebook belonged to the Socialist Party, not the defendants, he pointed out. Besides, "the notion that evidence even directly proceeding from the defendant in a criminal proceeding is excluded in all cases by the Fifth Amendment is plainly unsound."

With these two frivolous arguments out of the way, Holmes turned to the "real defence"—the claim that the defendants' convictions violated the constitutional guarantee of free speech. If Blackstone's view was still authoritative, the response to this claim would be straightforward: Schenck and Baer were punished *after* circulating the leaflets, not before, so they could not invoke the First Amendment as a defense. But Blackstone had taken a serious beating in recent months, beginning with Chafee's article in the *New Republic* and continuing with the briefs and arguments submitted by the defendants; even the government now seemed skeptical of his position. So Holmes had a choice to make. He could stand by his decision in *Patterson v. Colorado*, thus reaffirming the Blackstonian view and leaving speakers with almost no constitutional protection. Or he could overrule *Patterson* and dramatically expand the reach of the First Amendment. Neither option was very attractive. To overrule *Patterson* would be to admit that he had been wrong, a distasteful proposition for any judge, let alone one as eager for public recognition as Holmes. On the other hand, he had never been fully invested in Blackstone's position to begin with, having embraced it primarily in reliance upon his Massachusetts predecessor, Isaac Parker. And now that men like Chafee and O'Brian were questioning Blackstone's view, Holmes began to doubt its validity

himself. The trick was to distance himself from that view without calling attention to his own earlier mistake—a trick he managed quite
deftly. "It well may be that the prohibition of laws abridging the freedom
of speech is not confined to previous restraints," he wrote, "although to
prevent them may have been the main purpose, as intimated in *Patterson v. Colorado*." This was far from a candid admission of error.
There was the use of that qualifying phrase, "it well may be." And the
word "intimated" implied that *Patterson* had not fully embraced the
Blackstonian view, when in fact that is how every judge and commen-
tator had read the opinion. Still, it was enough to put Blackstone to rest
for good, and never again would a federal court dismiss a free speech
claim on the ground that the First Amendment guards only against
prior restraints.

Burying Blackstone was only the first step. For even if the First
Amendment went beyond the old English view, there was still the question of how far it went. Did it immunize all speech or writing, no matter how harmful or repugnant it might be? Was the First Amendment's
command that "Congress shall make no law . . . abridging the freedom of speech" to be taken literally, as meaning *no* law whatsoever?
To Holmes, the answer to these questions was clear: the right of free
speech was not absolute. Like every other right, it depended on context
and circumstance. But how could he convey the logic of this conclusion? How could he put it into terms that no one would dispute? Reading through the record in the *Debs* case, he had noted the example
used by Wertz in his address to the jury, an example that illustrated
both the dangers of free speech and the necessity of limiting its scope.
He now adopted that example as his own, stripping it down to its essence
and providing posterity with one of the most vivid and memorable
arguments against an absolutist interpretation of the First Amendment. "The most stringent protection of free speech," Holmes wrote,
"would not protect a man in falsely shouting fire in a theatre and causing a panic."

If free speech was not absolute, then what were its limits? In their
presentations to the Court, the two sides had offered competing theories. The defense attorneys cited Learned Hand's position in the *Masses*

case, arguing that speech was protected as long as it stopped short of direct incitement. O'Brian pushed back, pointing out that such an approach would leave the government "powerless to punish any incitement to lawlessness, however intentional and however effective, so long as it is concealed in veiled, indirect or rhetorical language." Instead, he argued, speech loses its protection whenever it threatens the public welfare. Reflecting on this debate, Holmes decided to read the *Masses* opinion himself, which he had not yet had occasion to do. His reaction was mixed. Although not persuaded by Hand's argument, he was impressed by its eloquence and decided to let Hand know. "I read your Masses decision," he wrote in late February, shortly after completing his own opinion in *Schenck*. "I haven't the details in my mind and will assume for present purposes that I should come to a different result, but I did want to tell you after reading it that I thought that few judges indeed could have put their view with such force or in such admirable form."

Hand wasn't the only source Holmes consulted in his effort to define the boundaries of free speech. For years, Laski had been singing the praises of John Stuart Mill, the British philosopher and member of Parliament who was famous for his liberal political views. Laski regarded Mill as one of the greatest thinkers of the nineteenth century, a man who understood the importance of the individual and the perils of the authoritarian state; he even hung a portrait of Mill on his office wall. Holmes was well acquainted with Mill. He had read several of his books during law school, and when he traveled to England after graduation he carried with him a letter of introduction from a friend of his father's. Holmes presented the letter at Parliament, and Mill responded by inviting him to dine at the Political Economy Club. Personally, Holmes found Mill dull and unimaginative, but he respected his scientific approach to philosophy and reread his work from time to time. Now, at Laski's urging, he returned to one book in particular, *On Liberty*, Mill's classic defense of personal freedom. Written in 1859, *On Liberty* introduced the harm principle—the idea that government is justified in restricting individual liberty only to prevent harm to others. The harm principle applied to all types of human activity, but the relevance of the book for Holmes was chapter 2, which focused on freedom of thought and discussion. Like Milton before him and Hand after him, Mill grounded his defense of free speech in the pursuit of truth and the fallibility of human judgment. Only by assuming we are infallible, he argued, can we justify the suppression of opinions we think false. "Yet it is as evident in itself, as any amount of argument can make it that ages are no more infallible than individuals—every age having held many opinions which subsequent ages have deemed not only false but absurd; and it is as certain that many opinions, now general, will be rejected by future ages, as it is that many, once general, are rejected by the present." This was essentially what Hand had said to Holmes the previous summer. Unlike Hand, however, Mill antici-pated Holmes's objection, which was that even though we are fallible, even though we can never be certain of the truth, we must still act. That was undeniable, Mill conceded. We must act, and we must assume, for the purpose of acting, that what we believe is true. But that does not mean we can assume our opinions are true for the purpose of sup-pressing speech. Just the opposite, in fact. For it is only because our opinions are open to challenge that we are justified in assuming their truth for purposes of action. "If even the Newtonian philosophy were not permitted to be questioned, mankind could not feel as complete assurance of its truth as they now do," Mill wrote. "The beliefs which we have most warrant for have no safeguard to rest on but a standing invitation to the whole world to prove them unfounded."

This was a powerful argument—and one that Holmes would adopt almost verbatim nine months later in his *Abrams* dissent. For now, however, it had little influence on him. Holmes was searching for a way to define the limits of free speech, not to justify its protection. And on the question of limits, Mill was much less helpful. His only acknowledgment that there *are* limits came at the beginning of chap-ter 3, where he shifted from freedom of speech to freedom of action. Explaining that the latter is more circumscribed than the former, Mill pointed out that "even opinions lose their immunity when the circum-stances in which they are expressed are such as to constitute their expression a positive instigation to some mischievous act." He then offered his own example of unprotected speech, writing that "an opinion that corn dealers are starvers of the poor, or that private property is robbery, ought to be unmolested when simply circulated through the press, but may justly incur punishment when delivered orally to an excited mob assembled before the house of a corn dealer, or when handed about among the same mob in the form of a placard." In many ways, this was a better example than shouting fire in a crowded theater, and it was certainly one Holmes could agree with. But it was an example, not a rule that courts could apply, which meant Holmes would have to look elsewhere for a way to define the limits of free speech.

The place he looked to was his own past. By this point in his career, Holmes had written about nearly every legal topic under the sun: contracts, torts, evidence, procedure, tax, bankruptcy, criminal law, constitutional law, administrative law. So when he stumbled upon some new problem, one he had not yet specifically addressed, his first instinct was to find an analogy in an issue he *had* addressed. In this way he had become almost a closed loop, repeating the old formulas over and over again in slightly new contexts. Thinking about the issue of free speech now, Holmes followed the same pattern. He searched deep in his memory for a suitable analogy, and the one he settled on was the crime of attempt.

Within the criminal law, attempt is an odd bird. Most crimes, such as murder, robbery, and arson, are committed when the actual harm occurs—when the victim is killed, when the money is stolen, when the barn is set on fire. Attempts are different. A person can be convicted of attempt even though the underlying crime has not yet taken place— even though no harm has occurred at all. In the language of the law, attempt is an inchoate, or uncompleted, crime. But most jurists agree that individuals should not be punished for the mere desire or intent to commit a crime; that would amount to punishing people for their thoughts. So courts have had to determine at what point *intent* is transformed into *attempt*. The traditional view was that a person is guilty of an attempt when he both intends to commit a crime and takes any step toward its completion—buying a gun, say, or casing a bank. Holmes disliked that approach. To him, it placed too much emphasis on the issue of moral guilt, which he had been working to extricate from the law for more than forty years. Why should we care if someone has a bad heart unless his actions pose a danger to society? For that reason, Holmes thought courts should require more than a mere preparatory step before a person could be convicted of attempt. "As the aim of the law is not to punish sins, but is to prevent certain external results," he wrote in an 1897 Massachusetts case, "the act done must come pretty near to accomplishing that result before the law will notice it." Thus, if a person lights a match next to a haystack with the intent to start a fire, he should be punished for attempted arson. But if he merely buys a box of matches with the same intent, the law should leave him be. This wasn't a precise, bright-line test, of course. There were many possibilities between these two examples, and it was unclear exactly how near to the result a person had to come before he was guilty of attempt. But Holmes didn't like bright-line tests anyway, since the answer in any given case would always depend on circumstances. As he wrote in another attempt case while on the Supreme Court, "It is a question of proximity and degree."

In Holmes's view, the issue posed in *Schenck* and the other speech cases was analogous to the issue raised by the crime of attempt. As with attempts, a person should not be convicted for the thoughts in his head or the feelings in his heart. But once he expressed those thoughts or feelings in a way that posed a sufficient danger to society, the protections of free speech ended. And the formula Holmes adopted for expressing this idea was strikingly similar to the formula he had adopted in the context of attempts. "The question in every case," he wrote in *Schenck*, "is whether the words used are used in such circumstances and are of such a nature as to create a clear and present danger that they will bring about the substantive evils that Congress has a right to prevent. It is a question of proximity and degree."

On its face, this formula appeared quite sensitive to the value of free speech. Most judges had analyzed Espionage Act cases by asking whether the speech at issue had a "bad tendency"—meaning there was *some* chance it might lead to harm at *some* point in the future. Holmes's formula, which was completely original, seemed to require much more.

The phrase "clear and present danger" suggested that a mere possibility of harm was not enough, that the likelihood of harm must be high. It also implied that the risk of *future* harm was insufficient, that the harm must be *imminent*. Had this standard been applied to the facts of *Schenck*, the convictions should have been reversed, since there was no evidence that Schenck and Baer posed a clear risk of imminent harm. But curiously, Holmes did not apply this standard to the facts. Though he had defended the right to petition the government in *Baltzer* and had renounced Blackstone just a few sentences earlier, he was not yet ready to embrace free speech in full. The issues were still too abstract to him, his instincts still too conservative. So instead of following the clear and present danger test to its logical conclusion—instead of thinking "through a difficult matter to the end," as Zane had put it— Holmes fell back on his old belief that individual rights are subordinate to the needs of the state. "When a nation is at war," he wrote, "many things that might be said in time of peace are such a hindrance to its effort that their utterance will not be endured so long as men fight and that no court could regard them as protected by any constitutional right." Then, with little further explanation, he affirmed the defendants' convictions.

Moreover, when he turned to the other two cases, he didn't so much as mention the words "clear and present danger." His opinion in *Frohwerk* conceded that the articles in the *Staats-Zeitung* were not inherently unlawful. He also acknowledged that unlike Schenck and Baer, who had mailed their leaflets to draftees, Frohwerk had not made "any special effort to reach men who were subject to the draft." And if the evidence showed that Frohwerk was a poor man turning out copy for a small newspaper, "there would be a natural inclination to test every question of law to be found in the record very thoroughly before upholding the very severe penalty imposed." But without a bill of exceptions, Holmes explained, the Court had to "take the case on the record as it is, and on that record it is impossible to say that it might not have been found that the circulation of the paper was in quarters where a little breath would be enough to kindle a flame and that the fact was known and relied upon by those who sent the paper out." This statement—with its speculation about unknown evidence and its reference to "a little breath" that might "kindle a flame"—was a far cry from the "clear and present danger" language of *Schenck*. And it suggested that Holmes had used that phrase casually, without intending to radically change the law.

His opinion in *Debs* only reinforced that impression. Holmes acknowledged that the main purpose of Debs's speech was to promote socialism, which the Espionage Act did not prohibit. "But if a part or the manifest intent of the more general utterances was to encourage those present to obstruct the recruiting service and if in passages such encouragement was directly given, the immunity of the general theme may not be enough to protect the speech." He then noted that Debs had told his audience he could not say all he wanted to, thus "intimating to his hearers that they might infer that he meant more." He also cited Debs's support of the St. Louis proclamation as proof that he had intended to obstruct the draft. Finally, Holmes endorsed the trial judge's statement of law to the jury. "We should add that the jury were most carefully instructed that they could not find the defendant guilty for advocacy of any of his opinions unless the words used had as their natural tendency and reasonably probable effect to obstruct the recruiting service, &c., and unless the defendant had the specific intent to do so in his mind." This was the strongest indication that Holmes was not trying to transform the law. The jury instructions were nearly identical to the bad tendency test. And if they were acceptable, then "clear and present danger" was, for now, merely a clever turn of phrase.

To the other members of the Court, the ambiguity of Holmes's opinions was nothing new. Although he was the most eloquent writer on the bench, he could also be the most obscure. In part, this was the result of working so fast and producing so many opinions. But it also had something to do with his general remoteness from the world. As Brandeis once complained to Frankfurter, Holmes didn't "sufficiently consider the need of others to understand or sufficiently regard the difficulties or arguments of others." If the other justices were troubled, however, they kept it to themselves. No sooner had Holmes circulated drafts of his three opinions than they wrote back to express their approval.

"Yea verily," responded Justice William R. Day.

"Direct as you usually are and as strong as direct," wrote Justice Joseph McKenna.

"Admirably well put," said the chief justice.

"Yes," added Justice Willis Van Devanter. "I think you have happily disposed of a bunch of unattractive cases."

Only Brandeis seemed at all uneasy. There was something about the cases that nagged at him, making him wonder whether the Court had done the right thing after all. But before he could think through the matter fully, Holmes had circulated his opinions and was preparing to hand them down. That was another problem with Holmes, Brandeis told Frankfurter. "He doesn't give a fellow a chance—he shoots so quickly."

7

Defending Sophistries

On the first Monday of March, the Court returned from a monthlong recess with more than two dozen decisions to announce. Reporters and lawyers filled the courtroom, listening attentively as each justice delivered the opinions he had been assigned to write, beginning with the most junior member of the Court, John Hessin Clarke, and proceeding up the ranks of seniority, to Brandeis, James C. McReynolds, Pitney, Van Devanter, Day, Holmes, McKenna, and White. Their styles of delivery were as different as their backgrounds and points of view—Pitney, the former congressman from New Jersey, reciting every word of his opinions as if addressing the House floor; Day, one of the few members of the Court without a law degree, swallowing his sentences with embarrassment; Brandeis, the People's Attorney, leaning over the bench to emphasize a point, his arguments clear and well ordered; and White, the chief justice, filling the room with his deep, round bass, his hands moving constantly before him. Holmes had a distinguished, efficient delivery. His voice was old-fashioned and plummy, like that of an English poet, and he enunciated each word with care. But he read only the essential parts of his opinions, omitting even those rhetorical gems he had worked hardest to polish.

Today, he announced the results in two cases, *Schenck* and *Panama*

Railway Company v. Bosse. Of the two, he was far more interested in the Panama case, which concerned the liability of employers for the negligence of their workers, an issue he had explored at length in *The Common Law.* To the journalists in the courtroom, neither case was particularly exciting. A few reported the outcome in *Schenck,* noting that it marked the first time the Court had ruled on the constitutionality of the Espionage Act. But Charles Schenck and Elizabeth Baer were small fish outside the world of Philadelphia socialists; the fact that their convictions had been affirmed was not exactly front-page news. *Debs* was the decision everyone was waiting for, and they would have to wait a bit longer. The ruling in that case, along with *Frohwerk,* would not be handed down until the following Monday.

In the meantime, Holmes reached another milestone. On Saturday, March 8, he celebrated his seventy-eighth birthday—"the foothills of 80." Three years earlier, when he turned seventy-five, the event had been grandly observed. Frankfurter organized a tribute in the *Harvard Law Review,* Walter Lippmann published an appreciation in the *New Republic,* and Fanny arranged a surprise party at home with a group of his young friends. She smuggled them in through the cellar after Holmes retired for the evening, then passed around bird callers she had bought from a street vendor. All at once the guests began blowing, and the house was filled with the song of robins and nightingales. When Holmes rushed downstairs to investigate, they burst out from the dimly lit parlor and greeted him with shouts and cheers. For a moment he was dismayed, fearing he had no food or drink to offer them. Then Fanny flung open the doors of the dining room to reveal a glorious spread, and Holmes stayed up till midnight, drinking punch, telling stories, and basking in the admiration of youthful eyes.

This year, the celebration was more subdued. Frankfurter was in Paris attending the peace talks, Lippmann was on vacation, and Laski was unable to interrupt his busy schedule in Cambridge. So after spending a dreary afternoon in conference with the other justices, Holmes paid a visit to the print shop, where he passed an hour jawing with Admiral Davis and showing off his new van Ostade. But if his friends could not be present, at least they were thinking of him. Hand telegrammed from New York, begging leave "to suggest upon the record that March Eighth is the anniversary of a day forever memorable in the annals of American Jurisprudence." The philosopher Morris Cohen wrote to say that he had "never seen the spirit of man defy time so chivalrously as in your case." And Laski sent an advance copy of his new book, *Authority in the Modern State*, which expanded on his theory of pluralism. Holmes had heard about the project frequently over the past two years but had not yet seen the manuscript. Thus, when he opened to the flyleaf and read the dedication he was unprepared for what he found:

TO

MR. JUSTICE HOLMES

AND

FELIX FRANKFURTER

THE TWO YOUNGEST OF MY FRIENDS

It was an inside joke, of course, and it couldn't have come at a better time. Rumors had been circulating that Holmes was on the verge of retiring—rumors planted, no doubt, by someone who thought he had outstayed his usefulness. Even Holmes sometimes wondered whether he was getting too old for the job. He had put that very question to Brandeis recently and was reassured by his colleague's reply. But no one could lift his spirits like Laski, and he sat down at once to express his gratitude. "The book arrived this morning," he wrote. "I trust that I need not tell you how much I am surprised and moved. Although I can believe little except your affection it makes me terribly proud that even for a moment I could elicit such an expression. I shall read the book as soon as may be—not just yet I fear—and write to you about that. Meantime my thanks and love to you both."

And the more Holmes thought about it, the more he realized Laski and Brandeis were right. Why shouldn't he stay on? He was in excellent health and could still manage the work, even if it was hard and sometimes took all his energy. There was no reason he couldn't continue for another few years, at least until he turned eighty. After that, who knew? He might even make it to ninety. The prospect pleased him so much he bought a new robe to silence the rumors of retirement. And when his niece wrote to ask whether it was true that he was stepping down, he sent her the following lines of verse in reply:

> I will sit in the seats of the mighty
> If I can until I am eighty (pronounced ity)
> And what I'll do then
> In the following ten
> I leave to the Lord God Almighty

Two days after his birthday the Court was back in session, and Holmes announced the decisions in *Frohwerk* and *Debs*. This time, the press took notice. The mainstream newspapers praised the rulings, declaring them a victory for patriotism and a rejection of anarchy. "Nothing has occurred since the beginning of the war which has contributed so materially to the vindication of the law in the United States as the trial and conviction of Debs," hailed the *Washington Post*. The *New York Times* described Debs as an enemy of the country and asked, "How, therefore, could he reasonably expect that it would fail to defend itself against him?" And the *New York Tribune* said the decision would be a warning to those "who try to shelter themselves behind Constitutional privileges which they appeal to in bad faith."

But progressives were outraged. Gilbert Roe, a prominent civil rights lawyer, claimed that Holmes had set back the First Amendment two centuries, while the *San Francisco Examiner* called the opinion "a perversion of the Constitution and a most dangerous and vicious invasion of our native and guaranteed liberties." In New York, a thousand people attended a meeting at the New Masonic Temple to protest the decision, and in Toledo riots broke out after city officials canceled a speech Debs was scheduled to give there. The defendant himself feigned indifference. When asked by reporters what he thought of the ruling, Debs responded, "I am not concerned with what those be-powdered, be-wigged corporation attorneys at Washington do."

Behind the scenes, an effort was made to override the decision. A group of prominent socialists, led by Upton Sinclair and Charlotte Perkins Gilman, petitioned the president for a pardon, citing Debs's age and long service to the cause of human freedom. Wilson, who was still in Europe at the peace conference, cabled his advisers in Washington that he was open to a pardon if the attorney general consented. But the attorney general, A. Mitchell Palmer, did not consent. In a telegram to Wilson, he argued that Debs had been given a fair trial and should serve his sentence. And so in early April, just four weeks after the Supreme Court issued its ruling, the government denied the pleas for clemency and ordered Debs to report to prison.

Holmes did not read the newspapers, of course, so he did not see the statements condemning his opinion or the debate about whether Debs should be pardoned. But he was made aware of the controversy by a stream of protests he received through the mail. A lawyer from California wrote that the decision was a "bold invasion of the cardinal principles of freedom and liberty which at all times should be jealously guarded against attack." The Central Labor Union of Bridgeport, Connecticut, complained that the Court had undermined rights "provided and guaranteed to every citizen by the Constitution." And the president of a Chicago hardware company predicted that Holmes's ruling would light a fire under the forces of revolution. "How long will even a benighted people continue to worship a fetish that fails to answer its prayers?" the man asked. "When law becomes an obstacle to progress, anarchy is the logical and inevitable sequence. It wipes the slate for a restoration of ideals."

This was not the first time Holmes had been denounced for an opinion he had written. And he was used to getting letters from cranks. But the intensity and volume of the criticism were unusual, and as the days wore on his nerves began to fray. "Just now I am receiving some singularly ignorant protests against a decision that I wrote sustaining a conviction of Debs, a labor agitator, for obstructing the recruiting service," he confided to his friend Lewis Einstein, then living in Italy. "They make me want to write a letter to ease my mind and shoot off my mouth; but of course I keep judicial silence."

If Holmes could not express his thoughts publicly, he could still defend himself to his friends, which is precisely what he did over the next several weeks. In letter after letter—to Einstein, to Laski, to Pollock, to the Irish historian Alice Stopford Green, even to his old crush, Baroness Charlotte Moncheur, the wife of the Belgian ambassador—he insisted that the decision in *Debs* was correct, that once the jury had found that Debs intended to obstruct the draft and might possibly have done so there was little the Court could do. But he also began to distance himself from the decision, explaining that he regretted having to write it and wondered why the government had pursued the case, "as the inevitable result was that fools, knaves, and ignorant persons were bound to say he was convicted because he was a dangerous agitator and that obstructing the draft was a pretence." Holmes couldn't speak for the jury, of course, but such talk was absurd as to the Court. "There was a lot of jaw about free speech, which I dealt with somewhat summarily in an earlier case, *Schenck v. U.S.*, also *Frohwerk v. U.S.*," he acknowledged. "But as I said, the powers of the Constitution certainly never supposed that the provision for it gave a man immunity for counseling a murder or falsely crying fire in a theatre, and if when a country is at war a man chooses to try to obstruct it and says things that tend directly to that result he can't complain if he is laid by the heels." "Now," he added, "I hope the President will pardon him and some other poor devils with whom I have more sympathy."

His friends responded diplomatically, assuring him that they did not hold the decisions against him while at the same time suggesting that perhaps he had dismissed the free speech claims too casually. "I read your three opinions with great care," wrote Laski, "and though I say it with deep regret they are very convincing." Holmes's point, he took it, was that the justices had no business interfering with the prosecutorial discretion of the executive branch, especially in light of their limited knowledge of the war situation. "I think you would agree," Laski added, "that none of the accused ought to have been prosecuted; but since they have been and the statute is there the only remedy lies in the field of pardon. Your analogy of a cry of fire in a theatre is, I think, excellent, though in the remarks you make in the *Schenck* case I am not sure that I should not have liked the line to be drawn a little tighter about executive discretion. The Espionage Act tends to mean the prosecution of all one's opponents who are unimportant enough not to arise [*sic*] public opinion. Wilson has been utterly damnable in the whole business."

Holmes did not reply to Laski's critique, but there was one letter he could not ignore. It came from Hand, who had continued to dwell on the issue of tolerance since their meeting the previous summer. Reading *Debs* and the other cases in New York, Hand was troubled by Holmes's test for evaluating free speech claims. In his own opinion in *Masses*, Hand had proposed a test that focused on the speaker's words. "Words are not only the keys of persuasion, but the triggers of action," he had written, and those that explicitly urge violation of the law "cannot by any latitude of interpretation be a part of that public opinion which is the final source of government in a democratic state." On the other hand, words that merely criticize the law without directly urging its violation should be immune from punishment. Hand favored this test because he thought it was precise and objective, leaving little room for guesswork. Holmes, by contrast, focused not on the speaker's words but on their likely result—whether, in the language of *Schenck*, they posed a "clear and present danger" or, in the less generous language of *Debs*, their "natural tendency and reasonably probable effect" was to cause harm. The problem with this approach, in Hand's view, was that it gave too much leeway to judges and juries. It permitted them to speculate about the dangers of unpopular speech, which he felt certain they would overestimate, particularly in periods of crisis. It also meant that decisions would turn on minor differences in circumstance that no one could predict ahead of time. "Once you admit that the matter is one of degree," he explained, "you give to Tomdickandharry, D.J., so much latitude that the jig is up at once."

But criticizing the opinion of a Supreme Court justice—especially one he admired as much as Holmes—was an awkward task. So Hand went about it with a deferential touch. Like Laski, he chose not to challenge the actual decisions reached by the Court. Instead he encouraged Holmes to think harder about the legal rule that lay behind those decisions, suggesting that it was not supported by history. He also questioned Holmes's reliance on the jury's finding of intent in *Debs*, arguing that such a focus on motive would chill valuable speech. Unfortunately, these points were obscured by Hand's effort not to offend Holmes, and the letter itself was a muddle:

> Dear Mr. Justice:
>
> I have read *Debs v. U.S.* and the other case and this is positively my last appearance in the role of liberator. I haven't a doubt that Debs was guilty under any rule conceivably applicable. As to the rule actually laid down my dying words are these, now already fast receding in the seas of forgotten errors, and a crazy Saragossa that would be, wouldn't it? All the mad freaks of past contrivance.
>
> The thing against which the statute aims is positive impediments to raising an army. Speech may create such by its influence on others' conduct. In nature the causal sequence is perfect, but responsibility does not go *pari passu* [hand in hand]. I do not understand that the rule of responsibility for speech has ever been that the result is known as likely to follow. It is not—I agree it might have been—a question of responsibility dependent upon reasonable forecast, with an excuse when the words, had another possible effect. The responsibility only began when the words were directly an incitement. If I am wrong about that, it is mere matter of history. I confess I have no present access to the history.
>
> Assuming that I am not wrong, then it was a question of extending the responsibility, and that was fairly a matter of better and worse. All I say is, that since the cases actually occur when men are excited and since juries are especially clannish groups—are they *societates perfectae*?—it is very questionable whether the test of motive is not a dangerous test. Juries won't much regard the difference between the probable result of the words and the purposes of the utterer. In any case, unless one is rather set in conformity, it will serve to intimidate—throw a scare into—many

a man who might moderate the storms of popular feeling. I know it did in 1918.

The rule coupled w. Burleson's legal irresponsibility certainly terrorized some of the press whose voices were much needed.

There, that is all! Absolutely and irrevocably all in *saecula saeculorum*! I bid a long farewell to my little toy ship which set out quite bravely in the shortest voyage ever made. . . .

Sincerely yours
L. Hand

Holmes was up to his eyes in work when Hand's letter arrived and could not give it the attention it required. The result showed. When he wrote back a few days later, it was clear that he did not understand the substance of Hand's test or how it differed from his own:

Dear Judge Hand

Since your letter came I have been so busy propagating new sophistries &c. that I haven't had time to defend the old ones. And now I am afraid that I don't quite get your point. As to intent under the Espionage Act I believe I have said nothing except to note that under the instructions the jury must be taken to have found that Debs's speech was intended to obstruct and tended to obstruct—and except further that evidence was held admissible as bearing on intent. Even if absence of intent might not be a defence I suppose that the presence of it might be material. Leaving that on one side, you say "the responsibility only began when the words were directly an incitement"—I am afraid I do not know exactly what history you have in mind—but I don't see how you differ from the test as stated by me [in] Schenck v. U S (March 3, 1919). "The question in every case is whether the words used are used in such circumstances and are of such a nature as to create a clear and present danger that they will bring about the substantive evils that Congress has a right to

prevent. It is a question of proximity and degree." I haven't time
even now to recur to your decision but I take it that you agree
that words may constitute an obstruction within the statute, even
without proof that the obstruction was successful to the point of
preventing recruiting. That I at least think plain. So I don't know
what the matter is, or how we differ so far as your letter goes.
With which I send you my blessing and don't hold you bound by
your adieu to this stage. . . .

Yours sincerely
O.W. Holmes

Once again, Hand had missed his mark. *I don't quite get your point*,
Holmes had written. And it was true. Holmes did not get the point. He
failed to see that while his test focused on predictions about the likely
effects of speech, Hand's test focused on the words actually spoken.
Nor did he see that Hand's test was designed to give speakers greater
protection by limiting the ability of judges and juries to act on their
prejudices. Perhaps the fault lay with Hand. Perhaps if he wrote again
and explained things more clearly, he might finally get his point across;
Holmes certainly seemed open to further discussion. But Hand was
finished. The resistance his views had met, combined with his own
natural self-doubt, led him to question whether his *Masses* decision
was right after all. "I kept up my hopes until the Debs case," he said
later, "and when the whole court affirmed that without laying down
anything like what I thought was the rule, I confess I began to wonder
whether I had not got some kind of wrong squint on the subject."
Events over the next year would soon give Hand reason to hope again,
and eventually he would receive credit for the courage he had shown
when everyone else was silent. For now, though, he decided to withdraw from the fight. If Holmes was to be won over, if the future of free
speech was to be secured, someone else would have to lead the charge.

8

Dangerous Men

Spring came early in Washington, which was one of the things Holmes loved about his adopted home. In Boston the winters dragged on and on, the blackened snow piling up in the gutters, the wind whipping around Beacon Hill. And just when you thought the end was near, just when the larches began to sprout and you spied "a bee toiling in sticky buds half opened," a snowstorm would blanket the earth, forcing the city back inside for another month. "It is snowing again. S'help me," you would sigh to your friend William James. In Washington, however, spring rushed in on the heels of autumn, so that it sometimes felt as if only a few weeks had passed between the dying of the last rose in November and the flowering of the first crocus on the White House lawn in March.

Holmes pushed hard to finish his opinions so that he might have a day or two free "to look at all the wild things in the country and the park." And then, when the work was done, he put down his pen and walked with his secretary, Lloyd Landau, down to the towpath that runs along the canal in Georgetown. A cardinal flitted across the path in front of them, and the air was filled with the sharp scent of boxwood—"the fragrance of eternity," his father once wrote. It was late when they returned home, and Fanny poured tea for Landau and herself. Holmes declined, not wanting to spoil his dinner, but he sat with them in the parlor, expounding on his philosophy of life. The universe is a mystery, he said. You can't know anything for certain— you can only place bets, which is why he called himself a bettabilitar-ian. Landau listened thoughtfully, sipping his tea and occasionally asking a question. Fanny, who had heard it all before, picked up her needle and began to sew. When she interrupted to ask Holmes for the scissors, he exploded in good-natured indignation. "You see," he told Landau, "just as I told you, women are all alike. You pour out your heart, your very soul, in the best of talk to them, the whole exciting philosophy of your being. And what do they say—pass the scissors, Wendell."

A few mornings later, Holmes and Fanny took the carriage down to Rock Creek Park, where they listened to the symphony of the tree toads and hunted for the first bloodroot of the year. Then on they rode to the Potomac Basin to stroll among the double flowering cherry trees—a recent gift from the mayor of Tokyo. Their pink and white blossoms stood out against the blue sky, Holmes wrote to Baroness Moncheur, "and as you looked ahead mist on mist of yellow and ten-der green and pink again—and song sparrows and red birds and a kingfisher and faint cawings of more distant crows." It had been years since he had enjoyed the arrival of spring so much, and when he asked himself, "How is this?" he quickly realized the answer: "Why the Armistice."

There were some things the armistice had not changed. After the ini-tial wave of relief and euphoria, the country had plunged back into a state of suspicion and anxiety. The fear of German spies and sympa-thizers that had given birth to the Espionage and Sedition Acts was now transformed into a fear of Bolshevists, who were said to be the kaiser's agents in disguise. A Senate committee investigating the loy-alty of German brewers during the war expanded its inquiry to include all forms of anti-American radicalism, particularly those with a Rus-sian accent. Led by North Carolina democrat Lee Slater Overman, the committee heard sensationalistic testimony about conditions under Soviet rule—reports of mass executions, of people being tied up and thrown into rivers to drown, of old men and women starving in the streets and young girls being raped by the Red Guard. Witnesses also testified that Bolshevism was alive and well in America. It was being preached in the Jewish ghetto on the Lower East Side of New York. It was being promoted in union halls and labor camps, to foreigners and Negroes. There had even been a meeting of Russian sympathizers at a Washington theater, with several congressmen in attendance. In short, the witnesses warned, a Bolshevik revolution was just around the corner.

As if to validate this prediction, a string of troubling incidents rocked the country in the early part of the year. First, on New Year's Eve in Philadelphia bombs destroyed the homes of the police superintendent, the president of the Chamber of Commerce, and the chief justice of the state supreme court. Then, two weeks later in Boston, a storage tank holding 2.3 million tons of molasses exploded, sending a wave of molasses twenty-five feet high crashing through the waterfront district. Twenty-one people were killed in the incident, which the owner of the tank blamed on "evilly disposed persons." In February, officials arrested fourteen Spanish immigrants on charges of conspiring to assassinate President Wilson, and in March and April police announced the discovery of violent plots to overthrow the government in Seattle, Chicago, and Pittsburgh.

In addition to the violence, the country was beset by mounting economic strife. Toward the end of the war, when military spending was keeping the economy afloat, management and labor had settled into a temporary truce. But the signing of the armistice placed new strains on an already tenuous relationship. No sooner had the fighting ceased than the government began canceling war contracts, forcing many industries to dissolve and others to shift rapidly to peacetime production. At the same time, the labor market was flooded with nearly four million soldiers returning from overseas and looking for work. Add to that stagnant wages and spiraling inflation (the cost of living had nearly doubled over five years), and conditions were ripe for class warfare. In an earlier period, labor would have been badly out-matched in this contest. But the reforms of the Progressive Era had sig-nificantly strengthened its hand. Laws protecting the right of collective bargaining had swelled union ranks; the American Federation of Labor alone had grown from half a million members in 1900 to more than four million in 1919. And now, with the European conflict over and its members hurting, the unions were ready to do battle at home.

The first showdown took place in Seattle in early February. After thirty-five thousand shipyard workers went on strike for higher wages and shorter hours, the Central Labor Council, an alliance of local unions, announced a citywide work stoppage. It was the first general strike in the United States, and it resulted in more than sixty thousand workers walking off the job. Though largely peaceful, the strike crip-pled the city, closing schools, suspending streetcar service, and shut-ting down restaurants, newspapers, and barber shops. City officials refused to give in to the union's demands, and the strike ended in failure after five days. But the press portrayed it as the first sign of the coming revolt, and it was followed by walkouts in nearly every part of the country affecting nearly every industry. In May alone there were 388 strikes, and by the end of the year there would be more than 3,600 strikes involving more than four million workers.

Events overseas also fed the hysteria. In the wake of the Russian Revolution, chaos was spreading across Europe. There were labor upris-ings in Germany, Bolshevik outbreaks in Poland, and communist takeovers of both Hungary and Bavaria. In addition, delegates from twelve countries formed the Communist International, an organiza-tion dedicated to the overthrow of world capitalism. Controlled by the Russian Communist Party, the Comintern, as it was known, launched an aggressive propaganda campaign aimed at radicals around the globe. In the United States, it circulated nearly five million copies of Lenin's notorious letter "To the American Workers," which urged the proletariat to throw off the shackles of capitalism and become foot soldiers in a universal crusade.

In reality, there was almost no chance of a Bolshevik takeover of the United States. In 1919, the American Communist Party had only seventy thousand members, less than one-tenth of 1 percent of the country's adult population. The Socialist Party, which opposed violent revolution, was scarcely any bigger. But government officials insisted the threat was real, and red hunting became a popular sport. Congress allocated $500,000 for an investigation of seditious activities. Attorney General A. Mitchell Palmer called for the enactment of a peacetime Espionage Act (the original act applied only during times of war). And the Overman Committee released a list of sixty-two radicals who were said to be enemies of the state. The list included such respected figures as Jane Addams, the social reformer from Chicago, Charles Beard, the Columbia University historian, and Frederic Howe, commissioner of immigration at Ellis Island. But the list, authorities made clear, was only the tip of the iceberg. Lurking just below the surface were thousands upon thousands of radicals who were spreading dangerous ideas across America. Many of these people, it was said, were teaching at universities, where they could corrupt the minds of the young. Many others were immigrants, particularly of Jewish ancestry. And for those unfortunate individuals who were both university professors and Jewish immigrants, well, the presumption of guilt was nearly automatic.

Holmes, of course, knew two men who fit just that description— Laski and Frankfurter. And as the witch hunt gathered momentum in the spring of 1919, both men found themselves under pursuit by the pack.

For Laski, the trouble had begun the previous spring when a complaint was filed against him at Radcliffe College, where he was teaching a course on economics. According to the mother of one of his students, Laski was a Bolshevist sympathizer who was indoctrinating the girls in socialist theory. Officials at Radcliffe forwarded the complaint to Harvard president A. Lawrence Lowell, who opened a file on the young instructor that would eventually include nearly a hundred letters from angry parents and alumni. Around the same time, a Harvard physics professor named Edwin H. Hall began telling anyone who would listen that Laski was a "poisonous influence" who was spreading leftist propaganda on campus. Hall's whispering campaign was successful enough that in January 1919 Laski offered to resign his position on the *Harvard Law Review* as a way to deflect criticism from the law school. But the situation only worsened that spring when he took part in a strike at the Lawrence textile mills, where more than thirty thousand employees had walked off the job after owners slashed their hours and pay. Laski also drew attention for his role in founding the Boston Trade Union College, a school designed to train workers in the ways of management. And then, of course, there was his new book, *Authority in the Modern State*, which laid bare, for all to see, precisely where Laski stood in the battle between us and them.

Like his earlier work, *Authority in the Modern State* began with the proposition that the state is not omnipotent and does not "represent in any dominant and exclusive fashion the will of society as a whole." Other associations, such as trade unions and churches, are also vital to human development, and the state has no automatic claim to supremacy over them. However, whereas Laski had previously held out hope that the state would grow more responsive to the concerns of labor, he now believed that a redistribution of economic strength could not be achieved through ordinary political means. The only way to advance the cause of labor was "to divide industrial power from political control." In practical terms, this meant the creation of industrial councils, elected bodies of workers that would decide all major manufacturing questions, from the length of the workday to the hourly wage to the method and rate of production. Laski was vague on the details of how this system would work. Nor did he explain exactly how it might be brought about—whether through a violent uprising or some sort of democratic process. But he was convinced that the solution to labor's problems was to shift power away from the central government and toward a federation of regional unions. "To admit the trade union to an effective place in government, to insist that it is fundamental in the direction of production, is to make the worker count in the world," he wrote. "He may be then also a tender of machines; but where his trade-union is making decisions in which his own will is a part he is something more than a tender of machines."

As radical as this proposal was, Laski was not yet a Marxist. For one thing, the centralization at the heart of the Russian experiment was antithetical to his theory of pluralism. He also placed far more emphasis on individual rights and freedom of thought than did the communists. In fact, his book was filled with the sort of libertarian rhetoric that conservatives would deploy against the Soviet Union for the next seventy years. "The only real security for social well-being is the free exercise of men's minds," he wrote. "Where the conscience of the individual is concerned, the state must abate its demands; for no mind is in truth free once a penalty is attached to thought." To old-line Bostonians, however, this hardly mitigated his sins. Laski was a foreigner, an English Jew who wore funny hats, smoked Canadian cigarettes, and welcomed students into his home while reclining on a sofa. As far as they were concerned, he was a Trotsky in their midst.

Frankfurter's reputation was not much better. Though more connected to the New England establishment than Laski, Frankfurter was still, at the end of the day, an outsider. Born in Vienna in 1882, he moved to the United States with his family at the age of eleven and settled in the Jewish ghetto on Manhattan's Lower East Side. His father was a struggling merchant who sold furs and silks out of the home, but the family came from a long line of rabbis and Frankfurter inherited their intellectual drive and ability. Unable to speak a word of English when he arrived, he was soon a top student at the local public school, graduated from college at the age of nineteen, and finished first in his class at Harvard Law School. With a record like that, getting a job should have been easy. But in those days most of the top law firms excluded Jews, and Frankfurter went from office to office in New York before finding work at Hornblower, Byrne, Miller and Potter. The partners had never hired a Jew before and were clearly apprehensive about doing so: during the interview, one of them took Frankfurter aside and suggested he change his last name.

Frankfurter didn't stay long at Hornblower. Shortly after joining the firm, he accepted an offer from Henry L. Stimson, the U.S. attorney for the Southern District of New York. The move changed Frankfurter's life. As a prosecutor, he learned how to build a case from the bottom up, paying close attention to the facts and presenting them in a manner accessible to juries. He befriended other public-minded lawyers and judges, including Learned Hand, who introduced him to Herbert Croly. Most importantly, he became Stimson's right-hand man, gathering evidence and preparing briefs in high-profile suits against the railroads and sugar trusts. And Stimson, in turn, became the first in a series of powerful men, including Holmes, Brandeis, and Franklin Roosevelt, whose coattails Frankfurter would eventually ride all the way to a seat on the Supreme Court.

The first step in that journey took place in 1911 when Stimson moved to Washington to become secretary of war under President Taft and Frankfurter went along as his chief assistant. It was in Washington that Frankfurter met Holmes. Carrying a letter of introduction from his former professor John Gray, he called on the justice shortly after arriving and soon became a regular for Monday afternoon tea. Like Laski, Frankfurter charmed and flattered the older man, listening reverently as Holmes recited his pet theories and trotting after him like a puppy down the broad sidewalks of the capital. He also introduced the justice to a growing group of young admirers at the House of Truth, the gathering place for lawyers, journalists, and diplomats in the capital. Guests mingled in a large room on the first floor that was furnished with a dining table and a long sofa. There they mixed cocktails, ate dinners of roast beef and salad, played cards, and smoked. But mainly they talked. And talked. And talked. About law, politics, literature, and art. And of course about truth, which was how the house got its name.

Frankfurter was at the center of all this, laughing loudly, exuding warmth, and putting everyone at their ease. "Wherever Frankfurter is, there is no boredom," said one friend. "As soon as he bounces in—he never walks, he bounces—the talk and the laughter begin, and they never let up." He was equally energetic in his professional life. As law officer for the Bureau of Insular Affairs (a division of the War Department), he represented the government in cases that came to the Supreme Court from Puerto Rico, Cuba, the Philippines, and other territories. In all, he appeared before the Court eight times over a three-year period, winning all but one of his cases. He also led the campaign to regulate power plants across the country, an effort that led to the creation of the Federal Power Commission and foreshadowed the rise of the regulatory state under the New Deal.

When Taft was defeated in 1912, Frankfurter remained in the War Department to ease the transition to a new administration. Without Stimson around to promote his ideas, however, he grew despondent, fearing he was stuck in a bureaucratic dead end. Fortunately, he was soon offered a way out. Harvard Law School asked him to return as a professor, and after consulting with Holmes (who advised against it) and Brandeis (who argued in favor of it), Frankfurter accepted. For the next several years he pursued the academic life, teaching classes, mentoring students, and writing scholarly articles. But he never abandoned the world of affairs completely. He assisted Brandeis on a series of cases defending progressive labor laws before the Supreme Court (and then took over the cases when Brandeis was appointed to the bench). He worked closely with the editors of the *New Republic*, attending board meetings and writing an occasional essay. And he stayed active in politics, endorsing Wilson in 1916 and building a network of allies in the administration. So when the United States entered the conflict in Europe and the War Department was looking for someone to manage the country's growing labor strife, Frankfurter was a natural choice. Receiving a telegram from Secretary of War Newton D. Baker in the spring of 1917, he requested leave from Harvard, packed his bags, and caught the next train down to the capital.

And that's when *his* troubles began.

The immediate question facing the War Department was how to deal with the textile mills of Massachusetts, which had threatened to disregard labor standards in the production of military uniforms. It soon became clear, however, that the crisis extended beyond the Northeast. Across the country, management and labor were at each other's throats, as each sought to take advantage of the war to advance its long-term interests. It was a volatile situation that threatened the nation's ability to mobilize for war. Already, strikes had paralyzed the copper mines of Arizona and the lumber mills of the Northwest. Now workers were threatening to walk off the job in the California oilfields, the Chicago meatpacking plants, and the telephone and telegraph lines of the Pacific coast.

Researching the situation in Washington, Frankfurter proposed that the president appoint an informal mediator to quietly attempt a resolution of the conflicts. Wilson ignored that suggestion and instead convened a high-profile commission to investigate the causes of the discord, with Frankfurter serving as secretary and legal counsel. Known as the President's Mediation Commission, the group left Washington in the fall of 1917 and spent several months traveling through Arizona and California, taking testimony, meeting with company officials and union leaders, and hammering out differences. The head of the commission, William B. Wilson, became ill midway through the trip, so the bulk of the work fell to Frankfurter, who was made for the task. His warmth and charm put people at their ease, while his persistence wore them down. Before long the strikes ended, and the two sides agreed to a tentative truce. From the president's perspective, the commission was a resounding success.

But Frankfurter got tangled up in two controversies. The first was an incident known as the Bisbee Deportation. During the copper strikes in Arizona, the town of Bisbee had emerged as a hot spot for labor strife, with widespread strikes and conflicts among various union factions. Amid rumors of violence, local officials asked the federal government to send in troops to keep the peace. When army officers arrived and saw no signs of violence, they denied the request. Frustrated with this response, mining officials and the local sheriff took matters into their own hands. Leading a massive vigilante force, they rounded up nearly twelve hundred strikers, loaded them onto cattle cars, and hauled them into the middle of the New Mexico desert, where they were stranded for two days without food or water. The army eventually rescued the strikers and moved them to a nearby town for safety, but the incident became a rallying cry for progressives. And although it was technically outside the commission's mandate,

Frankfurter persuaded the group to visit Bisbee and conduct a full investigation. For five days he interviewed witnesses and compiled evidence. On the sixth day, he drafted a report declaring the actions of local officials "wholly illegal" and recommending a process for resolving similar disputes in the future.

The second controversy stemmed from the case of Tom Mooney, the California labor leader who had been sentenced to death for allegedly planting a bomb that killed ten people and wounded forty others during a 1916 Preparedness Day march. After the trial, defense attorneys uncovered evidence suggesting that the primary witness against Mooney had perjured himself. But because they had already appealed to the California Supreme Court, the trial judge ruled that he lacked jurisdiction to reopen the matter. At the same time, the state Supreme Court indicated that it would consider only evidence that had been introduced at trial. This put Mooney in an impossible situation, with evidence undermining his conviction yet no court willing to hear it. The situation also proved embarrassing for the Wilson administration, which had gone to war to "make the world safe for democracy" yet now appeared unable to secure justice at home. Thus, before the commission began the journey west, Wilson instructed its members to investigate the case and report back on their findings.

As with the Bisbee affair, Frankfurter did most of the work, sifting through the evidence, interviewing the lawyers, and visiting Mooney in jail. He even dined with the archbishop of San Francisco, who assured him that although Mooney was a bad man he wasn't capable of murder. Frankfurter didn't go that far in his report for the commission. But he did conclude that the case was a miscarriage of justice that had weakened the country's credibility with its allies. To remedy the injustice, he proposed that Wilson urge the governor of California to grant Mooney a retrial—advice that Wilson followed, with mixed results. Instead of a new trial, the governor commuted Mooney's sentence to life in prison.

Made public within a few months of each other, the Bisbee and Mooney reports thrust Frankfurter into the national spotlight for the first time. Progressives cheered his efforts, embracing him as a new spokesman for their cause, while conservatives questioned his integrity, his motives, and even his patriotism. The most damning criticism came from Theodore Roosevelt, whose close friend the copper magnate Jack Greenway had spearheaded the Bisbee deportation. In a letter that was published in the *Boston Herald*, Roosevelt called the Bisbee report "as thoroughly misleading a document as could be written on the subject." He also accused Frankfurter of "excusing men precisely like the Bolsheviki in Russia, who are murderers and encouragers of murder, who are traitors to their allies, to democracy and to civilization, as well as to the United States."

Had Frankfurter lain low at that point, the attacks on him might have died down. Instead, in May 1918 he accepted a job as chairman of the War Labor Policies Board, a position that was even more divisive than the one he had just left. As secretary of the commission, his job had been to gather evidence and write reports. Now he was charged with imposing progressive labor standards, such as the eight-hour workday, on some of the most recalcitrant industries in the country. Frankfurter supported these reforms wholeheartedly, believing they would ultimately boost productivity. But the captains of industry viewed them as the first step to communism. When the chairman of U.S. Steel, Elbert H. Gary, met with Frankfurter in Washington, he complained that a shortened workday would destroy his company. He then spread a rumor that Frankfurter had threatened a federal takeover of the steel mills.

By the end of the war, then, Frankfurter was a controversial figure, closely identified with some of the most radical causes in the country. And the conservatives at Harvard were not pleased. In the spring of 1919, as the university launched a major fund-raising campaign, a group of influential alumni demanded that Dean Roscoe Pound remove Frankfurter (still on leave) from the faculty. When Pound refused, they demanded that *he* be removed. They also blocked the appointment to the faculty of Gerry Henderson, one of Frankfurter's former students, based on rumors that he was a Bolshevist. Distraught over the situation, Pound warned Frankfurter that their future at the school looked grim. But Frankfurter was in Paris attending the peace conference and could not defend himself in person. So Pound explained the situation to Brandeis, who had been a strong supporter in the past. And Brandeis shared the news with Holmes.

Holmes had little sympathy for the progressive causes that Laski and Frankfurter championed. He often said that "the crowd now has substantially all there is" and that reducing the luxuries of the rich would not significantly help the poor. He also had little patience with social reformers—"the upward and onwarders," he called them. They reminded him of the abolitionists of his youth, so dogmatic and cocksure. But although both Laski and Frankfurter fell into this category, Holmes was slow to find fault with his friends. Thus, when he heard that the two men were under attack for their views, he wasn't quite sure what to think.

"Every once in a while, faintly and vaguely as to you, a little more distinctly as to Frankfurter, I hear that you are dangerous men," he wrote to Laski in early April. "What does it mean? They used to say in Boston that I was dangerous. Have your writings as to sovereignty led people who don't read them to believe that you were opposed to law and order or what?"

Laski downplayed the attacks on himself. Yes, he had enemies, but they had not yet made his life difficult. Frankfurter, on the other hand, was in serious trouble. There was a movement afoot to run both him and Pound out of Harvard. Exactly who was behind the effort Laski couldn't say, though he suspected it was the work of Richard Hale and Thomas Perkins, two prominent Boston lawyers with close ties to the school. "Hale is abominable," he told Holmes. "He actually sent for the editor of the *Law Review* early in the year and warned him against Felix." Laski was also unsure about the motive behind the campaign, though again he had his suspicions, which revolved around anti-Semitism. In any case, he explained, Pound and his allies were taking a beating and could use some help. "If you ever get a chance to drop a hint to Hale or Perkins, you would do us all a great service."

Laski's suspicions were correct. Hale and Perkins *were* behind the attacks on Frankfurter, and anti-Semitism *was* prevalent on campus. Aside from Laski and Frankfurter, there were only three other Jews on the entire Harvard faculty, and one of those, a philosophy professor named Harry Sheffer, was also under pressure to step down. Even Lowell, the Harvard president, was an anti-Semite. Three years earlier, when Brandeis became the first Jew nominated to the Supreme Court, Lowell had circulated a petition among Boston's leading families to block his appointment. And three years later, he would plunge Harvard into one of the darkest moments in its history by proposing to cap the number of Jewish students admitted each fall.

Holmes did not share the anti-Semitism of Lowell and the rest of his peers. Indeed, for a Boston Brahmin descended from Puritan stock, he was remarkably unprejudiced. "It never occurs to me until after the event that a man I like is a Jew, nor do I care, when I realize it," he wrote to Pollock after receiving Laski's letter. And it was true, to a point. Many of his closest friends were Jewish—Laski, Frankfurter, Brandeis, Einstein, Lippmann, Morris Cohen, and the banker Paul Warburg. Yet he also recognized that he was drawn to Jews and often wondered why. He once asked Laski "whether loveableness is a characteristic of the better class of Jews," and then added, "When I think how many of the younger men that have warmed my heart have been Jews I cannot but suspect it." The truth is he saw something in these men that reminded him of himself when he was young: a fire, a curiosity, a disregard for received wisdom. Embracing them was a way of embracing his youth while also distancing himself from the parochial culture of his father's Boston.

So when Holmes received Laski's letter and learned that Frankfurter was the target of an anti-Semitic campaign, he naturally wanted to help. But what could he do? He was hesitant to confront Hale, a close friend of both his and Fanny's. And Perkins, he had been told, was impressed by Frankfurter when the two crossed paths in Washington. As for Laski, he was surprised to discover that such an agreeable young man had enemies. "I didn't know it and don't see why you should," he wrote. "Have you trod on toes?"

Laski again ignored the references to himself. If Holmes didn't know why he had enemies, there was no reason to spell it out for him. But he had to make the justice see the gravity of the situation for Frankfurter and Pound. "I understand your hesitation about writing to Hale," he responded, "and I am glad to have your remark on Perkins's attitude to Felix. The real truth is that there's a great fight on as to the future of the School and the older Tories are eager to make the place unbearable for Pound. He is a very great Dean and the students worship him and sooner or later the Law School Alumni Association has to step in and tell the world what Pound is counting for in scholarship and prevent this idle insistence on a status quo which has already lost its status."

Holmes, as Laski well knew, was president of the Law School Alumni Association. So his insistence that the association would have to step in was essentially a plea for *Holmes* to step in. And this time Holmes got the message. He had just received notice of the association's next meeting, he informed Laski two days later. "They ask for suggestions. Could I say anything to them? Answer quick. The letter comes from F. W. Grinnell, partner of Richard Hale."

This was the response Laski was hoping for, and he wasted no time taking advantage of it. "Only one word in very partial reply to a letter worth its weight in gold," he wrote back the next day. "If the Association would, *te movente*, record its appreciation of the way Pound kept the School going during the war it would help marvelously. That, *bien entendu*, if you felt so inclined. My love and great gratitude for that letter."

So that's what Holmes did. He sent a note to Grinnell repeating exactly what Laski had said. "Your letter invites suggestion and I venture one," he wrote. "I have a very strong conviction of the value and importance of Pound who I think has done much to maintain the superlative reputation of the School. If it were possible to pass a resolution expressing our appreciation of the way in which he has kept the School going during the war, or giving him encouragement in such form as is deemed best I should be much gratified. Perhaps you will call this to the attention of the meeting."

When Laski received a copy of this note from Holmes, he was

elated. "That is a most generous letter of yours about Pound and on his account, as well as my own, I am very grateful. It will give exactly the kind of help that is needed."

Pound was also pleased. Grinnell had shown him the letter, he wrote to Holmes, and it was "worth reams of resolutions." But he was still anxious about Frankfurter. "Unhappily most people hereabout seem to be chiefly concerned to push Frankfurter out of the school. If such a thing were to happen, it would be nothing short of a calamity. What I fear is that he will be made uncomfortable and will go."

Now Holmes was truly worried. It was one thing to hear vague and unsubstantiated rumors from Laski. But for Pound himself to voice concern about Frankfurter's future made the situation all the more urgent. He discussed the matter with Brandeis, who encouraged him to write directly to Lowell. After all, Holmes had known the Harvard president for more than four decades; it was Lowell, in fact, who had arranged for Holmes to deliver the Lowell Lectures in 1880. But Holmes was uncertain. Would it be proper for him to meddle in the affair? Or would it look like special pleading on behalf of a friend—and not just a friend but someone who had praised him lavishly in the pages of the *Harvard Law Review*? Still debating the question two days later, he wrote again to Laski:

> If the school should lose Pound and Frankfurter it would lose its soul, it seems to me. I hesitate because I know no details, but my convic-tion is strong. So far as Pound is concerned it is also disinterested, for I don't know his opinions except through his writings and so far as I know I never have come in for much credit in them. But there can be no doubt that he is a real focus of spiritual energy—and even if his presence has prevented subscriptions to the law school I can't but believe that the spark of inspiration is worth more than dollars. By Jove, I think I'll say that to Lowell. I am worried—and all the more that without my foreknowledge I was put in as president of the law school association—of course merely as figurehead—but I hate to feel King Log. With which I shut up as the barber is due to cut my hair. Does the movement threaten you? I am full of helpless anxiety.

In the end, Holmes did write to Lowell, explaining that he had a "very strong feeling that Pound and in his place Frankfurter have and impart the ferment which is more valuable than an endowment and makes a Law School a focus of life." He also suggested that Pound be given an honorary degree from Harvard, "as I believe he has from various other universities. He is one of the very few men whose work on legal subjects is referred to by Continental writers."

That seemed to do the trick. Lowell responded that he supported both Pound and Frankfurter and that neither was at risk of losing his job. Holmes forwarded that message to Laski with permission to show to Pound. "I have the notion that Pound thought Lowell's attitude to be different from this, and it may cheer him up," he wrote.

Holmes was cheered up as well. His friends had been in need, and he had come to their aid. Of course, one could never predict what the future might hold. The political climate was still turbulent, and in the months to come they might once again find themselves under attack. But for now, Laski and Frankfurter appeared to be safe.

9

"They Know Not What They Do"

If his friends were out of danger, Holmes himself was not. On Wednesday, April 30, a clerk at the General Post Office in New York was riding the subway home from work when an article in the newspaper caught his eye. The day before, a mail bomb had exploded at the apartment of Thomas Hardwick, a former U.S. senator from Atlanta. Wrapped in brown paper with the word "Novelties" stamped on the front and "Gimbel Brothers" printed in the return address, the bomb had been opened by Hardwick's maid, who lost both hands in the blast. It was the second attack on a public official in as many days—an identical bomb had been delivered to Seattle mayor Ole Hanson that Monday— and as the clerk read a description of the bombs, he was seized with fear. Earlier that week, sixteen similar packages had arrived at the main post office on Eighth Avenue and Thirty-third Street. Because the packages lacked sufficient postage, they had been placed in a storage room where, if the clerk was not mistaken, they were sitting at that very moment. Jumping up from his seat, he got off at the next stop and rushed back to the post office. Sure enough, the packages were still there and matched precisely the description of the bombs that had been sent to Hardwick and Hanson. They were small (about the size of a cigar box), harmless looking, and addressed to some of the most prominent businessmen and government officials in the country: J. P. Morgan, John D. Rockefeller, Attorney General A. Mitchell Palmer, Postmaster General Albert S. Burleson, Secretary of Labor William B. Wilson . . . and Supreme Court Justice Oliver Wendell Holmes.

In the days to come authorities discovered an additional eighteen bombs in post offices around the country, bringing the total number of targets to thirty-six. It was the largest assassination plot in United States history, and postal officials launched a massive investigation to identify the culprits, enlisting the aid of the Secret Service, the Department of Justice, the Bureau of Investigation, the New York Police Department, and even the federal Bureau of Mines, whose metallurgists examined the bombs for identifying features. Although no group claimed responsibility for the plot, suspicion immediately fell on the Bolshevists and Wobblies, since all of the men targeted had recently come under criticism from the radical left—Hardwick as the sponsor of an anti-immigration bill, Hanson as the man who broke the Seattle strike, and Holmes as the author of the *Debs* opinion. But there were few clues to go on: no fingerprints, no witnesses, not even a stray piece of thread or hair. And despite a series of confident statements from investigators and a handful of fruitless arrests, the perpetrators were never found.

Holmes's friends were shaken by the news and reached out to express their anger and concern. "I am writing you a brief note to say how shocked we are to hear of the outrageous attempt made on you and how thankful that it was frustrated," began a letter from Lewis Einstein. "My wife was wildly furious about it and there is little judicial in my judgment whatever else may remain—*noblesse oblige*! I can sympathize with Mrs. Holmes though I am sure she remained imperturbable and would keep cool in the crater of Vesuvius."

Ever the old soldier, Holmes also played it cool. "I haven't thought much about it except when reminded by letters," he responded to Einstein, "for, as I said to my wife, if I worried over all the bullets that have missed me I should have a job." He also played the martyr, suggesting that if the culprits knew his true feelings, they would not have put him on their list of targets. "I have said several times it brought home to me what, if we don't read into it what is not there, seems to me the greatest saying of antiquity—the words on the Cross: 'They know not what they do.'"

Three days later, Holmes came under attack again—this time in print. On Saturday, May 3, the *New Republic* published an article entitled "The Debs Case and Freedom of Speech." A month earlier, the magazine had printed a short paragraph that largely approved of Holmes's decision. "Eugene Debs has gone to the West Virginia Penitentiary to begin his ten year sentence," the editors had written. "There is no doubt about the legality of his conviction. His Canton speech clearly violated the Espionage act. But since that act ceases to have force when peace is declared, and since the emergency which might have justified it has passed, to let Debs serve his sentence would be both cruel and blind." This new piece, however, struck an entirely different note. Written by University of Chicago law professor Ernst Freund, it was a scathing critique of Holmes's decision, the Espionage Act, and the very notion of suppressing unpopular speech.

Freund began by doing what neither Laski nor Hand nor even the editors of the *New Republic* had been willing to do: challenge the validity of Debs's conviction. Here was a man sent to jail for little more than criticizing the war, he argued. "There was nothing to show actual obstruction or an attempt to interfere with any of the processes of recruiting." But it was not just the outcome of the case that troubled Freund. It was the way Holmes had justified that outcome. By relying on the jury's finding that Debs had intended to obstruct the draft—as well as its conclusion that his speech was likely to do so—Holmes had placed too much discretion in the hands of jurors. Like Hand, Freund thought this set a dangerous precedent. Not only would it empower juries to punish speakers they disagreed with; it would make it impossible for speakers to know ahead of time whether they could be punished for their words. And that, Freund believed, would chill all but the blandest political discussion. "To know what you may do and what you may not do, and how far you may go in criticism, is the first condition of political liberty," he wrote. "To be permitted to agitate at your own peril, subject to a jury's guessing at motive, tendency and possible effect, makes the right of free speech a precarious gift."

Freund also disputed the jury's finding that Debs's speech had in fact been likely to cause harm. After all, Debs had not directly urged his audience to obstruct the draft; at most, he had *in*directly encouraged them to do so by criticizing the war. And the likelihood that this encouragement would cause actual obstruction was "practically nil." Even Debs must have known this, Freund argued, "and he could hardly have intended what he could not hope to achieve. . . . Yet Justice Holmes would make us believe that the relation of the speech to obstruction is like that of the shout of Fire! in a crowded theatre to the resulting panic! Surely implied provocation in connection with political offenses is an unsafe doctrine if it has to be made plausible by a parallel so manifestly inappropriate."

Holmes did not see Freund's article when it first appeared on May 3. But the next Saturday he happened upon another article in the magazine denouncing the repressive policies of Postmaster Burleson. Finding himself in sympathy with that piece, Holmes told his secretary he was thinking about writing a letter of praise to the editor. Landau, who *had* seen Freund's article, then showed Holmes the earlier piece, which, naturally, the justice did not appreciate. It was one thing to portray Burleson as an intolerant reactionary; it was quite another to tar him with the same brush. And though he had dismissed similar criticism in the past as the work of knaves and fools, Freund was one of the most influential legal scholars in the country. He had helped to establish the University of Chicago Law School, practically invented the subject of administrative law, and was a friend to many of the men Holmes respected most, including Brandeis and Pound. Perhaps most troubling, the article appeared in the *New Republic*, a magazine Holmes had supported since its birth, a magazine that was home to Laski, Frankfurter, and all the other young men he adored, a magazine, in other words, that was like family. It was the second time in six months the family had taken a swipe at his views on free speech—Chafee's article the previous November was the first—and this time Holmes decided to swipe back. Two days after reading Freund's article, he sat down and drafted a letter to Herbert Croly that was quite different from the one he had initially intended to write:

May 12, 1919

My dear Mr. Croly:

On Saturday Mr. Hard's article on Mr. Burleson, Espionagent, fell under my eye. I do not know enough of the details of public affairs to have opinions about Mr. Burleson's conduct of his office but the general aspects of the article so stirred my sympathies that I want to express them. . . . As I spoke of it to my secretary and of my inclination to write to you he called my attention to the article on the *Debs* case which I had not seen. You had a short paragraph in an earlier number that struck me as exactly right. This article appeared to me less so if I understood its implications. The constitutionality of the act so far as the clauses concerning obstructing the recruiting service are involved was passed upon in *Schenck v. U.S.* and so all that was needed in the *Debs* case was to refer to that decision, and, given the finding of the jury, in my opinion it was impossible to have a rational doubt about the law. Freund's objection to a jury "guessing at motive, tendency and possible effect" is an objection to pretty much the whole body of the law, which for thirty years I have made my brethren smile by insisting to be everywhere a matter of degree. . . .

I hated to have to write the *Debs* case and still more those of the other poor devils before us the same day and the week before. I could not see the wisdom of pressing the cases, especially when the fighting was over and I think it quite possible that if I had been on the jury I should have been for acquittal but I cannot doubt that there was evidence warranting a conviction on the disputed issues of fact. Moreover I think the *clauses under consideration* not only were constitutional but were proper enough while the war was on. When people are putting out all their energies in battle I don't think it unreasonable to say we

won't have obstacles intentionally put in the way of raising
troops—by persuasion any more than by force. But in the main I
am for aeration of all effervescing convictions—there is no way
so quick for letting them get flat. . . . I write this letter only to
ease my mind, not to impose an answer on you.

> Very sincerely yours,
> O.W. Holmes

Of course it is only for your private eyes.

Like the earlier letters he had written to his friends, Holmes's note
to Croly was both defensive and defiant. He hated having to write the
Debs opinion, he insisted. Had he been on the jury, he likely would
have voted for acquittal, and he didn't understand why the government had pressed the case to a hearing. But as long as there was at least
some evidence to support the jury's verdict—which he thought there
was—he could not overturn that verdict simply because he might have
viewed the evidence differently. As for the constitutionality of the
Espionage Act, he explained, that question had already been put to
rest in *Schenck*. Of course, he neglected to add that he was the one who
had put it to rest; he cited his *Schenck* opinion as if it were the decree of
some superior tribunal he had nothing to do with. At the same time,
he took pains to downplay the implications of both *Debs* and *Schenck*.
He had only ruled on the *clauses under consideration*, he emphasized,
implying that other clauses—those in the 1918 Sedition Act, perhaps?—
might raise harder questions. He also signaled a new appreciation for
free speech, declaring that regardless of what the law dictated he personally favored the "aeration of all effervescing convictions"—not because
it promoted the search for truth or self-government, as Hand and
Chafee had argued, but because it was the best way to take the air out
of silly ideas.

When he finished the letter, Holmes put down his pen and thought
about what he had written. It occurred to him that it might be improper
to express his views so candidly on an issue that was likely to come

before the Court again. In fact, the justices had recently received another petition challenging the government's suppression of dissent, this one filed by a Russian immigrant named Jacob Abrams. If Holmes's letter to Croly became public, the parties to that appeal might claim he had prejudged their case. He was still debating the matter the next day when a letter arrived from Laski. "I am eager to hear if you read Freund in the *New Republic* of May 3rd and if you were at all influenced by his analysis," Laski wrote. Suddenly, Holmes had an idea. Instead of sending his letter to Croly, why not share it with Laski, who would surely convey its substance to the men at the *New Republic*? That way Holmes could protect his judicial integrity while still making his feelings known. Addressing an envelope to Laski, he slipped the letter inside and added the following note: "Yesterday I wrote the within and decided not to send it as some themes may become burning. Instead I trust it confidentially to you and it will answer your inquiry about Freund. I thought it poor stuff—for reasons indicated within."

Laski did not respond to Holmes's letter, and the two friends never mentioned Freund's article in writing again. But there was someone else who was eager to discuss it. Reading the piece in New York, Learned Hand saw Freund's analysis as a vindication of his own views and wanted to thank its author. "Your article in last week's 'New Republic' was a great comfort to me," he wrote Freund on May 7. "I had supposed that in holding such views about the Espionage Act I was in a minority of one in the profession, and that is rather too slim a party to carry a banner. You express my own opinion much better than I could myself and in your distinguished company I shall take heart of grace to believe I am right, even with the whole Supreme Court the other way."

In case Freund had not seen it, Hand also included the citation to his *Masses* opinion, which he hoped the professor might find useful. Then, almost as an afterthought, he closed with the following remark: "I own I was chagrined that Justice Holmes did not line up on our side; indeed, I have so far been unable to make him see that he and we have any real differences, and that puzzles me a little."

———

Another term was winding down. The briefs had all been submitted, the cases had all been argued; now it was just a matter of hashing out disputes among the justices, writing opinions, and announcing the last decisions of the term. Holmes had already finished his own opinions, of course, so the chief justice asked him to write one of his—"and has done it in such a kind hesitating way that even if I could have hesitated otherwise, which I shouldn't have done, I can't now." Once he took care of that, however, his work would be complete. Then he could forget about everything—the Court, the *New Republic*, Eugene Debs—and enjoy another summer at Beverly Farms luxuriating in ideas.

But Brandeis had other plans for him. It was the last full conference of the term, a cool overcast Saturday in May. The justices recorded their final votes, closed their docket books, and headed for home. Holmes and Brandeis walked together down the steps of the Capitol, past the Botanical Gardens, and across the Mall—a sprawling, wooded park carved up by narrow, winding paths, not the formal, rectilinear space it is now. As they strolled west toward the White House and Holmes talked eagerly about his plans for the summer, Brandeis offered a suggestion. Instead of contenting himself with philosophy and the abstract arts, Holmes should study something real and concrete, something with practical application. It would be good for his soul.

"You talk about improving your mind," Brandeis continued. "You only exercise it on the subjects with which you are familiar. Why don't you try something new, study some domain of fact. Take up the textile industries in Massachusetts and after reading the reports sufficiently you can go to Lawrence and get a human notion of how it really is."

It was a predictable suggestion from Brandeis, who lived by the maxim *ex facto jus oritur*—"the law arises out of fact." As a reformer, he had often used his superior command of the facts to embarrass his opponents. And when he appeared before the Supreme Court in 1908 to defend an Oregon law that limited the workday of women to ten hours, he devoted only two pages of his 113-page brief to the law. The remainder focused on facts, presenting a comprehensive survey of medical testimony, labor statistics, factory reports, and workplace statutes from sources as far away as the British House of Commons and the German Imperial Factory Inspectors. The "Brandeis brief," as it became known, was a revolution in the legal profession, ushering in a new style of advocacy. As a justice, too, Brandeis paid close attention to facts. He littered his opinions with charts, tables, and statistics that made them long and difficult to read. Laski and Pound both complained about this, asking Holmes if there wasn't something he could do to simplify his colleague's opinions. But Brandeis was unrepentant. After he and a clerk had worked hard to polish an opinion, he would often say, "Now I think the opinion is persuasive, but what can we do to make it more instructive."

In many ways, Brandeis owed his respect for facts to Holmes. By insisting that the life of the law has been experience, not logic, Holmes had paved the way for the sociological school of jurisprudence, which elevated social and economic data above precedent and formal reasoning. "For the rational study of the law, the blackletter man may be the man of the present," Holmes had written in "The Path of the Law," "but the man of the future is the man of statistics and the master of economics." Yet although Holmes recognized the value of facts, he personally despised them. It was one of the biases he inherited from his father, who complained that facts choked his windpipe when he talked. Holmes's objection was more theoretical. The world is divided into ideasts and thingsters, he told Laski, and he was an ideast. Brandeis, on the other hand, was a thingster. "If I wanted to be epigrammatic, I should say that he always desires to know all that can be known about a case whereas I am afraid that I wish to know as little as I can safely go on."

So Brandeis's suggestion that Holmes devote his precious time at Beverly Farms to studying the minutiae of the textile industry was disagreeable, to say the least. He would rather spend his time reading "this and that, that a gentleman should have read before he dies." Besides, he pointed out, he was too old to learn anything new.

This was true, Brandeis acknowledged. Holmes was "too old to acquire knowledge in many fields of fact." But he was "not too old to realize through one field what the world of fact was and to be more conscious and understanding of it. With his mind as an instrument, there wasn't anything he couldn't acquire."

Holmes did not commit to Brandeis's proposal that day. But as often happened when the two men spoke, his friend's words continued to gnaw at him afterward. Maybe Brandeis was right, he thought. Maybe he should learn some facts, if not for the good of his soul at least for the performance of his duties. Still, the prospect bored him stiff, and he wrote to Laski in search of sympathy:

> Talking with Brandeis yesterday (a big chap) he drove a harpoon into my midriff by saying that it would be for the good of my soul to devote my next leisure to the study of some domain of fact—suggesting the textile industry, which, after reading many reports &c, I could make living to myself by a visit to Lawrence.... Well—I hate facts—and partly because of that am impressed by Brandeis's suggestion. It was good for me that instead of philosophy I was shoved into the law. I suppose it would be good for me to get into actualities touching spindles—immigration—God knows what—but I would rather meditate on the initial push and the following spin.

For once, Laski was not sympathetic. He had been caught up in the growing labor crisis all spring, walking the picket lines in Lawrence, meeting with union leaders, and writing articles in defense of the strikers. Holmes's desire to ignore the facts, to not see what was really going on around him, struck a nerve, and he fired off an unusually critical reply:

> If I may say so, you come into contact with men of property on their very best side—the lawyer of ability appealing to your intellect, the great business man describing some fine achievement, the wife of a millionaire asking you to share some deeply-felt aesthetic enjoyment, Paul Warburg making marvelouslly [sic] simple some vast technical complexity. You don't see the obvious evils that one gets contact with among the trade unions—the blindness to pain, the hard obstinacy,

the relentless pressure, the unwillingness to experiment with the prospects of human nature. If you saw that Lawrence strike at first hand you would say (as I do) that almost any system must be better than one which gives some men economic power over others.

These were strong words to address to a man more than fifty years his senior, and a Supreme Court justice at that. But Holmes was impassive, refusing to be provoked or admit that he was wrong:

What you say to explain my opinions, while it confirms what I have long said, fails to hit me. For a quarter of a century I have said that the real foundations of discontent were emotional not economic, and that if the socialists would face the facts and put the case on that ground I should listen to them with respect. . . . My opinion, however, is based on the effort to think quantitatively not dramatically. I won't go over the old ground, but to my mind the notion that any rearrangement of property, while any part of the world propagates freely, will prevent civilization from killing its weaker members, is absurd. I think that the crowd now has substantially all there is—and that every mitigation of the lot of any body of men has to be paid for by some other or the same body of men—and I don't think that cutting off the luxuries of the few would make an appreciable difference of the situation.

He had said all of this before, to Laski and anyone else who would listen. But it felt good to say it again. And once he had, his resistance to Brandeis's proposal seemed to soften. "The temptation is strong to say that I am old enough to be entitled to leisure," he told Laski a few weeks later, "but I suppose that can't be while one is on the fighting line."

Then, before he could change his mind, he sent off to Congress for a report on the textile mills.

10

The Red Summer

The social unrest that had been building all year finally erupted that summer. It began on May 1, a traditional day for the celebration of labor that had recently become associated with the radical left. Enraged by the bomb plot against Morgan, Rockefeller, and other prominent figures, police and vigilante groups lashed out at socialists and immigrants around the country. In Boston, patrolmen used clubs and revolvers to disperse a crowd of May Day demonstrators outside the Dudley Street Opera House, while nearby a civilian mob trashed the headquarters of the Socialist Party. In New York, hundreds of returned soldiers and sailors took to the streets in search of Bolshevist sympathizers. They forced their way into the Russian People's House, a gathering spot for immigrants, then raided a reception at a socialist newspaper, destroying furniture, burning books, and beating the guests with sticks. The worst violence occurred in Cleveland, where a group of Victory Loan workers confronted a May Day parade and demanded that the marchers surrender their red flags. When the marchers refused, a mass brawl broke out in which the loan workers were badly outnumbered until mounted police arrived and charged the crowd. From there, the violence spilled over into Public Square, the site of a socialist rally, and then into the shopping district, where spectators smashed store windows and threw ink bottles, shoes, and other merchandise at rioters on the street. By the end of the day, one person was dead, more than a hundred were wounded, and scores of socialists were in jail.

The situation only grew worse at the beginning of June when bombs exploded in eight different cities within an hour of one another. Most of the targets were local officials unknown outside their jurisdictions: the mayor of Cleveland, a Massachusetts state legislator, a Pittsburgh police inspector, a Boston municipal judge. But one name on the list was familiar to everyone in the country: Attorney General A. Mitchell Palmer. A bomb exploded on the doorstep of his Washington home shortly after Palmer and his wife had retired for the evening. Neither was injured, though the explosion blew out the front of their house and shattered windows up and down the fashionable block. The first person on the scene was the assistant secretary of the navy, Franklin Delano Roosevelt, who lived across the street and had just returned from a party with his wife, Eleanor. Rushing out onto the Palmers' lawn, he encountered a grisly spectacle: blood splattered on the trees in front of the house and body parts strewn across the yard. Apparently, the culprit had blown himself up in the process of planting the bomb. Copies of an anarchist leaflet were also scattered about the street, leading authorities to conclude that the attack on Palmer, as well as the other explosions that night, had been coordinated by an anarchist group from Italy. But as with the bomb plot earlier in the year, investigators ran into a dead end and never identified the culprits.

Then came the mad, feverish days of July, when record-breaking temperatures combined with long-simmering racial tensions to ignite firestorms in two American cities. First, riots broke out in Washington after a newspaper reported that two black men had attacked a white woman walking home from work. This was not the first allegation of its kind in the capital. All summer, the local papers had been running inflammatory stories about sexual assaults by black men against white women. But this woman was the wife of a navy employee, and when word of the attack reached the shipyards a group of two hundred sailors set out to find and lynch her assailants. Marching into the south-west part of the city, they harassed and questioned black men and women as they went, grabbing them by the arms and sometimes slapping or punching them. When the sailors tried to chase one black couple into a house, police intervened and put a stop to the manhunt. The trouble was just beginning, however. Many blacks were fed up with their treatment since the end of the war. After helping defeat Germany—both in the factories and on the front lines—they had expected a new degree of respect and equality. Instead they had been accused of supporting Bolshevism and blamed for the lack of jobs for returning soldiers. They had also faced an increasing level of mob violence. Already that year, there had been twenty-eight lynchings of black men across the country, many of them prompted by allegations of sexual assaults on white women. So the next night when a white mob stoned a black man who had been arrested on a minor charge, blacks in Washington took matters into their own hands. Arming themselves with revolvers and knives, they fought back against the white servicemen patrolling the streets. Two days of riots and pitched gun battles followed, terrorizing the city and forcing President Wilson to mobilize more than two thousand federal troops. A combination of rain and cavalry eventually halted the violence, but not before six people were killed and one hundred injured.

The bitterness over these events had hardly subsided when an even more devastating incident occurred in Chicago. The trouble began on a scorching Sunday afternoon at a South Side beach segregated by race. A party of black sunbathers walking toward the water inadvertently crossed over to the white side of the beach. Angered, the whites began yelling and throwing rocks at the blacks, who retreated to their side. But moments later another group of black sunbathers appeared and a fight broke out, with each group hurling stones at the other. In the midst of this scuffle, a white sunbather began throwing bricks at five black boys swimming in Lake Michigan. One of the boys was hit in the head and drowned. When the other boys made it back to the beach and pointed out the culprit to a white policeman, he refused to arrest the man. Instead he arrested a black man on an unrelated charge and threw him into a patrol van, prompting a crowd of blacks to pelt the vehicle with rocks and stones. A black man then fired a revolver, hitting a white officer, and a black policeman fired back, killing the gunman. Soon word of the riot spread to nearby neighborhoods, and gangs of whites and blacks poured into the area, wielding guns, knives, and fists. The fighting continued until morning and then broke out again the next night as residents returned home from work. White mobs pulled black workers out of streetcars and beat them on the sidewalks. Other whites drove through black neighborhoods firing shots from their cars, while blacks gathered on the rooftops and returned the fire. It took three days and more than six thousand infantrymen to stop the violence. When it was over, 38 people were dead, 537 were wounded, and at least 1,000 blacks were homeless.

To those following the events in Washington and Chicago, New York and Boston, it seemed as if the entire country were engulfed in flames. Even Holmes, indifferent as he was to current events, could not help but notice the fires raging around him. After the bombing of the attorney general's house, he woke up to find a police officer stationed near his front door in Washington. And when he and Fanny arrived at Beverly Farms in mid-June, he discovered that their mail was being screened and that local police had been ordered to keep an eye on their home.

But Holmes had other concerns on his mind that summer. On the long train ride north, Fanny had fallen ill from the heat and fatigue and was now confined to her room. She lay in bed with the shades drawn, pale and lethargic, not interested in books or conversation or even getting up for dinner. Holmes worried she might have the flu, which had made a brief reappearance that spring, and called for a doctor to examine her. But the doctor could find nothing seriously wrong and assured Holmes she would eventually recover. In the meantime, he said, there was nothing to do but make sure she got plenty of rest and relaxation.

It was not the first time something like this had happened. Shortly after they were married, in 1872, Fanny spent several months in bed with what the family described to friends as rheumatic fever. She had another spell of the same sort in 1896, not long before Holmes left alone on a trip for England, and then at least one more, in 1908. The toll these episodes took on her was dramatic. Though she had never been beautiful, she had, as a young woman, possessed a certain sparkle and charm, with eyes that were bright and intelligent and a smile that was sly and sardonic. She had also carried herself with assurance and poise, in spite of a natural shyness. She was, after all, the oldest child of a respected Cambridge family. Her father, Epes Sargent Dixwell, ran a popular Latin school for boys (Holmes was one of his first students), and her grandfather was the author of a famous book on navigation. As a young woman, she had socialized with the sons and daughters of the Boston aristocracy, and in her early thirties she had distinguished herself as a skillful embroiderer, weaving silken landscapes of such beauty and subtlety that they were exhibited in museums. But as the years passed and she suffered through one breakdown after another, she became increasingly dour and eccentric. She gave up embroidery and burned all but a few samples of her work. She collected birds, marmosets, and squirrels, some of which roamed freely about the house. And she developed a strong sensitivity to light, pulling the rattan blinds on the porch at Beverly Farms down to the floor so that not a ray of sunlight penetrated inside. With Holmes and his young friends, she could still be pert and impish at times. She played practical jokes on April Fools' Day, placing a rubber ink spot on a freshly drafted opinion or hiding a fake cockroach in the flour barrel. And when Holmes was at Court she often slipped into the study to gossip with his secretaries, who universally adored her. For the most part, however, she had become a recluse, rarely going out in public, refusing to have her picture taken, and paying little attention to her appearance. Her eyes were now deep-sunken, her face colorless and gaunt. She kept her gray hair netted and pulled back tightly in a bun and wore dark dresses with high-boned collars. Next to Holmes, youthful and striking in his tailored English suits, she seemed old and frail, more like his mother than his wife. In the words of one Boston socialite, "she really did look like a monkey, with a long upper lip, darting black eyes and the restless manner of a small bird." Even Fanny described herself ruefully as looking "like an abandoned farm in Maine."

It was no surprise, then, that Holmes often sought the company of other women. He had always been something of a flirt, reveling in the attention of young women in Boston and Cambridge, especially after he was wounded in the war and came home to recover. "I admire and love ladies' society and like to be on intimate terms with as many as I can get," he told a female friend while at Harvard. The ladies admired him, too. Dashing in his officer's uniform, he charmed them with stories of the war and passionate talk about art, literature, and philosophy. Any young woman would have been happy to have him, but Holmes resisted the pressure to settle down, throwing himself into the study of law instead. Not until he was thirty-one and most of his friends were already married did he finally propose to Fanny, whom he described to one acquaintance as "for many years my most intimate friend." Even then, his eye continued to roam. He called regularly on several young wives in Boston and often attended dinner parties alone, finding the prettiest woman in the room and parking himself beside her. Society matrons gossiped about his behavior, and one husband threatened a divorce if his wife spent another evening in Holmes's company.

Fanny knew about all of this—it came with the territory of being Mrs. Oliver Wendell Holmes Jr. And naturally she didn't like it. She once turned up at the home of a woman Holmes was visiting and sent in a note that she was waiting in a carriage outside. On other occasions she rolled her eyes and mocked him for falling prey to the allurements of a pretty face. But as long as Holmes didn't cross the line, as long as his flirtations remained merely aspirational, she was willing to endure the pain and embarrassment they caused her.

What Fanny didn't know—what no one knew—was that one of those flirtations *had* crossed the line. In the summer of 1896, while traveling alone in England, Holmes, then fifty-five, began a romantic relationship with Lady Clare Castletown, an Anglo-Irish aristocrat who was married to Bernard Fitzpatrick, the second Baron Castletown

Courtesy of Historical and Special Collections, Harvard Law School Library

Lieutenant Holmes in 1861, shortly before the first of three injuries he suffered during the Civil War.

Courtesy of Historical and Special Collections, Harvard Law School Library

Fanny Holmes around the time of her marriage to Holmes in 1872. In later years, she refused to have her photo taken, lamenting that she looked like "an abandoned farm in Maine."

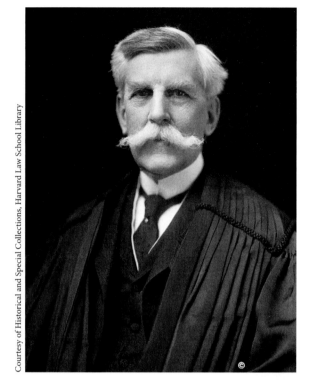

Holmes in 1915, the same year he upheld the conviction of a small-time anarchist for publishing a newspaper article inciting nude sunbathing.

The Holmes house in Beverly Farms, Mass., where Holmes and Fanny retreated each summer. From his study on the second floor, Holmes could glimpse the waves breaking just off the shore.

Learned Hand around 1920. It was a chance encounter with Hand on a train that prompted Holmes to begin rethinking his position on free speech.

Harold Laski with his wife, Frida, and daughter, Diana, in 1920, shortly before he left Harvard for a new post in England.

The members of the Supreme Court from 1916 to 1920. Seated, left to right: William R. Day, Joseph McKenna, Edward D. White, Oliver Wendell Holmes Jr., Willis Van Devanter. Standing, left to right: Louis D. Brandeis, Mahlon Pitney, James C. McReynolds, John H. Clarke.

Holmes's study in Washington, D.C. He liked to write his opinions at the upright desk in front of the window, explaining that "nothing conduces to brevity like a caving in of the knees."

Zechariah Chafee in 1920, the year his book *Freedom of Speech* was published. Though he came from a wealthy family and sympathized with men of capital, he wanted his side to "fight fair."

Louis Brandeis on the deck of the *Mauretania* in 1919, on his way to the Holy Land as de facto leader of the Zionist Organization of America.

Holmes around 1915. Still healthy and vigorous in his mid-seventies, he walked the two miles home from the Supreme Court each day.

Eugene Debs delivering the 1918 speech in Canton, Ohio, for which he was sentenced to ten years in prison.

Felix Frankfurter in 1925, on his way to becoming one of the most powerful and controversial liberals in the country.

The *Abrams* defendants (Samuel Lipman, Hyman Lachowsky, Mollie Steimer, and Jacob Abrams) posing for a photograph on the day of their deportation to Russia in 1921.

of Upper Ossory. He had first noticed her on a visit seven years earlier—a beautiful young woman with curly hair, dark eyes, and high cheekbones—but had managed little more than an introduction. On his return trip, however, he left his card at her London home and was soon rewarded with an invitation to lunch. That was followed by another lunch, a dinner, and a visit to the India Exhibition at the Empress Theatre. When the social season ended and the wealthy retreated to their country estates, Lady Castletown invited Holmes to Doneraile Court, her family's ancestral seat in the south of Ireland. Traveling by boat to Dublin and then by train and bus through the lush rolling hills of County Cork, he arrived in the middle of August to find that Lord Castletown was away and only a few other guests were on hand. For a week he and Lady Castletown were inseparable, strolling through the village streets, tramping through the wet fields, and baring their souls to each other in the privacy of the conservatory. By the time Holmes left to catch his ship back to America, he was helplessly in love. "It is the stopping so sudden that hurts," he wrote to her from the port of Queenstown, just before embarking. "I can only cling to your hand for a moment until the earth puts its shoulder between us—which is more than the world can do I hope in twenty years."

The journey home was dismal. The sky was gray, the sea leaden. Holmes passed the hours smoking cigars on deck and talking with an old Catholic priest who reminded him of Ireland. When the ship docked in Boston, he went to his house on Beacon Street instead of joining Fanny in Beverly Farms as planned. His solitude did not last long. Though it was almost midnight and she was by no means well, Fanny hired a carriage and traveled the thirty miles to Boston, arriving at one thirty in the morning. When Holmes awoke the next day and saw her sitting by his bedside, he was filled with shame that she had made the effort he had been unwilling to make himself.

But his feelings for Lady Castletown were greater than any sense of shame, and he continued the relationship by letter, writing her at least once a week, often while listening to arguments on the Massachusetts Supreme Court. "My Dear Lady," he would begin. Or "My Charmeress." Or "My Beloved Hibernia." And then, while the lawyers droned away, contesting the legality of a will or the validity of some cursed contract, he would pour out his heart to her, declaring his love, his devotion, and his desire to know everything about her, "to know every minutest movement of your mind—every thought and every whim and eat them." "I wish you would just pulsate onto the page and record the whole of yourself." He was tender and sentimental, full of small compliments and caresses. He got down on his knees, he kissed her hands, her feet. He sat with her in the conservatory and reminisced about the hours they had spent together. "I still carry in my pocket a handkerchief (one of my own) with a little infinitesimal dark smear upon it—with it I once rubbed away a—Do you remember? Isn't that a fool thing for a serious Judge?" But he was also insecure, jealous, and needy. He reproached her for the coolness he sometimes sensed in her letters and for her tendency to play coy. He asked about the other men in her life, fretting about one rival in particular. "Is he still in statu quo?" he inquired. "Has his importance grown? or how otherwise? or has he happily demised?" He waited anxiously for her letters, then scolded her for not matching his output. "Oh it is time that I heard." "*Please* don't let it be so long again." And he repeatedly expressed the fear that her feelings were not equal to his. "The thing to believe and take comfort in," he wrote, "is that we are not going to part company— and I am very sure that if we do it will not be I who does it—I am only less confident that it will not be you."

Holmes kept all of this secret from Fanny, instructing Lady Castletown to write to him at the courthouse and urging her to burn his letters, as he did hers. When she asked him for a photograph, he snuck off to have one made, then quickly destroyed the negative. Her own picture he kept tucked safely inside his wallet. It did not quite match his memory of her, but it helped to ease the pain of separation, unlike the tie pin she gave him for Christmas, which pricked his chin until he learned how to properly place it.

He returned to England two summers later to renew the affair in person. Apprehensive about the trip—Fanny was still ill, and the United States was on the verge of war with Spain—he sought assurance that it would be worth his while. "Do you swear that I should see a great deal of you if I come," he wrote to Lady Castletown in January, "or would it depend on chances which I will not seek to analyze more precisely?" He vacillated for months. In February, there was "very little doubt" he should come. In March, his prospects were "clouded." In April, they were "dim." May left him "hanging in exasperating uncertainty," and by June he was "nigh insane with the question of coming to England." In the end, he did what he had wanted to do all along. "Just settled sail Umbria June twenty five," he telegraphed a week before his departure.

He stopped first in London, where he dined with Lord Castletown, an affable sportsman who did not seem to mind the attentions paid to his wife by the American judge. Then it was on to Ireland, where he stayed for a few days at Granston Manor, Lord Castletown's family estate, before finally arriving at Doneraile Court. As on his earlier visit, it was just he, Lady Castletown, and a few trivial guests who could entertain themselves. Exhausted by the journey, Holmes came down with a painful and embarrassing case of shingles, which kept him awake at night. But the relationship deepened nonetheless, and when he returned to the States at the beginning of September his letters were as affectionate and optimistic as ever. "And now do you think that you can meet time and distractions and still care for me as much?" he wrote shortly after arriving back in Beverly Farms. "I believe you will. I firmly believe that time will make no difference to me. Oh my dear what joy it is to feel the inner chamber of one's soul open for the other to walk in and out at will. It was just beginning with you. Do not cut it off because of a little salt water."

True to his word, Holmes continued to write weekly, reaffirming his devotion with monotonous reliability. "Whatever you say or don't say I believe in you and trust you and love you dearly," he declared in the fall of 1898. "I long long long for you and think think think about you." The lady was less constant. As Holmes suspected, there was another man in her life—Percy LaTouche, a charming but feckless aristocrat whom she had been carrying on with for several years. And as the months passed and the distance between County Cork and Boston seemed to widen, she despaired of any future together with Holmes.

"It is *impossible* to really keep in touch," she wrote in May 1899, to which he responded, "Oh my dear it is possible to be unchanged after 20 years—I care for you just as much as when we were together and with every year new little roots grow out and bind you tighter. You don't mean anything to the contrary of that I am pretty sure. For you are a faithful wretch. But I hate any suggestion of less nearness. Write and say that you are not taking back anything that you said when I was there. . . . Tell me that you love me still the same."

A week went by without a response. Then another. And just when it began to appear that Lady Castletown *would not* write, Holmes found out that she *could not* write. Sometime in mid-May, she had fallen from a horse while out riding with LaTouche. She would survive, Lord Castletown informed Holmes in mid-June, but one eye was badly injured and she was in considerable pain. It would be months before she was fully recovered. And then, when she did recover, she was gone. War broke out between the English and the Boers, and Lord Castletown sailed for South Africa to join the fight, taking his wife with him. They stayed abroad for three years, not returning until the summer of 1901, at which point Holmes traveled to England to see Lady Castletown once again. By then the romance had faded. He was sixty, she was forty-six, and they were now dear friends as much as anything else.

Holmes paid three more visits to Doneraile Court over the next dozen years and continued to correspond with Lady Castletown the rest of her life (she died in 1927). But he did not see her again after 1913, when her husband was on the verge of bankruptcy and she was half blind. Nor did he replace her with anyone else. Though he continued to flirt, he never again let himself get carried away as he had with his beloved Hibernia. And these days his flirtations were mostly harmless. After all, he was nearing eighty and was not as virile as he had once been. So while he still wrote charming letters to Baroness Moncheur, occasionally called on John Gray's widow, Nina, and sometimes went for a carriage ride with his Beverly Farms neighbor Ellen Curtis, it was all much less exhilarating than when he was younger. And this summer, with Fanny bedridden and Holmes desperate to fill the emptiness of his days, he turned not to a woman but to a man. He turned, naturally, to Laski.

The young lad was happy to oblige. He had once again rented a cottage up the coast in Rockport, borrowing money from friends to help cover the expense. And as soon as he arrived for the summer, he telephoned Beverly Farms to say hello. Holmes missed his call ("I was in the house, but locked in the shrine") but responded at once by post. "I am afraid that I must put off seeing you as my wife is not very well," he wrote. "She is getting better I think but she had a pull down on coming on. I am dreadfully sorry as I long to see you." Two days later, his prospects had brightened. "Why shouldn't I call on you some afternoon this week," he proposed. "If yes, telephone to me Beverly Farms 14 what day suits you—or write—as most convenient.... Tell me where you are, with particularity—or I shall have to get the town crier."

That set the routine in motion. Once or twice a week for the next two months, Holmes would take a car or train to Rockport in the afternoon. He would stay an hour or more—preferably more—and they would sit on the terrace, sipping tea and canvassing all manner of esoteric subjects, from the religious feuds of the eighteenth century to the implications of Malthusian theory to the merits of the Socratic dialogues. Holmes confessed that he had never been impressed with Socrates's skills as a debater ("my impression is that an intelligent modern would have landed a sock dologer under his jaw in two minutes"), while Laski wondered once again who had been the greatest man of the nineteenth century. If that question was too subjective, as Holmes had argued the previous summer, perhaps they could at least agree on the twenty men who had had the greatest influence, starting with Napoleon, Bismarck, and Cavour, then moving on to Marx, Mill, Baur, Roscher, Ranke, Mommsen, Clark, and Maxwell. Holmes remained skeptical. "What influences are you going to count?" he wanted to know. "The man or men who made the bicycle possibly did more for human happiness, in my opinion, than a dozen Bismarcks or

Cavours." At any rate, could one really rank Mill over Bentham? And what about Alexander Hamilton, who "had a good deal of influence over the future of a pretty big piece of land"? "But I give it up," he concluded, "at least till next Saturday."

When Holmes was not visiting Laski (or arranging a visit, or following up on a visit), he was reading. He read over fifty books that summer—more than any year since he had joined the Court. The reports on the textile mills had not yet arrived, so he drifted back into the realm of ideas, indulging in philosophy, history, political theory, and belles lettres. As usual, Laski fed him a steady supply of material. He was already deep into the writing of his next book, a study of English political thought from Locke to Bentham, so most of his offerings came out of that research. In May, he gave Holmes a biography of Francis Place, the nineteenth-century British social reformer who had fought against the stamp tax on newspapers. In July, he passed along *The History of English Rationalism in the Nineteenth Century*, an account of the triumph of science and logic over religious dogma. In August, he presented Holmes with *The History of English Democratic Ideas in the Seventeenth Century*, a chronicle of the emergence of political liberalism during and after the English Civil Wars. Holmes protested weakly against Laski's generosity: "You are a bad boy to keep sending me pretty books." But he devoured each one as soon as it arrived and let it be known that he was hungry for more.

Of all the items Laski recommended that summer, there was one he especially wanted Holmes to read. It was an article by Zechariah Chafee in the June issue of the *Harvard Law Review*. Entitled "Freedom of Speech in War Time," the article repeated many of the arguments Chafee had made in the *New Republic* the previous fall, including his claim that the framers had rejected the Blackstonian view of free speech. But Chafee was not content merely to bring down William Blackstone. As he pointed out, Holmes had already done that in *Schenck*, though not before his earlier endorsement "had had considerable influence." What Chafee cared about now was filling the void left in Blackstone's wake. Many judges, he noted, had interpreted the First Amendment to protect the "use" of speech but not its "abuse," "liberty" of the press but not "license." Those formulas, however, gave little guidance to judges and speakers about what types of speech were protected. "Justice Holmes in his Espionage Act cases had a magnificent opportunity" to clarify the uncertainty, Chafee wrote. "He, we hoped, would concentrate his great abilities on fixing the line." Instead, like other judges, Holmes had taken aim at easy targets, such as the man who falsely shouts fire in a crowded theater and causes a panic. "How about the man who gets up in a theatre between the acts and informs the audience honestly but perhaps mistakenly that the fire exits are too few or locked?" Chafee asked. "He is a much closer parallel to Schenck or Debs. How about James Russell Lowell when he counseled not murder, but the cessation of murder, his name for war? The question whether such perplexing cases are within the First Amendment or not cannot be solved by the multiplication of obvious examples, but only by the development of a rational principle to mark the limits of constitutional protection."

What should that principle be? In private conversations, Chafee said that he favored the test proposed by Learned Hand in the *Masses* case, which protected all speech except explicit incitement to break the law. That standard, with its focus on the words actually spoken rather than their likely effects, was easy to apply and would provide clear notice to judges and speakers. But Hand's test had been rejected by the appeals court and ignored by the Supreme Court; there was little chance it would become the law of the land. A more plausible candidate was the bad tendency test that many lower courts had relied on during the war. To Chafee, however, this was the worst test of all. It allowed the punishment of speech that had only a remote possibility of causing harm, thus chilling any criticism of government. It also focused too much on the dangers of speech and not enough on its social benefits. When those benefits were properly taken into account, Chafee thought, speech should be punished only when "the interest in public safety is really imperiled, and not, as most men believe, when it is barely conceivable that it may be slightly affected."

But how could he endow that view with the authority of law? Reading Holmes's opinion in *Schenck*, Chafee found the answer he was looking for. "The question in every case," Holmes had written, "is whether the words used are used in such circumstances and are of such a nature as to create a clear and present danger that they will bring about the substantive evils that Congress has a right to prevent." *Clear and present danger.* That was exactly what Chafee had in mind. A requirement that speech pose a clear and present danger before it could be punished would protect much more speech than the bad tendency test. Prosecutors would have to show that the harm was real and imminent, not merely speculative and remote. And because the requirement had roots in the common law of attempts, it could be justified on the basis of precedent. There was only one problem. Holmes had not clearly indicated that the phrase "clear and present danger" was intended as a substitute for "bad tendency." Indeed, there was reason to think he was not introducing a new test at all but was simply using a different formula to describe the old test. For one thing, he had affirmed the defendants' convictions without explaining how their speech posed a clear and present danger to military recruitment. Furthermore, the language he used in *Debs*—"natural tendency and reasonably probable effect"—sounded suspiciously like "bad tendency." But Chafee ignored these facts and portrayed "clear and present danger" as a new standard designed to protect more speech than the old bad tendency test.

When it came to evaluating the results in the three cases, Chafee also disregarded the facts. Although he had earlier rejected the analogy between Schenck and a man who shouts fire in a crowded theater, he now asserted, somewhat inexplicably, that *Sugarman*, *Schenck*, and *Frohwerk* "were clear cases of incitement to resist the draft, so that no real question of free speech arose." The *Debs* case, however, was different. If the Supreme Court had applied the clear and present danger test to Debs's speech, Chafee argued, "it is hard to see how he could have been held guilty." It was true that a jury had convicted Debs, and equally true that the Supreme Court ordinarily does not second-guess a jury's factual conclusions. But the judge had not instructed the jury that a "clear and present danger" was necessary. In addition, the judge had allowed the jury to infer that Debs intended to obstruct the draft from the mere fact that he gave the speech. These were serious mistakes that had to be avoided in the future, Chafee argued. "If the Supreme Court test is to mean anything more than a passing observation, it must be used to upset convictions for words when the trial judge did not insist that they must create 'a clear and present danger' of overt acts."

Chafee's argument was inspired, if somewhat disingenuous. He had seized upon an isolated phrase in *Schenck*—a phrase used casually, almost carelessly, by Holmes—and held it out as announcing a new standard in First Amendment law. Then he had used that new standard to undercut one of Holmes's own opinions. Where most progressives had looked at *Schenck*, *Frohwerk*, and *Debs* and seen only disaster, Chafee had seen opportunity. As Hand put it to him in a letter two years later, "You have, I dare say, done well to take what has fallen from Heaven and insist that it is manna rather than to set up any independent solution."

In addition to turning Holmes's words against him, Chafee also faulted the justice for not paying adequate attention to the values underlying the First Amendment. "It is regrettable," he wrote, "that Justice Holmes did nothing to emphasize the social interest behind free speech, and show the need of balancing even in war time." Indeed, Chafee noted, Holmes's opinion in *Schenck*—with its assertion that "many things that might be said in time of peace . . . will not be endured so long as men fight"—suggested that he would "sanction any restriction of speech that has military force behind it, and reminds us that the Justice used to say when he was young 'that truth was the majority vote of that nation that could lick all others.' His liberalism seems held in abeyance by his belief in the relativity of values."

These were harsh words, reminiscent of Zane's attack on Holmes earlier that year. But Chafee softened their impact by praising the clear and present danger standard and noting that Holmes had contributed "some valuable suggestions pointing toward the ultimate solution." He also, like Zane, acknowledged the "habitual felicity" of Holmes's phrasemaking.

When Laski read Chafee's article that summer, he agreed with it completely. He sent a copy to Holmes and then had an idea that was almost as inspired as Chafee's article. Chafee was scheduled to spend a weekend with him in Rockport at the end of July. Why not invite Holmes to tea that weekend so that Chafee might make his argument in person? He broached the possibility with Holmes, who seemed open to the idea. Then, three days before Chafee was scheduled to arrive, Laski wrote to inform him of the plan:

July 23, 1919

Dear Zach,

    You won't forget that you are coming down on Saturday for the week-end. Holmes is coming to tea, and I want you to arrive in good time. For I have given him your article and we must fight on it. I've read it twice, and I'll go to the stake for every word. Bless you for it.

Yours ever,
HJL

Chafee did not forget. He took the train up from Cambridge and arrived in Rockport on Saturday morning. As planned, Holmes came by in the afternoon. It was a cool, drizzly day, and the little cottage was bustling. Diana, recently turned three, danced around the room while Frida served tea. There was also another woman present, whose face Holmes admired but whose name he did not catch. The party made small talk for a bit, debating the appeal of earlier eras versus their own. Then, when Holmes was comfortable and the time was right, Laski and Chafee presented their case.

It was essentially a rehash of Chafee's article, insisting on the need for a bright line between protected and unprotected speech, emphasizing the potential of the clear and present danger standard, and criticizing the Court's decision in *Debs*. Holmes listened patiently, conceding nothing outright but once again attempting to absolve himself of blame for the outcome in *Debs*. Yes, if he had been on the jury, he might have voted for acquittal, he told Laski and Chafee. But once the jury found that Debs had intended to interfere with the draft—and that his speech might likely do so—there was little the Court could do. He also seemed stung by some of Chafee's comments, particularly his suggestion that Holmes had fallen back on "obvious examples" instead of squarely addressing the limits of free speech. Wincing with embarrassment, Chafee made a mental note to tone down his language if he wrote about the issue again.

If Holmes was hurt, he quickly recovered. The next day he wrote Laski to thank him for the visit and pay tribute to his guests. "I was delighted with Chafee, admired the silently speaking face of the dame whose name I know not and got the expected joy from you and your family."

Still, Chafee was not optimistic. A few weeks later, he received a letter from Judge Charles Amidon of Fargo, North Dakota, one of the few judges who had kept his head during the war. Amidon praised Chafee's article, calling it the "ablest discussion of the First Amendment to the Federal Constitution which has been made" and predicting that it would ultimately sway judicial opinion on the subject. In response, Chafee explained that he had already discussed the article with Holmes but found that the justice was "inclined to allow a very wide latitude" to the government when it came to speech in time of war. He also noted that Holmes did not think it possible to draw a clear line between protected and unprotected speech; the best one could do was "simply to indicate cases on the one side or the other of the line. While I do not anticipate myself that any hard and fast line could be drawn, his failure, it seems to me, is the omission to state the principles by which decisions are to be placed on one side or the other."

"The greatest pity of all," he added, "is that Judge Learned Hand was reversed."

At the end of August, Laski returned to Cambridge and Holmes was left alone with Fanny, who had finally gotten out of bed but was still confined to the house. His days were quiet and dull. He slept late most mornings, read in bed for an hour or so, then walked to the post office in town. After a midday meal he napped, took another walk, ate supper and read aloud to Fanny or played solitaire (always five games in a row, each until he won). It was a dreary way to end his vacation, and the weather only made matters worse. It turned cold in late August and rained hard and steady throughout September. "Come back and bring the sunlight," he sighed to Ellen Curtis, who was away on a trip with her family.

The reports on the textile mills finally arrived, and Holmes forced himself to finish them, fighting off sleep as he did so. They were "not very enlivening," he told Nina Gray, "but still I hope it is good for my soul." Far more stimulating was *Mr. Standfast*, the latest spy thriller from John Buchan. "I got one leg on the fly paper and then I was caught. I read in bed till one and the next morning lay on the lounge from breakfast till dinner time (midday) and went down with shaking hands—not even having put on my shoes."

He also read, at Laski's suggestion, two more books that influenced his views on free speech. The first was *Essays on Freethinking and Plainspeaking* by Sir Leslie Stephen, the English author and critic who is best known today as the father of Virginia Woolf. Holmes and Stephen had once been close friends. They met in 1863 while Stephen was visiting Boston and Holmes was recovering from his third injury during the war, a bullet wound to the heel. Then, when Holmes traveled to Europe in 1866, he and Stephen spent several weeks together hiking through the Alps. In later years, after the death of his wife, Stephen became bitter and bereft, and the two friends drifted apart. But Holmes continued to regard him as one of the most penetrating thinkers of his generation and often returned to his work during periods of leisure. Earlier that summer, he had read *English Literature and Society in the Eighteenth Century*, a collection of essays published on the day of Stephen's death, in 1904. Now he turned to the present collection, a wide-ranging attack on the shallowness and insincerity of late nineteenth-century religious debate. A former clergyman turned agnostic, Stephen chastised those liberal but diffident clerics who tried to reconcile their hard-earned skepticism with the lazy fictions of faith. Instead of openly challenging antiquated Church doctrines—doctrines they knew could not withstand the scrutiny of science and logic—they "waste their power in an attempt to square circles." There is enough deceit and hypocrisy in the world without such misguided attempts at harmony, he argued. "Let us think freely and speak plainly, and we shall have the highest satisfaction that man can enjoy—the consciousness that we have done what little lies in ourselves to do for the maintenance of the truths on which the moral improvement and the happiness of our race depend."

The second book, *The Decline of Liberty in England*, was written by E. S. P. Haynes, a well-known British lawyer and author. Published in 1916, the book argued that individual freedom in England was being chipped away by growing state interference and an infatuation with German efficiency. Haynes focused most of his attention on social and moral issues, such as drinking, gambling, prostitution, divorce, and homosexuality, all of which he thought had been overregulated, usually to the detriment of the poor. But he also despaired over the future of free speech. Libel suits were on the rise, censorship was spreading, and a mob mentality was overtaking the country. Worse, judges had abdicated their responsibility and were deferring "to the wishes of the Executive without much attention to other considerations." Liberty of speech in England was still greater than anywhere else, including the United States, Haynes argued. But if judges failed to rein in the "unchecked power of the Executive" and if the public did not jealously guard this vital privilege, it would be swallowed up by the movement toward national militarism "and even more by an increasingly tyrannical collectivism which would destroy the freedom of the individual to discuss any problems except from the collectivist point of view."

Haynes's book was not a work of serious political theory like Mill's *On Liberty*. It was a polemic that Holmes found both verbose and obscure. Still, it made a strong impression on him, pushing him closer to a liberal view of the First Amendment. "The whole collectivist tendency seems to be toward underrating or forgetting the safeguards in bills of rights that had to be fought for in their day and that still are worth fighting for," he wrote to Pollock shortly after reading the book.

Then, foreshadowing the dissent he would write just a month later, he added, "We have been so comfortable so long that we are apt to take it for granted that everything will be all right without our taking any trouble. All of which is but a paraphrase of eternal vigilance is the price of freedom."

Before the summer ended, there was one final pleasure. On the third weekend of September, Laski and Frankfurter took the train out from Cambridge to visit for a day. As if on cue, the rain stopped, the clouds parted, and the sun shone briefly on Beverly Farms. Fanny was not yet strong enough to see callers, so Holmes received his guests alone. The cook served wine with lunch, and the three men sat together in the parlor, talking and laughing like old times.

For Frankfurter, the visit was a homecoming of sorts. He had been in Europe since March, attending the peace conference as a representative of the Zionist Organization of America. The organization was lobbying for a Jewish homeland in Palestine, and Brandeis had sent Frankfurter to serve as his eyes and ears. As usual, Frankfurter had found his way to the center of the activity, meeting with foreign ministers, helping to draft treaty language, and mediating disputes among Jewish leaders. The Wilson administration had also recruited him to evaluate the international labor standards that were being negotiated as part of the Treaty of Versailles. It had been a heady experience for the young professor, and as he related his adventures Holmes "listened dumb and admiring like a little boy."

When his guests departed, Holmes realized with embarrassment that he had forgotten to offer them tea. No matter. They gave him such happiness that nothing could undermine his pleasure in their visit— not Fanny's illness, not the chambermaid's remark that Laski was a saint to call on the old man so often, not even the weather, which turned wet and gloomy again as soon as his friends were gone.

"Your letter brings joy to my heart," he wrote later that week in response to a note from Frankfurter. "I do believe that your kindness for me has not been shaken by the sight you have had of so many impressive personalities in the old world. I listened to you in wrapt wonder and also with delight to see that it had not affected the naturalness and spontaneity of your thinking and your ways. You have brought a great deal of comfort and companionship to the natural loneliness of old age and I ask nothing better than that it may continue while I last."

11

"Workers—Wake Up!"

The trip back to Washington was difficult. Fanny was still weak and easily fatigued, so Holmes made the preparations himself. He booked a stateroom on the Federal Express, sent their trunks to the station, and gave instructions to the servants for closing down the house. His hands trembled as he thought of everything that could go wrong, his old train fever coming on again. "My apprehensive mind has contrived a catastrophe," he wrote to Baroness Moncheur on the morning of their departure. "I know it won't happen but I need to assure myself that it *hasn't*." They stopped first in Boston, where Holmes paid a call on Nina Gray, then continued south, passing overnight through New York, Philadelphia, and Wilmington. The train was delayed as usual, and when they finally arrived in the capital they were forced to check into a hotel because Fanny lacked the strength to mount the stairs at home.

Over the next two days, while Fanny recuperated from the journey, Holmes worked in his study, digging through the piles of books and pamphlets that had accumulated over the summer. He was joined by his new secretary, a Harvard Law graduate named Stanley Morrison. With Frankfurter in Paris the previous spring, Holmes had asked Laski to recommend a man for the job. George Osborne, the president of the *Law Review*, was "passionately anxious to come," Laski responded. But Osborne was lame, and Holmes decided that a man on crutches would not do ("though I grieve"). So the job went to Morrison, an editor on the *Law Review* and a first lieutenant in the army. He arrived at the house on the appointed morning, and the two men worked until dinnertime, filing the books Holmes wanted on his shelves and tossing the rest into the fireplace.

Brandeis stopped by in the midst of their labors, full of good cheer and news from the recess. Like Frankfurter, he had spent the summer overseas, traveling to Palestine as part of a Zionist delegation. It was his first trip to the Holy Land, and he talked excitedly about the experience. For his part, Holmes confessed that he had made little progress in his study of facts. What with Fanny's illness and a delay in getting the proper reports, the whole project had simply been too much for him. He was sorry, he said, he had meant to do more. Brandeis waved off the apology. Gracious and understanding as always, he said not to give the matter another thought. And after he had left, Holmes reflected once more on the warmth and kindness of his friends.

But mostly he was glum. Even after he and Fanny moved back to the house, a sense of futility and despair hung over him. "I don't feel the usual glow in getting back to my books and etchings," he wrote to Laski. "It hardly seems as if I had been away—whether preoccupation, age or accident I don't know."

Detecting the note of pessimism in Holmes's letter, Laski did his best to reassure him. "I hope that is not your feeling," he responded. "There is no one living who has the right to look back as you can with the clear sense of great work greatly done." As if to prove the point, he proposed that they publish a collection of the justice's legal papers. Holmes had already put out a compilation of his speeches in 1891, a thin little curio that had been reprinted four times, most recently in 1913. But that collection was purely ornamental, a hodgepodge of Memorial Day addresses, university orations, and tributes to deceased colleagues. What Laski had in mind was something more substantial—a volume that would bring together Holmes's most important contributions to legal theory since *The Common Law* appeared almost forty years earlier. It would include "The Path of the Law," of course, and Holmes's two-part lecture on the law of agency. His survey of early English equity, published by Pollock in the *Law Quarterly Review*, would also make the cut, as would "Legal Interpretation," "Executors," and "Privilege, Malice and Intent," all originally printed in the *Harvard Law Review*. Then there were his appraisals of Montesquieu and John Marshall, along with his review of Holdsworth's *History of English Law*. And for good measure, why not throw in his two most recent essays, "Ideals and Doubts," from 1915, and "Natural Law," from the year before?

As Holmes contemplated the project, his enthusiasm grew and his spirits revived. He made a list of all the pieces to be considered and sent it off to Laski, along with copies of the ones in his possession. These were simply suggestions, he insisted in an accompanying note. As for the final selections, "I leave it all to you."

Then came the plunge into work. With the flu epidemic officially over, the Court began its term promptly this year, on the first Monday of October. There was much work to be done and many cases on the docket. The government's antitrust suit against U.S. Steel had finally made its way to the Court after eight long years of litigation. That would be argued first and would last nearly a week. Then the justices would hear a boundary dispute between Minnesota and Wisconsin over the Saint Louis Bay, an important harbor at the base of Lake Superior. There were also a handful of railroad cases, myriad tax appeals, and a challenge to the War-Time Prohibition Act. Finally, the Court would once again consider several petitions to set aside convictions under the Espionage and Sedition Acts.

The first of these was *Schaefer v. United States*, an appeal from the editors and officers of a German-language newspaper called the *Philadelphia Tageblatt*. Founded in 1877, the *Tageblatt* was known primarily as a "society" paper, not because it covered the well-heeled and glamorous but because it reported on the activities of all the local societies—the building associations, the singing groups, the gymnastics clubs—that were at the center of German immigrant life. When war broke out in Europe, the editors decided to expand their coverage of national and international events. The problem was they had no way of getting this news. With a small staff and a limited budget, they could afford neither to send their own reporters overseas nor to subscribe to the wire services. Instead they copied articles from other papers, both English and German, and printed them as their own, usually rewriting the headlines or changing a sentence or two to make the stories fit onto the page. In the fraternity of cash-strapped and harried newspaper editors, this was a common practice. But eventually it led to the *Tageblatt*'s downfall. For when government agents began reading the paper in the summer of 1917, they concluded that many of the changes made to the reprinted articles were favorable to the German cause. They therefore charged the editors with making false reports with intent to hinder the war, a violation of the Espionage Act.

On its face, this was a curious charge to bring. Prosecutors did not allege that the articles themselves were false; that would have been a daunting task, since much of the war news was difficult to verify. Rather, they claimed that by altering the text of dispatches that had been printed in other papers, the *Tageblatt* editors had conveyed a false impression of what those dispatches initially said. What made the case especially strange was that despite the "false reports" charge, the prosecutors made no attempt to compare the articles as they appeared in the *Tageblatt* with the original wire dispatches. They showed only that the defendants had not printed the articles exactly as they appeared in other German-language papers that were under government surveillance—papers that, most probably, had themselves edited the wire reports to make those stories fit better on *their* pages.

As if that weren't dubious enough, the alterations made by the *Tageblatt* editors were so minor as to be almost laughable. In one article about the German capture of Riga, a Russian city on the Baltic Sea, they had omitted a single sentence reading, "From this it can be concluded that the fall of Riga has united the opposing political factions in Russia." In another article, about the demand for political reforms in Germany, they had deleted a reference to the country's "increasingly bad economic conditions." The changes to the headlines were equally trivial. "Suicides in Pershing's Army" had become "Many

Suicides in Pershing's Army Reported," while "Sarrail's Troops in Great Attack" had turned into "Sarrail's Troops Beaten" (which they had been). The most serious alteration appeared in a story about Robert La Follette, a Wisconsin senator closely allied with Brandeis. La Follette had given a speech arguing that the war should be paid for not through bonds but through a tax on companies that were profiting from it. In the original dispatch, he was quoted as saying that if inflation continued to rise there would be "bread lines" the following winter. In the *Tageblatt*, he was quoted as saying "bread riots." But even that change might not have been as sinister as it appeared. According to the testimony of one of the editors, the German-language paper from which he copied the article had used the made-up word *Brotreihen*, which literally means a line or row of bread. Since La Follette surely wasn't predicting that inflation would result in lines of bread, the editor claimed, he had used the German word *Brotriot* instead to convey what he thought the senator meant.

Perhaps recognizing the weakness of their case, prosecutors also charged the defendants with obstructing recruiting, the same offense alleged in *Schenck*, *Frohwerk*, and *Debs*. But this charge was just as questionable as the other. It rested on two editorials and an article published during the summer of 1917. The first, an editorial on July 4, argued that England had always been hostile to the United States and that it was therefore a mistake to rescue it now. The second, an article entitled "Yankee Bluff," quoted a German professor who mocked American promises of military support to the Allies, suggesting that the country lacked the stomach for war. And the third, an editorial captioned "The Failure of Recruiting," claimed that the lack of volunteers for the military was evidence that "the overwhelming majority of the people here do not approve of waging this war for the benefit of England."

Under normal circumstances, the government's case against the *Tageblatt* would have collapsed of its own flimsiness. But circumstances were not normal. The defendants were tried in September of 1918, at the height of the Allied counteroffensive. Anxiety was running high, and the government was pulling out all the stops to ensure cooperation with the war effort. Just weeks earlier, officials had rounded up more than ten thousand men in New York City for failing to produce their draft cards. A new drive for war bonds was also under way, and the Justice Department was vigorously enforcing the Espionage and Sedition Acts. So much importance did the department attach to the *Tageblatt* prosecution that it dispatched Owen Roberts, a rising young lawyer who would later sit on the Supreme Court, to try the case. The result was predictable. After a three-day trial, a jury convicted all five defendants, and a judge sentenced them to prison terms ranging from one to five years. The defendants appealed to the high court, and the government, as it had done in the other cases, asked for an expedited hearing.

If *Schaefer* was one of the weaker cases brought under the Espionage and Sedition Acts, the second case before the Court that term was one of the stronger. Titled *Abrams v. United States*, it centered on a group of five Russian Jews in New York City ranging in age from twenty-one to thirty-three. All five had arrived in the United States between 1908 and 1913 and joined the anarchist movement then flourishing in the immigrant communities on the Lower East Side and in Harlem. Their leader was Jacob Abrams, a short, compact man with long dark hair, prominent ears, and a mustache in the shape of an upturned V. Born in the Ukraine in 1886, Abrams displayed a rebellious streak at a young age, taking part in the wave of strikes and revolts known as the 1905 Russian Revolution and serving time in Siberia. He soon moved to the United States and found work as a bookbinder in one of the dingy, foul-smelling plants that littered downtown Manhattan. But his passion remained social revolution and the emancipation of the working class. He met his wife at a May Day parade, served as president of the local bookbinders union, and earned a reputation as a hard-hitting militant who would confront anyone who disagreed with him. It was this reputation that attracted the loyalty of three other radicals: Jacob Schwartz and Hyman Lachowsky, who also worked as bookbinders, and a furrier named Samuel Lipman. Abrams also won the admiration of a young woman named Mollie Steimer. Twelve years younger than Abrams, Steimer did not exactly look like a dangerous anarchist. She was four foot nine, weighed ninety pounds, and had the round, soft features of a child. But five years crouching over a sewing machine in a shirtwaist factory had convinced her that capitalism was a corrupt system that offered no hope for the future. And in spite of her frail figure—the anarchist leader Emma Goldman called her "a slip of a girl"—she was tough, stubborn, and not scared of anyone.

Like most other anarchists, the members of the group opposed the United States' involvement in the war, believing it was motivated by nothing more than capitalist greed. "The only just war," they declared in the masthead of their short-lived newspaper, *Freedom*, "is the social revolution." But unlike the German socialists in *Schaefer*, Abrams and his comrades had no sympathy for the Central Powers. To the contrary, they loathed German militarism as much as American capitalism. So it wasn't until the United States turned its sights on *their* homeland that they decided to take action.

It happened during the summer of 1918, less than a year after the Russian Revolution and just months after the newly installed Bolshevik government had signed a peace treaty with the kaiser. That treaty dealt a major blow to the Allied cause. In addition to freeing up German troops that could be redeployed to the Western Front, it stranded seventy thousand Czech soldiers who had been battling German and Austro-Hungarian forces in the Ukraine but were now forbidden from fighting on Russian soil. Eager to reach France and rejoin the war, the Czechs made their own agreement with the Bolshevists: in exchange for safe passage out of Russia, they would lay down their arms and not take part in the counterrevolution that was sweeping across the country. But that agreement broke down after the Czechs clashed with freed German prisoners making their way back to the front. Believing that the Bolshevists had armed the prisoners, the Czechs refused to give up their weapons and began seizing control of Russian towns and villages along the Trans-Siberian railroad. Anti-Bolshevist forces soon rallied to their side, and by June the Czech legion and the Red Army were locked in full-scale combat.

From the perspective of the Wilson administration, the conflict was an incredible stroke of luck. American officials had been looking for an excuse to intervene in Russia ever since the Bolshevists made peace with Germany. Now they had one. At the urging of a Czech delegation, Wilson ordered five thousand troops to northwestern Russia and another seventy-five hundred to Vladivostok on the Sea of Japan. The purpose of their mission, he insisted, was not to interfere in the battle between the Red Army and the counterrevolutionaries. Instead they would assist the Czech soldiers in making their way safely out of the country, defeating any German soldiers they met on the way, and eventually joining the Allied armies on the Western Front. To American radicals who had cheered the Russian Revolution—and even to some conservatives who hadn't—that explanation didn't quite wash. To them it seemed clear that the goal of the mission was to destroy the fledgling Bolshevik government.

At least that's how Jacob Abrams and his followers saw things. Wilson had betrayed them, they believed. After initially voicing support for the revolution and waxing poetic about national self-determination, he was now sending American soldiers to kill their dreams, and perhaps their friends and family too. Something had to be done. Someone had to expose the president for the fraud he was. And the anarchists were just the ones to do it. Earlier that summer Abrams had rented a six-room apartment on East 104th Street, where members of the group had begun living and meeting. He had also rented a basement store a few blocks away on Madison Avenue that he stocked with a printing press and several cases of type. Thus, when Wilson announced the deployment of troops on August 3, the members of the group were ready for action. Gathering in their East Harlem apartment, they agreed to print and circulate two leaflets condemning the intervention in Russia. The first, drafted by Lipman and written in English, was titled "The Hypocrisy of the United States and Her Allies." In stilted and strident language, it denounced Wilson as a liar who had deceived the country about the real purpose of the Russian expedition. "He is too much of a coward to come out openly and say: We capitalistic nations cannot afford to have a proletariat republic in Russia. Instead, he uttered beautiful phrases about Russia, which as you can see, he did not mean, and secretly, cowardly sent troops to crush the Russian Revolution. Do you see now how German militarism combined with allied capitalism to crush the Russian revolution?"

This was nothing new, the leaflet continued. The tyrants of the world always fight one another until they see a common enemy in working-class enlightenment, at which point they join forces to smash it. That's what they had done to the French Revolution in 1815, and that's what they were doing now. For the workers of America, there was really only one question:

What have you to say about it?

Will you allow the Russian Revolution to be crushed?
YOU: yes, we mean, YOU the people of America!

THE RUSSIAN REVOLUTION CALLS TO
THE WORKERS OF THE WORLD FOR HELP.

The Russian Revolution cries: "WORKERS OF THE WORLD!
AWAKE! RISE! PUT DOWN YOUR ENEMY AND MINE."

Yes friends, there is only one enemy of the workers of
the world, and that is CAPITALISM.

It is a crime, that workers of America, workers of Germany, workers of
Japan, etc., to fight THE WORKERS' REPUBLIC OF RUSSIA.

AWAKE! AWAKE! YOU WORKERS OF THE WORLD!

REVOLUTIONISTS

P.S. It is absurd to call us pro-German. We hate and despise German militarism more than do your hypocritical tyrants. We have more reasons for denouncing German militarism than has the coward of the White House.

The second flyer, written by Schwartz in Yiddish, sounded many of the same themes. "Workers—Wake Up!" it blared across the top before decrying the hypocrisy of "his Majesty, Mr. Wilson and the rest of the gang, dogs of all colors!" But whereas the first leaflet was addressed to the people of America, this one targeted a more specific audience: "Workers in the ammunition factories, you are producing bullets, bayonets, cannon, to murder not only the Germans, but also your dearest, best, who are in Russia and are fighting for freedom." And in place of the first leaflet's vague call to rise up and "put down your enemy and mine," this one proposed a more concrete plan of attack:

> Workers, our reply to the barbaric intervention has to be a general strike! An open challenge only will let the government know that not only the Russian worker fights for freedom, but also here in America lives the spirit of Revolution.

> Do not let the government scare you with their wild punishment in prisons, hanging and shooting. We must not and will not betray the splendid fighters of Russia. Workers, up to fight.

> Three hundred years had the Romanoff dynasty taught us how to fight. Let all rulers remember this, from the smallest to the biggest despot, that the hand of the revolution will not shiver in a fight.

> Woe unto those who will be in the way of progress. Let solidarity live!

THE REBELS

Working in the basement store on Madison Avenue, Abrams printed five thousand copies of each leaflet on thin sheets measuring four-and-one-half inches by twelve. Then, on Thursday, August 22, members of the group began scattering them from the rooftop of a building on the Lower East Side. A shopkeeper, angered by what he read, rushed upstairs to investigate, only to see several men running north across the roofs of adjoining buildings. The police fared little better. After being notified by the shopkeeper, they went door to door in the neighborhood looking for clues, all to no avail. The next day the headline in the *New York Tribune* read, "Wilson Attacked in Circulars from Roofs of East Side." That same morning, around quarter to eight, a group of men and boys were gathered at the intersection of Crosby and Houston Streets, waiting for the doors of their workplace to open. Suddenly the sky was filled with slips of paper that floated down and landed in the street and gutters. Like the shopkeeper the night before, the men were outraged by what they read and notified the police. When officers arrived to investigate, they learned that a man named Hyman Rosansky had arrived for work early that morning, around the time the circulars appeared. They also learned that Rosansky was an anarchist with a history of trying to stir up trouble among his coworkers. Searching his coat pockets, police discovered several copies of the leaflet, which Rosansky claimed he had found on the fire escape. When they escorted him home they found additional copies, along with a stash of radical literature and a loaded revolver. And when they took Rosansky to the station house for questioning, he told them everything he knew. The leaflets had been printed by a group of anarchists he had met several weeks before. They had given him a stack to throw from the window at work, and he had arrived early that morning to avoid being seen. Except for Lachowsky, he couldn't remember their names . . . Oh, and one thing more: he was scheduled to meet them at their apartment on 104th Street after work.

The scene in East Harlem that night was chaotic. Police had shut down a socialist meeting at a nearby hall, and hundreds of radicals marched through the streets singing Russian songs and passing out copies of the group's leaflets. When officers tried to arrest the leaders of the demonstration, the crowd swarmed around them, pushing and screaming. Billy clubs came out, a brick flew through the air, hitting a policeman in the head, and paddy wagons rushed in to restore order. In the middle of the commotion, eight detectives crouched in the shadows and doorways of East 104th Street, their eyes trained on building number 5. Rosansky stood out front, waiting nervously for the anarchists to arrive. At seven thirty, Mollie Steimer walked up, exchanged a few words with Rosansky, and went inside. The others appeared soon after, some of them carrying bundles of leaflets, and Steimer came back outside to join them. As they headed to a nearby restaurant, the detectives swooped in to arrest them. They carted Steimer, Lachowsky, and Lipman down to the station but ordered Abrams and Schwartz to show them inside the apartment. There, in rooms sparsely furnished with cots and wooden packing boxes, they found hundreds of leaflets, an assortment of anarchist literature, a bill of sale for a printing press, and another loaded revolver. They threw Abrams and Schwartz into a taxicab, hurried downtown to join the others, and questioned the suspects one by one.

They began with Lachowsky, the only person Rosansky had identified by name. Where had the leaflets come from? they demanded. Who had written them? What role had Mollie Steimer played in the scheme? Lachowsky admitted that he gave the circulars to Rosansky and planned to distribute some himself, but he refused to implicate the other members of the group. Not satisfied with this response, the detectives called in Inspector Thomas J. Tunney, the head of the New York Bomb Squad. Although technically an explosives expert, Tunney had gradually expanded his jurisdiction to cover all radical and anarchist activities. In fact, a year earlier his unit had been transferred from the police department to the army's Military Intelligence Division. Tunney had a reputation for dealing harshly with subversives and for not following formal procedures. So when he arrived at the interrogation room that night, the situation quickly turned ugly. According to Lachowsky, the lights went out and someone punched him in the face. Then he was pulled into an adjoining room, where four detectives with blackjacks surrounded him. They dragged him about by his hair and put a gun to his chest, threatening to shoot him if he didn't tell the truth. They used similar tactics on Schwartz and Lipman and threatened Abrams with the same. The only one spared the third degree was Steimer, but she was willing to talk anyway. By dawn, all five suspects had confessed.

For the federal prosecutor in New York, Francis G. Caffey, the case of the Russian anarchists posed a challenge. Unlike many of the radicals prosecuted under the 1917 Espionage Act, the anarchists had not attacked the legality of the draft or its administration. As a result, it would be difficult to convict them for obstructing recruiting or inciting disloyalty in the military. Caffey sidestepped this problem by indicting them instead under the 1918 Sedition Act, which cut a far broader swath than its predecessor, banning almost any speech critical of the government. In four separate counts, he charged them with conspiring to willfully publish scurrilous language about the form of the United States government, bring that form of government into disrepute, incite resistance to the war against Germany, and curtail the production of weapons and ammunition. In light of the defendants' call for a strike in the munitions factories, this last count appeared to be especially strong. But there was one small wrinkle. As John Lord O'Brian, head of the Justice Department's war division, reminded Caffey after the indictments were handed down, advocating the curtailment of weapons production was only a crime under the Sedition Act if done with the intent to hinder the war against Germany. And the anarchists, of course, were focused not on the German war but on Wilson's intervention in Russia.

The trial took place in October 1918 in federal district court in Manhattan. The senior judge on that court was Learned Hand, which might have given the defendants hope they would receive a fair trial. If so, they were soon disappointed. Owing to a backlog of cases, Hand had asked several judges from other districts to pitch in that fall. And because he wanted his visitors to feel useful, he made a point of giving them a full plate of interesting cases. So when Abrams and the other defendants walked into the courtroom for their first appearance, they were met not by the free speech champion Learned Hand but by an Alabama bigot named Henry DeLamar Clayton Jr.

Clayton was no stranger to the spotlight. Born into a distinguished Alabama family—his father was a major general in the Confederate army and later president of the state university—he had a long history of public service. For seventeen years, he represented Alabama in Con-

gress, serving as chair of the House Judiciary Committee and author-
ing the landmark antitrust law that still bears his name. Before that, he
had been a state legislator and federal prosecutor in Montgomery. In
many ways, Clayton was the picture of a genteel nineteenth-century
politician. He lived on a plantation, avoided controversy, and won
reelection every two years without spending more than a few hundred
dollars. But his gentility carried with it a set of deeply ingrained prejudices. For one thing, he was an apologist for slavery, which he thought
had been unfairly portrayed by its critics. Most Southerners, he insisted,
were not like Simon Legree, the tyrannical slave owner in *Uncle Tom's
Cabin.* Instead they were benevolent and caring folk who took good
care of their slaves. And most slaves, he argued, were docile creatures
who loved their masters and were happy with their lot in life. Clayton's
prejudices were not limited to race, however. He opposed suffrage for
women on the grounds that his wife did not want to be burdened with
the duty of voting. He also believed in literacy tests for immigrants
and deportation for radicals and subversives. "I have no sympathy
with any naturalized citizen who is given to carping criticism of this
Government or who cannot say that he loves America first, last, and
forever," he told the *New York Times* in 1916.

If Clayton had no sympathy for citizens who criticized the government, there was little chance he would sympathize with the *Abrams*
defendants, none of whom had even applied for citizenship. Nor was
he likely to sympathize with their opposition to the war: his brother, a
colonel in the army, had died five months earlier in the trenches of
France, and Clayton wore a black armband in mourning. Sure enough,
when the defendants walked into court for their first appearance, in
mid-September, Clayton's hostility quickly revealed itself. In response
to a comment by Mollie Steimer that she and her friends were being
prosecuted for exercising their right to free speech, he snapped, "Freedom of speech is one thing, and disloyalty is another. What you term
free speech does not protect disloyalty. I am sorry for the people of
New York that have to deal with individuals who have no more conception of what free speech is than a billy goat has of the gospel."

The prosecution was led by John M. Ryan, an assistant U.S. attorney who had previously worked for Caffey in private practice. Ryan called twenty-two witnesses to the stand over four days in an effort to prove one central fact: that the anarchists had printed and distributed the leaflets in question. He called the workmen who had picked up the leaflets thrown by Rosansky, the landlords who had rented the apartment and basement store to Abrams, the shopkeeper who had sold him the printing press and cases of type, and an expert who could link that type to the leaflets. He also questioned the police officers who had handled the case, walking them through each step of their investigation, from the moment they arrived at the corner of Houston and Crosby Streets until the moment, three days later, when they discovered the printing press in the basement store on Madison Avenue. Finally, he called to the stand a police stenographer who read into evidence the defendants' confessions. Aside from pointing out that the defendants tried to hide what they were doing (and thus knew that it was wrong), Ryan made no effort to prove that they intended to interfere with the war or were likely to succeed. As far as he was concerned, it was enough to show that they had printed and circulated the leaflets.

The defense lawyer, Harry Weinberger, did not challenge this contention on cross-examination. Instead he sought to expose the abuse his clients had suffered at the hands of the police. Staring down the officers with all the intimidation he could muster (though only five foot four, he prided himself on being a good fighter), Weinberger asked them one by one whether they had dragged Lachowsky around the room by his hair, whether they had punched and kicked Lipman, whether they had hit Schwartz in the chest. These questions bore directly on the legal issues in the case. If Weinberger could establish that the police had forced his clients to confess, the judge might rule their statements inadmissible. There was also another purpose behind his inquiry. The day before the trial began, Jacob Schwartz had died in a prison ward at Bellevue Hospital. Although the official cause of death was pneumonia, Weinberger believed the police were ultimately responsible. Schwartz had long suffered from a defective heart, and the blows from the officers, he believed, had weakened him to the point that he was susceptible to an infection. Surely that information would influence the jury if Weinberger could only get it before them. But Clayton thwarted his plan, stopping his questioning before he could make any progress and lobbing the officers a few softballs of his own. Not surprisingly, they denied having laid a finger on any of the defendants.

The anarchists then took the stand themselves. Like Debs before them, they readily admitted having done what they were accused of. Yes, they had printed the leaflets, and yes, they had circulated them among the immigrants and factory workers of Manhattan. So what? They had not criticized the *form* of the United States government, as the indictment alleged; they had merely criticized the current leaders of that government. Moreover, as O'Brian had pointed out to Caffey, they could be convicted on the munitions charge only if they had intended to interfere with the war against Germany. And that they denied. They despised Germany as much as the next person. Hadn't they said so in the postscript to the first leaflet? Hadn't Abrams himself volunteered to go to Russia and fight on the Eastern Front? What they objected to was Wilson's intervention in Russia, not the war against Germany. But Clayton again frustrated their defense. When Weinberger asked Abrams about his background as a way of establishing his hostility to the kaiser, the judge ruled the questions out of order and took over the examination himself. Where had Abrams studied anarchism? he inquired. How many other anarchists were living in New York? If they all disliked the United States so much, why didn't they go back to Russia? When Weinberger interjected that his clients would be happy to return to their homeland, Clayton shot back, "Well, I wish these people were over there now, if I may be allowed to have a wish!"

Clayton was especially hostile to Steimer, who refused to stand up each time he entered and exited the courtroom. Interrupting her testimony, he asked whether, as an anarchist, she believed in the laws prohibiting murder. When she responded that in a just society there would be no crime and thus no need for laws, Clayton asked what she thought about the laws regarding morality and marriage. Wouldn't such laws still be necessary even in a just society? Not at all, she replied. People should marry for love, not for moral or economic reasons. "And when the love grows cold, you think they ought to end the marriage relation; that is your idea?" Clayton sneered. "Well, I do not think that this has anything to do with this trial," answered Steimer.

When the testimony was over, the attorneys made their closing arguments, with Ryan stressing the fact that the defendants had urged a strike in the munitions plants and Weinberger shifting his focus to the issue of free speech. His clients, he told the jury, were no different from other figures throughout history who had been punished for their beliefs. Like Jesus and Socrates, they had simply spoken the truth as they saw it, and for that they had been arrested, beaten, and thrown in jail. Weinberger spoke for more than two hours, defending the cause of anarchism and the value of nonconformity. He even quoted a statement from President Wilson that "a man that is afraid of the truth is afraid of life." He was wasting his breath. The jury deliberated for less than an hour before returning a verdict of guilty on all four counts.

Two days after their conviction the defendants were back in front of Clayton to be sentenced. Weinberger announced that his clients wished to say a few words to the court, and Abrams stood up to speak. "I do not want any mercy," he began before Clayton interrupted: "That being the case, there is no further need of any talk on your part." He cut short the other defendants as well and launched into a two-hour diatribe in which he recounted the trickery and deceit of German spies, defended the Sedition Act as a measure of national self-defense, and mocked Weinberger's attempt to paint his clients as martyrs. "Did anybody ever hear such rot?" he said. "Yet I sat here and listened, ad nauseum, because I did not wish by any act of mine to influence the jury. He tried to bring Christ in here and put him on the same level with these miserable defendants! Did you ever hear such a profanation? I never did." When the rant was over, he sentenced Abrams, Lipman, and Lachowsky to twenty years in federal prison, the maximum penalty allowed under the law. Steimer, in spite of her clashes with the judge, got off easy: fifteen years in the state penitentiary.

After the sentencing, Weinberger declared his intention to appeal directly to the Supreme Court and asked that his clients be released on bail. Ryan objected, arguing that the defendants were too dangerous, and Clayton, eager to close the matter and return to Alabama, agreed. Weinberger then petitioned the Supreme Court to set bail, asserting that his clients had promised not to leave New York or engage in further propaganda. He had gotten to know them well, he said, and could "vouch for the honesty of their promise." That was good enough for the Court. On November 11, 1918—the day of the armistice—it set bail for each defendant at $10,000. Ordinarily that would have been beyond the means of a group of poor anarchists. But the trial had generated significant publicity in progressive circles, and Weinberger had little trouble raising the funds from a combination of friends, family, and enlightened philanthropists.

Keeping his word to the Court proved more difficult. The defendants might have promised not to publish more leaflets, but that didn't mean they were willing to abandon their cause entirely. Steimer, in particular, tested her attorney's patience and goodwill. In March 1919, she was one of 164 people arrested in a raid on the Russian People's House. She spent five days at Ellis Island before Weinberger managed to win her release. In September, she was arrested for throwing copies of the *Anarchist Soviet Bulletin* from the roof of a building on Canal Street. Again she was released, this time on $500 bail. In mid-October, while attending the trial of two other anarchists, she was taken into custody for refusing to stand when the judge entered the courtroom. After a lecture from the judge, she was barred from ever entering his courtroom again. Three days later, she was arrested when police spotted her mailing copies of a flyer entitled "Arm Yourselves," which included veiled threats against state officials. Weinberger somehow got her out on bail again, but within a week immigration officials had picked her up and taken her once more to Ellis Island, where she promptly began a hunger strike.

In the meantime, the anarchists' appeal was moving forward at the Supreme Court. Because the two cases raised similar issues, the justices combined *Abrams* and *Schaefer* (along with a third Espionage Act case involving only procedural questions) and set a hearing date for October 21, 1919. For a weary and beleaguered Weinberger, it couldn't come soon enough.

12

A Plea for Help

While Weinberger was fretting over the fate of Molly Steimer and her friends, Holmes received his own bit of disturbing news. Trouble had flared up again at Harvard, and this time Laski was at the center of it. Sticking his neck out in support of a strike by the Boston police, he had incurred the wrath of the entire New England establishment—the conservative press, the Back Bay gentry, the Harvard overseers. Now he was fighting for his professional survival, and there was no guarantee he would come out alive.

It had all started that summer when a labor dispute erupted between the Boston police force and city officials. Like police in many other cities, Boston cops had long complained about the conditions of their employment—the long hours, the low pay, the vermin-infested station houses, and the absence of a formal grievance system. For many years, however, they lacked the leverage to do anything about it. The American Federation of Labor did not accept police into its membership, and the informal unions established by the cops were not powerful enough to negotiate better terms. That changed in 1919 when, after repeated requests, the AFL finally agreed to admit policemen into its ranks. Sensing an opportunity to improve their bargaining position, the Boston police voted that August to form an official union and apply for a charter with the AFL. To the commissioner of police, Edwin Upton Curtis, this was tantamount to mutiny. Membership in the AFL, he believed, was incompatible with the duties of a police officer and would make the men answerable to the interests of labor instead of to him. So when the AFL issued a charter to the force a few days later, Curtis suspended nineteen of the union's newly elected officers for violating a department rule against joining outside groups. Then, when the officers threatened to strike over the suspensions, he called for volunteers to patrol the streets in the event of a walkout—a call that was quickly answered by Edwin H. Hall, the Harvard physics professor who had been hounding Laski. Writing in the *Boston Herald*, Hall declared that he would help keep peace and order in the city and urged Harvard students to return to school early to join him. "Come back from your vacations, young men," he entreated. "There is sport and diversion for you right here in Boston."

As tensions escalated and the two sides headed for a showdown, Boston mayor Andrew James Peters appointed a committee to mediate the dispute. Led by a Harvard overseer and investment banker named James J. Storrow, the committee recommended that the policemen be given higher wages, that the suspended officers be reinstated, and that the force be permitted to form a union as long as it did not affiliate with the AFL. Peters quickly endorsed the compromise, as did the police officers. But Commissioner Curtis rejected it. And so at 5:45 p.m. on September 9, the Boston police went on strike for the first— and last—time in the city's history.

The first night of the strike was tense and turbulent. Gangs of hooligans roamed the streets, stealing spare tires from parked cars, overturning fruit stands, pulling fire alarms, smashing the windows of stores and looting the goods inside. Riots broke out in Scollay Square, and gamblers flocked to Boston Common for all-night games of dice and revelry. A ragtag band of volunteers, including several hundred Harvard students, attempted to quell the disorder. But the students were untrained and ill prepared, and when an angry crowd pelted them with mud they quickly retreated to the safety of Harvard Yard. The next day the Massachusetts State Guard was called up, and five thousand soldiers marched into the city with sabers drawn and machine guns at the ready. Confronting a mob in South Boston, they opened fire, killing two men and a boy. Clashes elsewhere in the city brought the death toll to nine, and it was not until the third night of the strike that calm was finally restored.

By that time, the fate of the nearly twelve hundred striking policemen was largely sealed. The officers had hoped to receive support from the Boston Central Labor Union and the AFL. But public outrage over the strike—and the turmoil it caused—was more intense than they anticipated. Newspapers branded the policemen as radicals, Bolshevists, traitors, and deserters. President Wilson called the walkout "a crime against civilization." And Senator Henry L. Myers of Montana warned that if the police succeeded the United States would be under communist control within two years. Under these conditions, it was no surprise that the Central Labor Union was reluctant to stand in solidarity with the policemen. Fearing a repeat of the failed Seattle strike that spring, its members voted down a proposal for a citywide strike. The AFL also lost its nerve. Returning from a tour of Europe and recognizing the strike for the disaster that it was, AFL president Samuel Gompers urged the police to return to work and submit the dispute to mediation. It was too late. Commissioner Curtis had the upper hand now and wasn't about to show mercy. On September 13, he announced that the city would not reinstate the officers and would hire a replacement force instead. When Massachusetts governor Calvin Coolidge endorsed that decision, declaring that "there is no right to strike against the public service by anybody, anywhere, any time," the police officers knew they had lost.

It was at this point that Laski was drawn into the controversy. The police strike represented a crucial test of the theories he had put forward in his book *Authority in the Modern State*. Although much of his discussion focused on private sector unions, he extended his argument to public employees. Indeed, he dedicated the final chapter of the book to an analysis of the French civil service and its demand for the right to organize, which Laski fully supported. Yes, the civil service had a reputation for inefficiency and idleness, he acknowledged. But it also had legitimate grievances. Corruption was rampant, nepotism commonplace, and the entire administration so top-heavy and hierarchical that there was little room for autonomy or initiative. The only way to salvage the system was to give public employees the same rights as their industrial counterparts, including the right to organize, to bargain collectively, and, most importantly, to strike. "The class struggle is no less real there," Laski wrote. "The humbler civil servant there, as in industry can free himself only by his own efforts. His triumph will come only from the strength and power of his associations, which must more and more attempt the domination of the services to which he belongs. By the strength of those groups he can attain the desired reforms, if not peaceably, then by the accepted methods of direct action. The result will be the transformation of the state."

Of course, the Boston police were no ordinary civil servants. They were responsible for keeping the public safe and secure, and even the editors at the *New Republic* thought they had gone too far in walking off the job. But Laski wasn't willing to abandon his theories simply because the consequences might be unpleasant; in his book, he had referred approvingly to earlier police strikes in London and Lyon. So when the Harvard *Crimson* asked for his thoughts on the situation in early October, he stuck to his guns. Every man has the right to affiliate with a union, he told the *Crimson*, no matter who his employer or what his vocation. Moreover, the blame for the crisis rested squarely on the shoulders of Commissioner Curtis, since he knew the officers were planning to strike yet did little to protect the city. Laski also pointed out that the replacement force was being hired under an agreement that "fulfills practically all of the strikers' requirements," thus proving that "the demands of the striking policemen were justified." "The best thing that can be done now," he concluded, "is to take these improvements as a basis for negotiations and to see if the reinstatement of the men will not act as a curative for the atmosphere of ill-feeling that now exists on both sides."

The reaction to these comments was swift and severe. A professor of government told the *Crimson* that Laski was nothing more than a "boudoir Bolshevist," while an undergraduate wondered whether

Laski would also support "the striking of soldiers who were dissatisfied with their pay or conditions." The *Crimson* itself, though it agreed with Laski's assessment of Curtis, mocked his support for the strikers. And several prominent alumni wrote to President Lowell, complaining that Laski was corrupting the student body with his radical views and barbarian manners.

The real uproar was still to come. On October 15, Laski was invited to address a meeting of the wives, sisters, and mothers of the displaced policemen at Boston's Fay Hall. Standing before an audience of twenty-five hundred women, he blasted Curtis's handling of the situation, asserting that it was the commissioner's inflexibility and refusal to negotiate with the officers that had caused the strike. "We are told the police are deserters," Laski told the crowd. "The deserter is Commissioner Curtis, who was guilty at every point of misunderstanding his duties and failure to perform his functions. The people are waking up to the fact that 1,200 men are never entirely wrong. If the men had given in to the commissioner, he would have continued in his old methods. The commissioner has learned that labor is more unified than ever as a result of this issue. Labor will never surrender."

Printed in the newspaper the next day, these remarks sparked a furious backlash. In a letter to the *Boston Herald*, Professor Hall accused Laski of glorifying Bolshevism and attempting to intimidate those who disagreed with his radical doctrines. The only consolation, he said, was that, like a rattlesnake, Laski was dumb enough to announce his presence. The *Boston Evening Transcript* also denounced the speech. "It is not too much to ask," the newspaper wrote, "whether the Harold J. Laski who addressed last night's meeting at Fay Hall is an instructor in or lecturer upon American Government or Soviet Government. The parents of the sons entrusted to his tutelage are entitled to know. The followers from Maine to California of straight Americanism will, we think, insist upon knowing."

And they did want to know. The trickle of letters to Lowell turned into a flood. Harvard was in the midst of a $15 million fund-raising campaign, and many of the writers threatened to withhold their contributions unless Laski was fired. How could the school retain such a menace, parents and alumni wanted to know. He was a "carrier," a "Typhoid Mary of governmental disease." It would be one thing if he taught mathematics or physics. But Laski taught history and government, the very subjects a Bolshevist was least suited to teach. "Is it not, Mr. President," asked one writer, "like selecting an atheist to teach our boys religion?"

For Lowell, the Laski affair was a major headache, which he estimated cost the school $300,000. But he refused to give in to the pressure. Academic freedom was sacred, he explained in letter after letter to the critics. The real danger to America was not Laski or Bolshevism but the erosion of free thought and inquiry. If Harvard represented only one point of view, "it would be stagnant."

Lowell's statements quieted some of the furor and even won the university a few new friends. Julian Mack, a federal appeals judge in Chicago, sent Lowell a check for $50,000 from a man named Max Epstein. Although not a Harvard graduate, Epstein had been persuaded by Mack, Frankfurter, and Pound to make a donation to the law school. Without mentioning Laski by name, Mack underscored the motivation behind the gift, stating that he hoped it would "tend to check any discouragement that may come from the refusal of other wealthy men to subscribe to the fund except under the condition that Harvard forsake her fundamental principles of academic freedom."

Not everyone was so easily mollified. If Lowell didn't have the stomach to fire Laski, perhaps the board of overseers should do it for him. "Why not clean house and get rid of the foreign propagandist," a Wall Street millionaire named Paul Tuckerman wrote to several board members after Lowell rebuffed him. Prompted by this complaint and others, the board agreed to take up that very question at its next meeting, on October 27.

On October 21, then, when the Supreme Court heard arguments in *Schaefer* and *Abrams*, Laski's fate was very much up in the air. The arguments lasted two days and covered a range of issues. The attorneys in *Schaefer*, one of whom had also appeared in *Schenck*, argued that the government had failed to prove a violation of the Espionage Act. Although it was true that their clients had altered reports appearing in other papers, they had done so mainly for reasons of space, a standard practice in the newspaper business. Moreover, the government had failed to prove that any of the *Tageblatt* articles were false or conveyed a false impression of the original wire dispatches. The only thing prosecutors had shown "was that the articles which were published differed from the articles in the papers from which they were copied." And that, the attorneys maintained, was not a crime.

Arguing for the *Abrams* defendants, Harry Weinberger offered a more general theory of the First Amendment. In his view, free speech was absolute and protected all discussion of public policy, no matter how inflammatory or subversive. Even speech harmful to the public welfare could not be suppressed as long as it did not "break out into overt acts against peace and good order." His argument was forceful and impassioned, punctuated with quotes from Milton and Jefferson. But in light of the Court's rejection of similar reasoning in *Schenck*, he did not stake his entire case on it. He also asserted that his clients had not violated the Sedition Act when they called for a strike in the munitions factories because they had no intent to hinder the war against Germany. Citing their testimony at trial and their avowed hostility to German militarism, Weinberger maintained that their sole intent was to stop the Russian intervention by arousing public opinion against it. "Russia had been surrounded by a stone wall of lies," he told the justices, "and these young defendants protested against the lies and against military intervention in Russia—not to help Germany—not to hurt America—but to bring America back to its idealism—back to the road it had travelled since its revolutionary birth." This was not the sort of rhetoric likely to sway the conservatives on the Supreme Court. Nonetheless, Weinberger thought he had struck a chord and was optimistic about his chances. "The argument here looks good for a favorable decision," he wired an associate shortly after the hearing.

John Lord O'Brian did not appear on behalf of the government this time. He and his assistant, Alfred Bettman, had resigned in May when the Justice Department closed down its war division. From the defendants' perspective, this was about the worst thing that could have happened. In spite of their willingness to defend the Espionage and Sedition Acts (even in cases, like *Debs*, that they initially opposed), O'Brian and Bettman were two of the most progressive lawyers in the department. They believed strongly in free speech and spent much of their time in office reining in the repressive impulses of prosecutors across the country. Before stepping down, they also urged Wilson to pardon or commute the sentences of many who had been convicted under the acts, including Jacob Frohwerk, whose prison term was reduced from ten years to one. Bettman, in particular, took seriously the government's responsibility not to trample on the First Amendment. Just a month before the Supreme Court heard arguments in *Schaefer* and *Abrams*, he had written to Zechariah Chafee congratulating him on his article in the *Harvard Law Review* and explaining that, with a few qualifications, he agreed "most heartily with all that you say."

What made the resignations of O'Brian and Bettman especially unfortunate was who replaced them: Robert P. Stewart, the U.S. attorney from South Dakota who had prosecuted the defendants in *Baltzer*. Stewart took a dim view of radical rhetoric and seditious speech. Whereas O'Brian and Bettman accepted the Espionage and Sedition Acts as necessary evils and enforced them in spite of some misgivings, Stewart seemed to derive personal pleasure from prosecuting the anarchists and agitators who were besmirching the country's good name. He had made this clear earlier in the year when Weinberger proposed that the government drop the charges against his clients in exchange for their return to Russia. Although Attorney General Palmer initially seemed receptive to this idea, Stewart quickly shot it down. In a memo to Palmer, he described the defendants as "typical supporters of the proletarian republic or Bolsheviki government in Russia" who had "called for the overthrow of the present form of Government." They had been properly convicted, he added, and deserved no special treatment now.

His position before the Supreme Court was equally hard-nosed. In defending the convictions in *Schaefer*, Stewart argued that it didn't matter whether the articles in the *Tageblatt* were false in any real or objective sense. What mattered was that they differed from the articles from which they were copied. The reasoning behind this assertion was murky, but it had something to do with the fact that the Espionage Act prohibited both false "statements" and false "reports." According to Stewart, this was significant because although a "statement" could be false only if inconsistent with reality, a "report" could be false if it did not accurately reflect the information provided to the person making it, even if the report itself was metaphysically true. This interpretation raised an obvious question: why would Congress have banned reports that were "false" only in this technical, make-believe sense? Again, Stewart's answer was murky. He appeared to maintain that newspapers are particularly adept at ascertaining the truth and that readers rely on this fact when forming their opinions. Therefore, when a newspaper falsifies a report received by it, the foundation of public opinion is undermined. "Whether the false 'report' is true as a matter of fact, or is nearer the truth than the facts as ascertained by the reporter, is immaterial, since the reader is entitled to make up his own mind," Stewart argued. Of course, the *Tageblatt* was a newspaper too, so one might have thought it was entitled to the same presumption of reliability as other papers. Stewart did not consider this possibility. In his view, if the *Tageblatt* editors did not think the reports they received correctly represented the facts, "they must, if they wish to avoid making false 'reports,' confine their opinions to the media of editorial or other comments."

Stewart's argument in *Abrams* was more straightforward. Two of the charges against the defendants—conspiracy to incite resistance to the war and curtail production of munitions—were similar to the charges upheld in *Schenck*, he claimed. Therefore, "it follows necessarily" that they were "equally constitutional." The other two charges—conspiracy to publish scurrilous language about the United States and to bring the country's form of government into disrepute—simply defined the offense of seditious libel, which was part of the common law of England when the First Amendment was adopted. And because the First Amendment was merely intended to "fix the liberty of the press" in place, so that it would be no more and no less than it had been prior to 1791, Stewart insisted that those charges were also constitutional. As for Weinberger's claim that his clients had not intended to hinder the war against Germany when they called for a strike in the munitions factories, Stewart could barely conceal his disdain. "We are entirely willing to take the judgment of any fair-minded reader upon the question," he wrote. Besides, as long as the jury reasonably could have concluded that the defendants had the requisite intent, the Court lacked the power to overturn its verdict.

Holmes listened carefully to the attorneys, leaning over the bench and jotting down notes in his black copybook. He was particularly intrigued by Weinberger's argument on the issue of intent. In *Debs*, he had accepted the jury's finding of intent as conclusive. But now, after being warned of the dangers of that approach by both Hand and Freund, he began to think more critically about the issue. Had the anarchists really wanted to hinder the war against Germany? Wasn't it more accurate to say that they simply objected to the intervention in Russia? And even if they did intend to interfere with the war, what chance did they have of succeeding? In his *New Republic* article, Freund had argued that not even Eugene Debs could have hoped to hinder the war effort. If that was true—if the leader of the Socialist Party, one of the most eloquent speakers alive, was impotent in the face of the nation's war machine—was it really possible that five unknown Russians living on the fringes of society had posed a danger?

When the justices met in conference that Saturday, October 25, Holmes shared his thoughts with the rest of the Court. Brandeis, not surprisingly, seconded his concerns, and Clarke agreed that some of the charges in *Schaefer* were troubling. But that was it. The other justices voted to uphold the convictions in both cases. To them—as to most observers—the defendants' free speech claims were no stronger than the ones Holmes himself had rejected in *Schenck*, *Frohwerk*, and *Debs*. Chief Justice White assigned the opinion in *Schaefer* to McKenna and the majority in *Abrams* to Clarke. If Holmes wanted to formally change his stance on free speech, he would have to do so not as the author of the Court's opinion but in dissent.

———

There was no time to write anything now, however. When the conference was over, Holmes hurried home to change into evening clothes. There was a new British ambassador in town, and Holmes and Fanny had been invited to dine at the embassy that night. Then Sunday morning he was up early reviewing the opinions his colleagues had circulated from prior weeks. As usual, it was a frustrating experience. Whereas he always got straight to the point, the other justices tarried around the edges, belaboring the obvious and responding to every absurd argument of counsel. They also had an annoying fetish for certainty. Holmes had noticed this often over the years and saw it again in one of the opinions he read this morning. Responding to an argument by counsel, the opinion had fallen back on the old formula "Where are you going to draw the line?" That question, Holmes explained in reply, ignored the fact that all decisions are a series of points tending to fix the shadow of a line. "The admission of an antithesis between extremes necessitates it. North and South Poles import an equator."

He glanced at the clock on the mantel, which read 11:35. But daylight savings had ended overnight, so perhaps it was only 10:35. In either case the days would now grow shorter and darker, and winter would soon arrive. Sighing with regret, he picked up the latest letter from Pollock, which had arrived a month before and still had not been answered. After three years of hearing about Laski, Pollock had finally read his first book, *Studies in the Problem of Sovereignty*. His impression was not favorable. "On sovereignty in general," Pollock wrote, "Laski seems to me confused, and likely to be confusing to novices." He blurred the distinction between legal sovereignty and political supremacy, his portrait of the legal philosopher John Austin was "a figment," and his depiction of the theologian Thomas Erastus was "often loose and sometimes erroneous." Overall, Pollock concluded, "L's mind seems to me quite un-legal." Holmes knew there was merit in what Pollock said. He had made many of the same points to Laski himself, explaining that it was a matter of fact, not morality, that the state would punish those who defied its claim to authority. On the other hand, Holmes responded to Pollock, that didn't mean the state—or any other institution with power—was obligated to exercise that power.

Take the recent strikes in the steel industry. "I believe that this country like yours, if the issue is pressed too far, will crush those who set themselves against it, but I regret the persistence of the head of the Steel Co. in refusing to deal with the unions, and should be sorry to see the issue take that form."

Finishing his letter to Pollock, Holmes turned next to Laski. He had heard about his involvement in the police strike and was naturally concerned. He was also sympathetic—not to Laski's view of the strike, which Holmes had only a vague notion of, but to Laski's desire to express that view. Sixty years earlier, as a student editor of the *Harvard Magazine*, Holmes had had his own run-in with the authorities on campus. Eager to prick the complacency of the establishment, the magazine had published a series of provocative articles on abolition, atheism, and women in college (the young men wanted them). Holmes, caught up in the idealism of his own youth, had added his voice to the chorus, urging readers not to avoid "books of an agitating tendency." "We *must*, will we or no, have every train of thought brought before us while we are young, and may as well at once prepare for it." Angered by this article and others, the faculty appointed a committee to consider whether the magazine should be shut down. The Harvard president even wrote to Holmes's father, asking him to have a word with his son. But Holmes did not back down then and saw no reason for Laski to do so now.

The question was whether he, long since a member of the establishment himself, would come to Laski's defense. And it was a question he could not avoid answering. For earlier that week—on Wednesday, in fact, the very day the Court heard arguments in *Abrams*—something curious had happened, something that has never before been revealed and that sheds new light on Holmes's actions that fall. Furious not only with the attacks on Laski but with the general atmosphere of intolerance in the country, Frankfurter had paid a visit to the office of Ellery Sedgwick, editor of the *Atlantic Monthly*, member of the Harvard board of trustees, and descendant of one of the oldest families in New England. As Frankfurter described it in a newly discovered letter to his fiancée, Marion Denman, "I bearded the great editorial lion in his den yesterday—Ellery Sedgwick to shake him to some plain speaking. . . . He *wants* to be a liberal and is considerably one." In fact, Sedgwick had agreed to "print a blast on tolerance" if Frankfurter could solicit one from a member of the old guard, somebody like Holmes or Charles Norton Eliot, the former president of Harvard—in other words, Sedgwick had said, "somebody who counts." Frankfurter responded that "everybody counts who has courage & speaks sense," but he was intrigued by Sedgwick's proposal nonetheless and apparently mentioned it to Laski, who in turn mentioned it to Holmes. It was a shame that Holmes could not take Sedgwick up on his offer, Laski wrote to the justice later that week, or could he? An article by someone of his stature would go far toward silencing the forces of intolerance.

Though awkwardly phrased, Laski's letter was essentially a plea for help, much like his request earlier that year on behalf of Frankfurter. But Holmes did not initially see it for what it was. Only after he had finished writing to Pollock and read Laski's letter again did he realize exactly what was being asked of him. And his response, though equally awkward, revealed just how far Holmes had come in his thinking over the past year:

> I didn't till this moment read your letter correctly and realize that it asked if I would write. I thought it expressed a regret but assumed that I couldn't—I can't—I am too much beleaguered with duties. I infer that you have had trouble, I hope not serious, because of your criticism of Curtis. I gather from what I have seen that you didn't uphold the strike (which I think impossible) but pitched into Curtis's behavior, of which I know little but which I should think was at least open to discussion. I fear that we have less freedom of speech here than they have in England. Little as I believe in it as a theory I hope I would die for it and I go as far as anyone whom I regard as competent to form an opinion, in favor of it. Of course when I say I don't believe in it as a theory I don't mean that I do believe in the opposite as a theory. But on their premises it seems to me logical in the Catholic Church to kill heretics and the Puritans to whip Quakers—and I see

nothing more wrong in it from our ultimate standards than I do in killing Germans when we are at war. When you are thoroughly convinced that you are right—wholeheartedly desire an end—and have no doubt of your power to accomplish it—I see nothing but municipal regulations to interfere with your using your power to accomplish it. The sacredness of human life is a formula that is good only inside a system of law—and so of the rest—all of which apart from its *banalité* I fear seems cold talk if you have been made to feel popular displeasure. I should not be cold about that—nor do I in any way shrink from saying what I think—but I can't spare the energy necessary to deal with extra legal themes.

Of all the letters Holmes wrote during this period, none captures so clearly both the extent to which his views on free speech had evolved since the previous June and the extent to which he was still wrestling with the issue. Indeed, with its internal contradictions and sudden swerves of direction, Holmes's letter to Laski suggests a man on the verge of a momentous decision, vacillating between the dictates of reason and the pull of emotion, between the voice in his head and the one in his heart. On the one hand was the logic of persecution, which still had a powerful hold on him. From a moral standpoint, he could see no difference between the punishing of dissenters and the killing of Germans during the war. Both rested on the same "justifiable self-preference" he had identified as long ago as *The Common Law*. "If a man is on a plank in the deep sea which will only float one, and a stranger lays hold of it, he will thrust him off if he can," Holmes had written. "When the state finds itself in a similar position, it does the same thing." On the other hand, Holmes himself had taught that logic wasn't the only aspect of the law. There was also experience, "the felt necessities of the time," "even the prejudices which judges share with their fellow-men." And it was those aspects of the law that were most relevant to him now. For what had been merely an abstract question for Holmes over the past year was, suddenly, concrete and personal. The face of free speech was no longer Eugene Debs, the dangerous socialist agitator. It was his good friend Harold Laski, and Holmes's views shifted accordingly—and dramatically. He still did not have a theory of free speech that satisfied him, but he now declared himself willing to die for it, just as he had been willing to die for the cause of the Union six decades earlier. Moreover, he realized now how his blustery comments about the logic of persecution might seem "cold talk if you have been made to feel popular displeasure," as of course Laski had been. "I should not be cold about that," Holmes insisted. Nor was he afraid to speak his mind. Nonetheless, he claimed, he was too busy at work to write outside the job.

When Laski received Holmes's letter, he might justly have been disappointed. After all, he had offered to defend Holmes against Zane earlier in the year. He had also printed Holmes's essay on natural law, had dedicated his second book to Holmes, and had found a publisher for the justice's collected legal papers. Surely it was not too much to ask for something in return. Surely a man who declared himself willing to die for free speech could find time to write an article for a friend. For all his faults, though, Laski was not a bitter or petty man. He took Holmes's rejection in stride and on October 28 reassured him that everything would work out fine:

> I have had a fight here, but am, I think, out of danger. Lowell was mag-
> nificent and I felt that I had a president in him I would fight for. My
> protest in the police strike was against the stupidity of dealing in
> absolutes. It is useless to say you are *für oder gegen* the union. The
> problem is what conditions led to its formation? Could they have been
> remedied? Was an attempt made to remedy them? My insistence was
> that Curtis & Coolidge bungled the whole situation and the Republi-
> cans, naturally did not like it. But the atmosphere is clear again and
> I don't think there will be any difficulties over academic freedom in
> the future.

It was a brave thing for Laski to say, but it was far from true. The board of overseers had met the day before to consider the complaints against him. And although no action had been taken, the consensus was that Laski's behavior warranted further investigation. The overseers therefore appointed a subcommittee to interview Laski at the Boston Harvard Club and report back to the full board, which would decide at its January meeting what to do about the troublesome instructor.

13

"Quasi in Furore"

Holmes received Laski's letter at the end of October. At almost the exact same moment, he began writing his dissent in *Abrams*. Although Justice Clarke had not yet circulated the majority opinion, Holmes liked to prepare his dissents ahead of time; that way he could send a draft to his colleagues as soon as the majority arrived. So he read back over the briefs, reviewed his notes from the hearing, and thought out what he wanted to say. Then, moving to his familiar spot at the upright desk in the corner of his study, he wrote twelve paragraphs that would change the history of free speech in America.

He began modestly enough, listing the charges against the defendants and describing the leaflets at the center of the case. They were "abusive," he conceded, and full of the "usual tall talk"—attacks on President Wilson, charges of hypocrisy, and appeals to the solidarity of the working class. But nothing in the leaflets could be interpreted as assailing the *form* of the United States government, which was what the first two counts of the indictment alleged. Nor could they be construed as encouraging resistance to the war against Germany, the basis of the third count. As to the fourth count, which charged the defendants with inciting the curtailment of military supplies, it was true they had advocated a strike in the munitions factories. To violate the Sedition Act, however, something more was required; they must have *intended* to interfere with the war. And in Holmes's view, the defendants never had that intent. They were not German sympathizers who hoped the Allies would lose the struggle in Europe. They were Russian immigrants who wanted Wilson to keep his nose out of their homeland's affairs. They had said as much in the postscript to the English leaflet, and even in the Yiddish leaflet "it is evident from the beginning to the end that the only object of the paper is to help Russia and stop American intervention there against the popular government."

Of course, the jury had convicted the anarchists on all four counts, which meant it *did* think they intended to hinder the war against Germany. And in defending his *Debs* opinion, Holmes had insisted that the Court lacked the power to overrule the jury's findings of fact. So why was he willing to set aside the jury's decision now? He did not say. Was the jury's finding of intent so at odds with the evidence as to be unreasonable and hence subject to judicial second-guessing? Possibly, although that explanation still fails to distinguish *Debs*, since one might have said the same thing about the jury's finding of intent in that case. A more likely explanation is that, thanks to the arguments of Hand and Freund, Holmes was simply no longer willing to grant juries the same latitude as before.

At any rate, Holmes's argument on intent invited a more fundamental objection. As prosecutors had pointed out at trial, the legal definition of intent differs from its lay meaning. In ordinary usage, to say that a person intends a result means that he desires to bring that result about. In the language of the law, however, a person is generally deemed to have intended whatever results he knew (or should have known) were likely to follow from his actions. Applied to the *Abrams* case, this distinction was crucial. Because the anarchists knew (or should have known) that curtailment of munitions would hinder the war against Germany, prosecutors argued that they possessed the necessary intent, even if their real motive was simply to stop the intervention in Russia.

Holmes was well aware of the distinction between legal intent and lay intent. It was a distinction he himself had advocated four decades earlier in *The Common Law*. Seeking to rid the law of its focus on moral guilt, he had written that, for legal purposes, intent was "perfectly consistent with the harm being regretted as such, and being wished only as a means to something else." So how could he now conclude that the anarchists did not intend to hinder the war against Germany? By arguing that Congress had used the word "intent" in the Sedition Act not in this sweeping legal sense but in the more narrow lay one. "I am aware of course that the word 'intent' as vaguely used in ordinary legal discussion means no more than knowledge at the time of the act that the consequences said to be intended will ensue," he wrote. "But, when words are used exactly, a deed is not done with intent to produce a consequence unless that consequence is the aim of the deed. It may be obvious, and obvious to the actor, that the consequence will follow, and he may be liable for it even if he regrets it, but he does not do the act with intent to produce it unless the aim to produce it is the proximate motive of the specific act, although there may be some deeper motive behind."

Congress must have used the word "intent" in this way, Holmes continued, because the Sedition Act would be absurd otherwise. To illustrate his point, he offered a hypothetical: "A patriot might argue that we were wasting money on aeroplanes, or making more cannon of a certain kind than we needed, and might advocate curtailment with success, yet even if it turned out that the curtailment hindered and was thought by other minds to have been obviously likely to hinder the United States in the prosecution of the war, no one would hold such conduct a crime." It was an imperfect analogy, since the defendants in *Abrams* had advocated a complete shutdown of the munitions factories, not just a redistribution of resources. Even Holmes was forced to "admit that my illustration does not answer all that might be said." But "it is enough to show what I think and to let me pass on to a more important aspect of the case. I refer to the First Amendment to the Constitution that Congress shall make no law abridging the freedom of speech."

Halfway through his opinion, Holmes had now reached the heart of the matter. Even if the anarchists were guilty under the Sedition Act, did their convictions nonetheless violate the First Amendment? Could Congress punish those who criticized the government and advocated violation of the law? Or was such expression protected by the principle of free speech?

In the nine months since he had written *Schenck*, *Frohwerk*, and *Debs*, Holmes had come under considerable pressure to rethink his answer to these questions. He had been attacked in the pages of the *New Republic* and the *Harvard Law Review*, challenged in correspondence with Hand, confronted over tea by Chafee. Laski had fed him one book after another espousing a liberal view of free speech, and Frankfurter had tried to arrange for him to write a piece on tolerance in the *Atlantic Monthly*. Even Brandeis's suggestion that he spend the summer studying facts was, at bottom, a criticism of the conservatism and indifference reflected in Holmes's First Amendment opinions. In short, Holmes had been the target of an intense lobbying effort on the part of his closest friends and admirers. And now, at the very moment one of those friends was under attack for his own radical views, that effort bore fruit. For although Holmes purported to stand by his earlier opinions ("I never have seen any reason to doubt that the questions of law alone that were before this Court in the cases of Schenck, Frohwerk, and Debs were rightly decided," he wrote), the remaining six paragraphs of his dissent made it nearly impossible to take him at his word.

For starters, he disavowed the notion—suggested in *Schenck* and criticized by Chafee—that free speech is inapplicable during times of war. The government's power to restrict speech "undoubtedly is greater in time of war than in time of peace because war opens dangers that do not exist at other times," he wrote. "But as against dangers peculiar to war, as against others, the principle of the right to free speech is always the same." What was that principle? Was it the clear and present danger test he had articulated in *Schenck* and then seemingly abandoned in that very case? Or was it the bad tendency test he had appeared to fall back on in *Frohwerk* and *Debs*? That summer, Chafee had pushed Holmes strongly toward the former position, and the justice now assented. "It is only the present danger of immediate evil or an intent to bring it about that warrants Congress in setting a limit to the expression of opinion where private rights are not concerned," he wrote. "Congress certainly cannot forbid all effort to change the mind of the country."

Holmes's embrace of the clear and present danger test was a triumph for free speech. Whatever confusion his earlier opinions had generated was now cleared away. He was rejecting the bad tendency test and staking his reputation on a radical new standard that would protect all but the most immediately dangerous speech. As evidence of his commitment to this new standard, he used the words "immediate" or "imminent" seven times in his opinion—three times in one sentence alone. And because he had initially announced the clear and present danger test for a unanimous Court in *Schenck*, he could even claim that it—and not bad tendency—was the law of the land. Indeed, that is precisely what he and Brandeis would argue in one dissent after another over the next decade.

Just as important as Holmes's embrace of the new test was his application of it. In *Schenck*, he had made no attempt to assess whether the defendants posed a clear and present danger. Instead, consistent with his general indifference to facts, he had simply concluded that the First Amendment did not protect their speech. In *Abrams*, by contrast, he focused on the actual circumstances of the "crime." And although the circumstances were similar to those in *Schenck*, Holmes's conclusion was quite different: "Now nobody can suppose that the surreptitious publishing of a silly leaflet by an unknown man, without more, would present any immediate danger that its opinions would hinder the success of the government arms or have any appreciable tendency to do so." Publishing the leaflet for the purpose of obstructing the war might have indicated a greater danger, he added, and would have qualified as an attempt. But as he had already explained, and as he repeated now, the defendants had not intended to interfere with the war against Germany.

Finally, Holmes took the unusual step of criticizing Judge Clayton's handling of the trial and the sentences handed down, neither of which was at issue before the Court:

> In this case sentences of twenty years imprisonment have been imposed for the publishing of two leaflets that I believe the defendants had as much right to publish as the Government has to publish the Constitution of the United States now vainly invoked by them. Even if I am technically wrong and enough can be squeezed from these poor and puny anonymities to turn the color of legal litmus paper; I will add, even if what I think the necessary intent were shown; the most nominal punishment seems to me all that possibly could be inflicted, unless the defendants are to be made to suffer not for what the indictment alleges but for the creed that they avow—a creed that I believe to be the creed of ignorance and immaturity when honestly held, as I see no reason to doubt that it was held here but which, although made the subject of examination at the trial, no one has a right even to consider in dealing with the charges before the Court.

Holmes might have ended his opinion there. Having explained why the defendants had not violated the Sedition Act and why their speech did not pose a clear and present danger, he was under no obligation to say anything further. And had he stopped there, his dissent might have faded into the fog of history, another well-intentioned yet ultimately futile attempt to curb the excesses of popular government. But Chafee, in his article that summer, had also faulted Holmes for failing to emphasize the social value of free speech. So Holmes now responded to that critique, setting forth a philosophical justification for the opinion he had just reached. He was still at his desk in the corner of the study, his knees beginning to ache. In the garden below he could see a cluster of yellow chrysanthemums and beyond them the autumn leaves, glistening in the sunlight. As he stood there looking out the window, the power of his argument overtook him and he wrote the concluding paragraph, he reported to Frankfurter, "*quasi in furore*"—as if possessed.

The opening lines of that paragraph came easy, being merely a variation of what he had been saying for years and had written almost verbatim to Laski a week before:

> Persecution for the expression of opinions seems to me perfectly logical. If you have no doubt of your premises or your power and want a certain result with all your heart you naturally express your wishes in law and sweep away all opposition. To allow opposition by speech seems to indicate that you think the speech impotent, as when a man says that he has squared the circle, or that you do not care whole heartedly for the result, or that you doubt either your power or your premises.

What came next was more difficult. If persecution for the expression of opinions was perfectly logical, how could Holmes insist on a policy of tolerance? He might emphasize the fallibility of human judgment, as Hand had done in his letter seventeen months earlier. Because we cannot be certain we are right, Hand had written, we must be tolerant of conflicting opinions. "Tolerance," in his words, "is the twin of Incredulity." But that argument would get Holmes only so far. As he had responded to Hand at the time, we are always acting on the basis of a provisional hypothesis. We can never be sure we are right. Yet that doesn't stop us from acting. So why should we let the possibility that we are wrong stop us from suppressing speech?

It was at this point that Holmes's extensive reading came into play. For John Stuart Mill had asked and answered this very question in *On Liberty*, which Holmes had reread at Laski's suggestion earlier that year. The reason we cannot suppress speech on the same theory that we act on in general is because "complete liberty of contradicting and disproving our opinion is the very condition which justifies us in assuming its truth for purposes of action." Since we can never be sure we are right, in other words, we can only rely on the fact that we have heard every argument and considered all points of view. But that premise collapses once we start suppressing speech. "If even the Newtonian philosophy were not permitted to be questioned, mankind could not feel as complete assurance of its truth as they now do," Mill had written. "The beliefs which we have most warrant for have no safeguard to rest on but a standing invitation to the whole world to prove them unfounded."

Mill's argument provided Holmes the answer he was looking for. It also fit nicely with his description of himself as a bettabilitarian. As he had told his secretary, Lloyd Landau, that spring, the universe is a mystery. We can never know anything for certain; we can only place bets one way or another. Like any gambler, however, we should gather as much information as possible before wagering our money or our lives. Only then can we be confident in the bets we have made.

All of this depended, of course, on the assumption that truth is more likely to emerge under conditions of free and open debate than under a regime of government regulation. And that assumption was by no means self-evident. By definition, freedom of speech means that individuals are free not only to speak the truth but to spread lies, misinformation, and unintentional falsehoods. It is therefore incumbent on any advocate of free speech to explain why a system of tolerance will promote truth instead of error. In *Areopagitica*, Milton had answered this challenge by invoking the metaphor of combat. "And though all the winds of doctrine were let loose to play upon the earth, so Truth be in the field, we do injuriously by licensing and prohibiting to misdoubt her strength," he wrote. "Let her and Falsehood grapple; who ever knew Truth put to the worse in a free and open encounter?" Laski had also employed the language of battle in *Authority in the Modern State*: "Yet in the clash of ideas we shall find the means of truth," he wrote. "There is no other safeguard of progress."

As an old soldier, Holmes was not averse to the use of martial imagery; indeed, war was the defining metaphor of his life. In *Abrams*, however, he chose a different metaphor, one that would reframe the debate about free speech and ultimately become a part of our cultural lexicon. And once again, he drew inspiration from his extrajudicial studies. For in addition to the books he had read on tolerance that summer, he had also read a biography of Adam Smith, the Scottish economist and founder of free market capitalism. It was not Holmes's first introduction to Smith. He had read *The Wealth of Nations* years earlier and, like all good Republicans, admired both its author and his theories. But the biography, written by the British journalist Francis Hirst and loaned to him by (who else?) Laski, was helpful to Holmes in two respects. First, it emphasized the extent to which Smith believed not just in economic liberty but in political liberty, including free speech and religious tolerance. Second, Hirst disputed the revisionists who had tried to invoke Smith's name in support of governmental regulation of the economy. Although Smith accepted the need for some regulation, Hirst argued, he believed strongly that a policy of "free trade" would produce the greatest good for the greatest number. "*The Wealth of Nations* is a forest of full-grown arguments for free trade," Hirst wrote. "Smith's name can no more be dissociated from free trade than Homer's from the siege of Troy." In all, Hirst used the phrase "free trade" more than twenty times in his book, including as a chapter title. So it was only natural that Holmes, when casting about for a metaphor to explain the value of open debate, should seize on the idea of free trade, or, as he put it, "free trade in ideas."

These, then, were the elements of Holmes's argument for tolerance: an acknowledgment, based on experience, that human judgment is fallible; a recognition, thanks to Mill, that free speech is the necessary predicate on which our bets about the universe must be based; and a conviction, inherited from Smith, about the power of free trade and competition to promote the greater good. Weaving these various threads together, Holmes responded to the logic of persecution in one rich, profound, and unforgettable sentence:

> But when men have realized that time has upset many fighting faiths, they may come to believe even more than they believe the very foundations of their own conduct that the ultimate good desired is better reached by free trade in ideas—that the best test of truth is the power of the thought to get itself accepted in the competition of the market, and that truth is the only ground upon which their wishes safely can be carried out.

To those acquainted with Holmes's jurisprudence, his invocation of free trade in this sentence would be jarring. Although Holmes believed in free markets as much as any other member of his class, he had previously mocked his brethren for reading laissez-faire into the Constitution. In *Lochner v. New York*, a 1905 case involving a maximum-hour law for bakers, he dissented from the Court's ruling that due process bars government from interfering with private business arrangements. Noting that the case had been decided "upon an economic theory which a large part of the country does not entertain," Holmes chastised the majority for injecting its own views into the Constitution. "A constitution is not intended to embody a particular economic theory, whether of paternalism and the organic relation of the citizen to the state or of laissez faire," he wrote. "It is made for people of fundamentally differing views, and the accident of our finding certain opinions natural and familiar, or novel, and even shocking, ought not to conclude our judgment upon the question whether statutes embodying them conflict with the Constitution of the United States."

Holmes's dissent in *Lochner*, more than any other opinion, had made him a hero to progressives. And the position he had taken there was well on its way to becoming the majority view among judges and scholars. So there was some irony—if not hypocrisy—in his reliance on laissez-faire to justify his defense of free speech. But Holmes, as his critics had long said, was more of an aphorist than a system builder. He believed that legal decisions, like art, should include only what is essential. "'The point of contact' is the formula—the place where the boy got his fingers pinched," he once explained to Frankfurter. "The rest of the machinery doesn't matter. So the Jap. master puts five dots for a hand, knowing they are in the right place, and the etcher elaborates what he wants you to see and leads up to it with a few scrawls." Thus, Holmes's metaphor of a "free trade in ideas" was not intended to import an entire economic theory into the realm of the First Amendment. He was not claiming that there is a literal "marketplace of ideas" or that free speech magically produces an objective and verifiable truth via the mechanism of the invisible hand, as some of his more obtuse detractors have argued. He was drawing a picture to help us see the way in which free and open debate promotes the ultimate good even if there are short-term costs, just as there are costs when government abandons protectionism and opens its markets to competition. And at that level—the level of art, not mechanics—his metaphor surely succeeded. More than that, by invoking the language of free trade, he provided a justification for free speech that even conservatives could not fail to appreciate.

One problem remained. As an advocate of judicial restraint, Holmes could not simply impose his views on the country. He had to ground his belief in "the free trade in ideas" in some superior source of authority; he had to ground it in the Constitution. This would be the most questionable part of his analysis, since he simply stated it baldly, as a matter of accepted fact:

> That at any rate is the theory of our Constitution. It is an experiment, as all life is an experiment. Every year if not every day we have to wager our salvation upon some prophecy based upon imperfect knowledge. While that experiment is part of our system I think that we should be eternally vigilant against attempts to check the expression of opinions that we loathe and believe to be fraught with death, unless they so imminently threaten immediate interference with the lawful and pressing purposes of the law that an immediate check is required to save the country.

Perhaps recognizing the weakness of this claim, Holmes bolstered it with an argument from history. Lurking in the background all year had been a debate about the Sedition Act of 1798. The government argued that it had been clearly constitutional, while Chafee and the defense lawyers maintained that it was repudiated by history. Although Holmes had little basis for choosing between these two claims, he now embraced the latter reading and relied on it as support for the clear and present danger standard:

> I wholly disagree with the argument of the Government that the First Amendment left the common law as to seditious libel in force. His-

tory seems to me against the notion. I had conceived that the United States through many years had shown its repentance for the Sedition Act of 1798 by repaying fines that it imposed. Only the emergency that makes it immediately dangerous to leave the correction of evil counsels to time warrants making any exception to the sweeping command, "Congress shall make no law abridging the freedom of speech."

Holmes took great pride in his writing and worked hard to make every sentence shine. Believing that judicial opinions should be agreeable to the ear when read aloud, he tried to end each paragraph with a short word or an accent on the final syllable, "so that the axe may fall and the head drop. When you end on a polysyllable, it gives a squashy feeling." He had not always been confident of his abilities. A few years after taking his seat on the Court, he confessed to Pollock that his sentences sometimes seemed "as if they had been written by a schoolboy on a slate." But over the years he had grown into his style and was now the most assured writer on the Court.

Still, he worried that his dissent in *Abrams* was not good enough, that he had not made his point with sufficient force or clarity. So he ended the paragraph—and his dissent—with an apology, a rare public acknowledgment of his anxieties and insecurities:

Of course I am speaking only of expressions of opinion and exhortations, which were all that were uttered here, but I regret that I cannot put into more impressive words my belief that in their conviction upon this indictment the defendants were deprived of their rights under the Constitution of the United States.

Whatever his uncertainties, Holmes had no cause for regret. Like Lincoln at Gettysburg, he had produced a document that far exceeded his own estimation and would survive long after he was gone. Moreover, he had done it with style. The opinion had all the qualities that made his voice as a judge distinctive. It was direct and provocative, written in an almost aggressively colloquial style. At the same time it was elusive and oracular, suggesting hidden depths and complexities. And it incorporated nearly all the major themes of his life—his belief in the supremacy of experience over logic, his strange combination of confidence and doubt, his commitment to Darwinism, his bettabilitarianism, his taste for battle. There were new ideas too, ideas he had picked up over the past year, from Hand and Chafee, Mill and Smith, Freund and Laski. It was almost as if Holmes had been working toward this moment his entire career, and now in one opinion—in one paragraph of that opinion—it had all come together in a brilliant expression of constitutional faith.

14

Adulation

When Holmes finished his dissent, he sent a draft to the printer so it would be ready to distribute when the majority opinion arrived. Then he picked up a letter he had received from Frankfurter earlier that week. Like Laski, Frankfurter had inquired about the possibility of Holmes's writing an article on tolerance. Not ready to respond at the time, Holmes had put the letter aside while he completed his work. But now, with *Abrams* out of the way and his other opinions circulated, he sent the following reply:

November 1, 1919

Dear Frankfurter,

Your letter gave me great pleasure to know that all is
going well. But the same causes that have delayed my answer
make it impossible for me to write outside the job. I am too
busy. Just now I am full of a tentative statement that may
see light later on kindred themes to your subject but I don't
yet know whether what I have written *quasi in furore*, as
Saunders says, is good enough. And ahead of me is a string of
cases to be remediated and that drives me mad. I already had

told Laski that the notion of my writing an article was
no go. . . .

Affectionately Yours,
O.W. Holmes

Although Holmes did not know it at the time, Frankfurter was not
in Cambridge when this letter was posted. He was en route to Washington with good news, and the next day he showed up unexpectedly
on Holmes's doorstep to share it. He was engaged to Marion Denman,
a bright and attractive young woman he had met six years earlier at
the House of Truth. The daughter of a Congregationalist minister,
Denman had graduated from Smith College and worked for a while at
a private girls' school in Manhattan. Now, after a long and rocky
courtship, she had agreed to become Mrs. Felix Frankfurter, and the
groom was bursting with pride. There was only one problem: he had
not received parental approval. His father had died three years earlier,
and his mother opposed the match because Denman was a Gentile. So
Frankfurter sought Holmes's blessing instead, which the justice readily gave. Then, springing up from his chair, Holmes called to Fanny, who
shuffled feebly into the room. "Tell her! Tell her!" Holmes commanded,
to which Frankfurter replied, "I'm going to marry Miss Denman."
Without saying a word, Fanny left the room as the two men exchanged
embarrassed glances. A minute later she returned, holding her fists
out in front of her. "Which do you think she would like?" she asked
Frankfurter, opening her hands to reveal an amber stone in one and a
fragment of jade in the other. "This, I think," said Frankfurter, pointing to the amber, which Fanny placed in his hand before shuffling
away again in silence.

Four days later, on Thursday, November 6, Justice Clarke circulated
the majority opinion in *Abrams*. It was just as Holmes expected, and
he had no one to blame but himself. Clarke dismissed the anarchists'
First Amendment claim, asserting that it had been "sufficiently discussed and is definitely negatived" in *Schenck* and *Frohwerk*. He also
rejected the argument that the anarchists lacked the intent to interfere

with the war. "Men must be held to have intended, and to be account-able for, the effects which their acts were likely to produce," he wrote. "Even if their primary purpose was to aid the cause of the Russian Revolution, the plan of action which they adopted necessarily involved, before it could be realized, defeat of the war program of the United States." Having already anticipated this argument, Holmes saw no need to revise what he had written. Instead he called for the messenger and handed him eight copies of his dissent, one for each of his col-leagues. Then, anxious as always as to how they would react, he picked up his pen and wrote to Pollock:

> Today I am stirred about a case that I can't mention yet to which I have sent round a dissent that was prepared to be ready as soon as the opinion was circulated. I feel sure that the majority will very highly disapprove of my saying what I think, but as yet it seems to me my duty. No doubt I shall hear about it on Saturday at our conference and perhaps be persuaded to shut up, but I don't expect it.

Holmes was right; his colleagues did disapprove. But they didn't wait until Saturday to voice their displeasure. On Friday, November 7, three of them—Van Devanter, Pitney, and a third whose identity has been lost to history—appeared at his home with a request that he withhold his dissent for the sake of national security. Pitney had already sent Holmes a note indicating the basis of his disagreement. "I think there was a case for the jury," he had written. But the discussion in Holmes's study focused less on the merits of the case than on the poten-tial impact of his dissent. The country was in turmoil. The unrest that had erupted that summer had continued into the fall. The Boston police force had been disbanded, the steelworkers had gone on strike. In the Capitol, the Senate was locked in a bitter fight over the peace treaty Wil-son had negotiated in Paris. The president, meanwhile, had suffered a stroke and lay incapacitated at the White House, his wife reportedly running the show. At a time like this, with the future of the country at stake, it was important for the Court to speak with one voice, the justices told Holmes. Even Fanny, his own wife, agreed with them.

Regardless of what he thought of them as judges, Holmes was fond of both Pitney and Van Devanter, with whom he sometimes played hooky to see the cherry blossoms in spring. And he was not above holding his tongue for the sake of peace on the Court. Two years earlier, in a case out of Louisville, he had initially opposed the Court's decision to strike down a law forcing blacks and whites to live in separate parts of town. He had even prepared a dissent that he circulated to his colleagues. But when the Court announced its decision the following Monday, he quietly withdrew his opinion and made the result unanimous.

This time, he felt different. Having written the opinions in *Schenck*, *Frohwerk*, and *Debs*, Holmes felt he had a duty to limit the effect of those decisions. There was also the matter of his friends. Hadn't he already told Frankfurter that he was "full of a tentative statement that may see light later on kindred themes to your subject?" Hadn't he assured Laski that he did not shrink from saying what he thought? To remain silent now would be an act of cowardice, of betrayal. So no, Holmes told his colleagues regretfully, he would not withdraw his dissent. He could not do as they wished.

The only justice who agreed with his decision was Brandeis. Returning a draft of Holmes's opinion, he scribbled across the bottom, "I join you heartily & gratefully. This is fine—very."

That evening at 8:45 a convoy of police cars quietly approached the headquarters of the Union of Russian Workers on East Fifteenth Street in Manhattan. When the building was surrounded and the signal had been given, federal agents and local officers poured out of the cars and stormed inside. Swinging blackjacks and shouting commands, they rounded up the two hundred occupants and dragged them into the street, many injured and covered in blood. While paddy wagons transported the suspects downtown for questioning, the agents searched the building from top to bottom, breaking down doors, ripping open desks, and tearing up carpets. When they were done, they filled two army trucks with membership books, account ledgers, and radical literature and hauled them away for inspection.

The roundup in Manhattan was just one of a dozen carried out that night by the Department of Justice. Across the country, federal agents and local police raided workplaces, meeting halls, and homes in search of anarchists, Bolshevists, and other radicals. They arrested 150 people in Newark, 50 in Detroit, 33 in Hartford, and 30 in Philadelphia. In all, more than 500 people were arrested nationwide.

Although authorized by Attorney General Palmer (and hence known as the Palmer Raids), the operation was actually the work of a twenty-four-year-old official named John Edgar Hoover. A graduate of George Washington Law School, Hoover had joined the Justice Department two years earlier as a member of the enemy aliens section, which was responsible for registering German nationals during the war. Smart and hardworking, he moved quickly up the ranks and was soon the department's leading expert on alien affairs. So when Palmer went looking for someone to lead the crackdown on radicals after the bombings of 1919, Hoover was the obvious choice. He was promoted to special assistant to the attorney general and put in charge of the newly created Radical Division, a unit of the Bureau of Investigation (precursor to the FBI). Over the next several months he immersed himself in research, poring over anarchist pamphlets, studying the communist movement, and collecting the names of alleged radicals. Having put himself through law school as a clerk at the Library of Congress, he had much practice cataloging, which he now put to new use, creating a massive index of every disloyal or suspicious person in America. By mid-October, when Congress demanded to know what steps Palmer was taking to exterminate the red menace, Hoover was ready. Drawing on his research, he obtained deportation warrants for six hundred members of the Union of Russian Workers, an anarchist group based in New York City. Then, working with local police departments, he planned a series of raids for the night of November 7, the second anniversary of the Russian Revolution.

The raids themselves were a fiasco. In addition to the violence and

property damage, police seized many people who were entirely inno-
cent. Of those arrested in New York, only thirty-nine were ultimately
charged with deportable offenses; the rest were released, though not
before some spent weeks or even months in jail. Nonetheless, Hoover
had achieved his goal, which was to send a message to the radicals—
and the country—that dissent would not be tolerated. In case that
message wasn't clear, he arranged for a navy ship to transport 249
aliens back to Russia just before Christmas, then began organizing an
even larger and more audacious roundup for the first week of January.

Hoover wasn't the only one lashing out at the radical left. In New
York, a committee led by state senator Clayton R. Lusk had been investigating communists and anarchists all year. When word of the federal
raids spread, the committee launched its own sweep. On Saturday,
November 8, state and local police raided seventy-three meeting halls,
editorial offices, and printing shops in New York City, arresting more
than five hundred suspects. Like the federal operation, this one was
violent and indiscriminate. Many of those arrested had been attending
concerts or receptions and had no idea why they were picked up. After
being thrown into patrol wagons and taken to police headquarters,
they were herded into a gymnasium while they awaited interrogation.
Then, once they produced proof of citizenship or were otherwise cleared,
officials sent them home as though nothing had happened.

Politicians and the mainstream press hailed the raids that weekend, declaring them overdue. "Too long the government pursued the
policy of waiting until some overt act was committed before taking
steps against the anarchists, and it is now a source of satisfaction to the
public to see in operation the new policy of exerting every possible
effort to prevent deeds of violence," wrote the *Washington Post*. To
those troubled by the climate of fear and paranoia, however, the raids
were an ominous sign. In just one year, all of the goodwill and unity
generated by the armistice had vanished. The witch hunt was in full
stride, and no one in a position of authority seemed willing to stop it.
If ever a call for tolerance was needed, now was the time.

———

Monday, November 10, 1919. The justices line up outside the court-room, in the corridor of the Capitol. The clock over the bench strikes noon, and the marshal recites his familiar lines: "Oyez, Oyez, Oyez . . ." As the audience rises, the nine members of the Supreme Court file into the chamber and take their seats. All eyes turn to Chief Justice White, who stares down at the papers before him and says nothing. Instead a voice from the end of the bench breaks the silence. It is Justice Clarke, the most junior member of the Court, who delivers his opinion first. "I am authorized to announce the judgment of the Court in *Abrams v. United States*," he says before reading a summary of the case and an excerpt from the majority opinion.

When he is finished, Holmes clears his throat and looks out into the audience. It is a typical crowd—members of the bar, a handful of reporters, a few secretaries and congressional aides. These are the people who will hear his words, but his dissent speaks not just to them. It speaks also to the men down the hall who enacted the Espionage and Sedition Acts, to the prosecutors who enforced the laws, to the judges who presided over the trials, to the jurors who sat in judgment, to the editorialists who demanded tougher penalties and swifter retribution, and perhaps most importantly to later generations who may, in their own moment of crisis, be tempted to sacrifice the principles of free-dom to the cause of hysteria.

And this, once again, is what he says:

Persecution for the expression of opinions seems to me perfectly logical. If you have no doubt of your premises or your power and want a certain result with all your heart you naturally express your wishes in law and sweep away all opposition. To allow opposition by speech seems to indicate that you think the speech impotent, as when a man says that he has squared the circle, or that you do not care whole heartedly for the result, or that you doubt either your power or your premises. But when men have realized that time has upset many fighting faiths, they may come to believe even more than they believe the very foundations of their own conduct that the ultimate good desired is better reached by free trade in ideas—that the best test of truth is the power of the thought to get itself accepted in the competition of the market, and that truth is the only ground upon which their wishes safely can be carried out. That at any rate is the theory of our Constitution. It is an experiment, as all life is an experiment. Every year if not every day we have to wager our salvation upon some prophecy based upon imperfect knowledge. While that experiment is part of our system I think that we should be eternally vigilant against attempts to check the expression of opinions that we loathe and believe to be fraught with death, unless they so imminently threaten immediate interference with the lawful and pressing purposes of the law that an immediate check is required to save the country. I wholly disagree with the argument of the Government that the First Amendment left the common law as to seditious libel in force. History seems to me against the notion. I had conceived that the United States through many years had shown its repentance for the Sedition Act of 1798 by repaying fines that it imposed. Only the emergency that makes it immediately dangerous to leave the correction of evil counsels to time warrants making any exception to the sweeping command, "Congress shall make no law abridging the freedom of speech." Of course I am speaking only of expressions of opinion and exhortations, which were all that were uttered here, but I regret that I cannot put into more impressive words my belief that in their conviction upon this indictment the defendants were deprived of their rights under the Constitution of the United States.

On paper and in the courtroom, these words could be regarded as merely an abstract defense of free speech. To Holmes's friends, however, to the men who had come under attack for their views during the past year, they had a more personal meaning. To Laski and Frankfurter, to Hand and Pound, even to the editors of the *New Republic*, Holmes's words read as if they were a defense of *them*, as if in writing his *Abrams* dissent he was not just protesting the conviction of five anarchists he had never met but was also standing up for his friends. Holmes may have been unwilling to write an article on tolerance, but what he *had* done for them was far more significant. And one by one, in heartfelt letters, they let him know how thankful they were:

Nov. 12, 1919

My Dear Mr. Justice,

In the midst of a feverish week, I want just to say in so many words that amongst the many opinions of yours I have read, none seems to me superior either in nobility or outlook, in dignity or phrasing, and in that quality the French call *justesse*, as this dissent in the Espionage case. It is a fine and moving document for which I am deeply and happily grateful.

Ever affectionately yours,
H.J.L.

Nov. 12, 1919

Dear Justice Holmes,

And now I may tell you the gratitude and, may I say it, the pride I have in your dissent. You speak there as you have always spoken of course. But "this time we need education in the obvious" and you lift the voice of the noble human spirit.

The times also make me especially shy about my personal happiness and yet I should be less than healthy and honest did I not say how you send me off—somehow gladder than I thought anybody but Marion now could make me. If I came to Mrs. Holmes and you no less humble than your knight of romance in not caring a damn what anybody thought (tho' I know I can afford this gesture of indifference), knowing that you would be glad and yet happy that you were happy, blame yourselves and all the good angels of mercy.

Faithfully,
F.F.

Nov. 13, 1919

My Dear Judge Holmes:

Am I allowed to thank you for your dissenting opinion in the Steimer case? Somehow I would like you to know that there exists profound gratitude to you, coupled with a pretty clear sense not to abuse in any way what you have vindicated.

We are printing the opinion in full in next week's issue.

Devotedly yours,
Walter Lippmann

Nov. 13, 1919

Dear Mr. Justice:

I have just seen the complete text of the minority opinion in the case under the Espionage Act which has been handed down by the Supreme Court. I was so deeply moved by it that I cannot forbear to write you and tell you what a profound piece of legal and political reasoning it seemed to me to be. I feel sure when the history of our time comes to be written it will be ranked among our most influential political documents.

Faithfully yours,
Herbert Croly

Nov. 26, 1919

Dear Judge Holmes:

Opportunity to read your opinion in the Abrams case has only just come—but if I had known what was in store for me I should have pushed everything to one side and given it the right of way. It is worthy to stand with your opinion in the Lochner case as one of the classics, yes one of the landmarks, of our laws. May it come to its own as quickly as did the position you took in the Lochner case! Perhaps we may forgive those responsible for the unhappy situation of today for that they have also brought forth indirectly a document of human liberty to keep up the succession from the Apology of Socrates, the Areopagitica, and Mill on Liberty.

Yours very truly,
Roscoe Pound

When the first wave of appreciation had subsided, another out-pouring of praise followed in its wake.

From Laski:

I told you what a glorious opinion that was. I'm not a collector but if you hadn't the habit of putting your MS in the wastepaper basket I'd have put in a formal requisition for it. Croly will write a piece on it; we all feel that you have restated the case for liberalism as even you have hardly ever done.

From Frankfurter:

I still read and rejoice over your dissents and Pound has stolen from me when he says your paragraphs will live as long as the Areop-agitica.

Morris Cohen is here and he and Laski and I are boxing the com-pass many times round the cosmos. You are the only monistic prin-ciple among us.

And of course from Hand, whose chance encounter with Holmes on a train seventeen months earlier began this story:

Nov. 25, 1919

Dear Mr. Justice

I was greatly pleased with your dissent in the Abrams case, especially with the close which, if I may say so, was in your very highest vein. I am quite confident that whether it is avowed or

not, in the end your views must prevail, after people get over
the existing hysteria. It will not be the first time that you have
formed the law by a minority opinion. I also agree with
enthusiasm with your analysis of motive & intent about which
there has been much too meagre discussion in the books. It was
with a strong emotion that I read your words, stronger because I
had found so little professional support for my own beliefs which
would always have been expressed so, had I had the power to
express them. I cannot help feeling like thanking you, even
though I recall the annoyance it gives me when anyone undertakes
to thank me for what I may say in an opinion. I always want to
answer, "You fool, *I* didn't do it, it just came that way, quite
simply and inevitably. If you thank me, you only show that you
haven't the remotest idea of what I am doing." So I shall
refrain—expressly anyway.

Meanwhile the merry sport of Red-baiting goes on, and the
pack gives tongue more and more shrilly. I really can't get up
much sympathy for the victims, but I own to a sense of dismay
at the increase in all the symptoms of apparent panic. How far
people are getting afraid to speak, who have anything really
worthwhile to say, I don't know, but I am sure that the public
generally is becoming rapidly demoralized in all its sense of
proportion and toleration. For men who are not cock-sure about
everything and especially for those who are not damned
cock-sure about anything, the skies have a rather sinister
appearance.

Faithfully Yours,
Learned Hand

For the most part, Holmes accepted the gratitude of his friends in
silence. As pleased as he was by their affection, there was something
embarrassing about the effusiveness of their letters. To Hand, however, he felt obligated to reply:

Nov. 26, 1919

My dear Judge,

   Your letter gives me the greatest pleasure and I am very much
obliged to you for writing to me. Sympathy and agreement
always are pleasant but they are much more than that when they
come from one that I have learned to think of as I do of you.
Accept my thanks.

                                      Ever Sincerely Yours,
                                      O.W. Holmes

   Then, with that obligation fulfilled, he returned to his familiar
pose of detachment. Writing to Frankfurter at the end of November,
he mentioned that Brandeis had passed along a rumor that Thomas
Perkins, the Harvard trustee, was down on his dissent. "I have supposed that that would be the point of view of the conservative but, as
yet, I have heard nothing of it," he wrote. "However that is ancient history, and I am thinking about other cases now."

15

"Alone at Laski"

If Holmes had moved on from the *Abrams* decision, others had not. Encouraged by his dissent, the Harvard Liberal Club held a meeting in early January to protest the government's suppression of speech. Chafee, who was the club's adviser, invited Holmes, Brandeis, and Hand to address the gathering, but all three declined, citing previous commitments and the impropriety of appearing at a partisan event. Not wanting to disappoint the audience entirely, Holmes sent Chafee a short message to be read aloud in his absence. "For obvious reasons I should not care to speak upon your subject except as from time to time I have to," the message stated. "I see no impropriety, however, in suggesting the isolated reflection that with effervescing opinions as with the not yet forgotten champagnes, the quickest way to let them get flat is to let them get exposed to the air." It was the same metaphor he had used in his letter to Herbert Croly the previous spring, but of course that letter had never been sent. Or rather, it had been sent to Laski, whose amusement at the comparison was not diminished upon a second hearing. "Only you could have written that letter to the Harvard Liberal Club," he wrote Holmes two days after the meeting. "Felix and I chuckled with effervescent joy."

Holmes's dissent also spurred Harry Weinberger to action. In

March, he persuaded Frankfurter, Chafee, Pound, and two other Harvard faculty members to sign a petition urging President Wilson to pardon his clients. Echoing Holmes's opinion, the petition insisted that the leaflets had been "the honest expression of a Russian citizen on Russian intervention" and were not intended to hinder the war against Germany. It also asserted that because the defendants were willing to be deported to Soviet Russia, "the United States could in no way be harmed by an amnesty at this time." (Wilson rejected the petition, but the government ultimately commuted the defendants' sentences and deported them to Russia in November 1921.)

Not everyone was pleased with Holmes's dissent, of course. Although the public response had initially been muted, the critics soon made their voices heard. Writing in the *Yale Law Journal*, Princeton University professor Edward S. Corwin quarreled with Holmes's interpretation of the word "intent": "In law, as in ethics and in common sense, men must be held to intend, if not the usual consequences of their acts, certainly the necessary means to their objectives." Day Kimball, a student editor on the *Harvard Law Review*, disputed Holmes's claim that awareness of our own fallibility justifies protection of seditious speech. Pushed to its ultimate conclusion, toleration "becomes impotence, self-destruction," Kimball argued. "We may not believe that the truths we hold are immutable, but for some of them at least we must stand ready to fight." And C. W. German, writing in the *University of Missouri Bar Bulletin*, described Holmes's opinion as "a positive menace to society and this Government" and predicted that radicals would invoke it to justify their propaganda. "I am unable to conceive how a man with the antecedents, education, learning, attainments and experience of the learned author of this dissenting opinion can refer to the circulars involved as 'a silly leaflet' and later as 'poor and puny anonymities.'"

The most vicious attack came from a friend. In early spring, Holmes heard rumblings about an article by John Henry Wigmore, a professor at Northwestern Law School whom he had known and corresponded with for nearly thirty years. Inferring that the article concerned his *Abrams* dissent, Holmes asked Frankfurter if he had heard anything about it. "If you do know of such a piece, please let me know what and where it is," he wrote. "I always want to see what Wigmore says."

Frankfurter did know of such a piece, and soon so did Holmes. Entitled "Abrams v. U.S.: Freedom of Speech and Freedom of Thuggery in War-Time and Peace-Time," the article appeared in the March 1920 issue of the *Illinois Law Review*. Actually, to call what Wigmore wrote an "article" is charitable. It was more like a screed, a spitting, sneering, snarling screed. If Holmes had written his dissent "as if possessed," Wigmore must have written his critique as if enraged. From beginning to end, it throbbed with anger and arrogance, contempt and condescension. Not once did it pause to offer a conciliatory word or consider the possibility that anyone other than its author might have a valid point of view.

Its target, of course, was Holmes. But perhaps because of their long friendship and Wigmore's earlier extravagant praise of him ("our greatest American or English analyst and jurisprudent," he had written in 1894), he did not once mention the justice by name. Indeed, he did not refer to any of the justices by name, relying instead on the bloodless designations "majority" and "minority." Of the majority opinion, Wigmore was almost entirely silent. After quoting a brief line, he remarked simply, "There is here nothing further to say as to the majority opinion." The minority opinion could not be so easily dispensed with. "It is shocking in its obtuse indifference to the vital issues at stake in 1918, and it is ominous in its portent of like indifference to pending and coming issues," Wigmore wrote. "That is why it is worth analysis now."

To analyze the minority opinion, however, one would need to understand it. And according to Wigmore, the dissent was so elliptical and obscure "that its exact point is difficult to gather." He also doubted whether the justices in the minority were even open to argument and analysis. "The opposite interpretations of the majority and the minority were due, not to genuine ambiguities in the language," he argued, "but to differences of temperament and attitude towards the issues involved. A pre-existing attitude of the minority disinclined them to interpret the facts as the majority did. You cannot argue with a state of mind. But you can point out its nature and its portent."

So that's what Wigmore proceeded to do. The great fault of the minority opinion, he explained, was its ignorance of the military situation in August 1918, when Abrams and his comrades had circulated their flyers. To demonstrate his own knowledge of that situation, he reviewed in patronizing detail the crisis the country had faced during that decisive summer. America had gone to war, he reminded his readers, to stop a "ruthless military caste" that sought to "dominate the world by force, at any cost of life, treasure, honor, and decency." Although there was "no need to rehearse its revealing incidents," Wigmore did just that with a long list of "the countless unscrupulous inhumanities which marked every step of Germany's warfare": "the burning of Louvain, the devastation of Belgium, the bombing of field hospitals and the torpedoing of hospital ships, the Lusitania, the Sussex, the enslavement and debauchment of women-civilians, the 'sunk without a trace,' the bayoneting of the wounded, the crucifixion of prisoners." The war thus presented a clear moral issue, probably the clearest issue in the history of mankind, he argued. Yet in the spring of 1918 the outcome of that issue was in doubt. The withdrawal of Russia and a series of German offensives threatened to crush the Allied cause once and for all. Only a massive influx of American troops had staved off defeat, and only a further influx could turn defense into offense, bringing the war to a successful conclusion. But those troops could not fight barehanded. They needed arms—rifles, machine guns, artillery, and ammunition. And to produce those arms, the munitions factories needed workers, tens of thousands of them, laboring day and night with feverish intensity. "There was danger in a single day's lapse at a single factory or a single work bench," Wigmore warned. "What nerved each man to his task was the thought that on his performance, multiplied by that of every other man, depended the fate of America and her allied civilized nations."

It was the fate of those nations that the Russian anarchists had threatened, "alien agents" and "parasites" that they were. Through their

"cowardly" and "dastardly" actions, they had jeopardized the future of
the entire civilized world. It was so obvious that even a child could see
it. Everyone could see it except the minority, which "was blind to the
crisis—blind to the last supreme needs of the fighters in the field, blind
to the straining toil of the workers at home, obtuse to the fearful situation which then obsessed the whole mind and heart of our country."
Instead of opening its eyes to that reality, the minority had delivered a
civics lecture on truth and tolerance that was "sadly out of place": "In a
period when the fate of the civilized war hung in the balance, how
could the Minority Opinion interpret law and conduct in such a way as
to let loose men who were doing their hardest to paralyze the supreme
war efforts of our country?"

The answer, according to Wigmore, lay in the minority's "mis-
placed reverence for freedom of speech," its "overanxiety" and "touch-
iness in this tender doctrine." And all for no reason. Ignoring the two
thousand prosecutions that had been brought under the Espionage
and Sedition Acts, the magazines and newspapers that had been shut
down, the vigilante campaigns that had been waged against dissenters, Wigmore proclaimed that the battle for free speech had been won
long ago. "Is there not in Anglo-America today an irrevocably established free trade in every blasphemous, scurrilous, shocking, icono-
clastic, or lunatic idea that any fanatical or unbalanced brain can
conceive? I firmly believe that in these days the tender champions of
free speech are, like Don Quixote, fighting giants and ogres who have
long since been laid in the dust."

Not that all ambiguities about the scope of the First Amendment
had been resolved. There was still the question of where the line should
be drawn so that "Freedom of Speech does not become Freedom of
Thuggery." But the minority opinion, with its vague standards and
indefinite language, did not provide the answer. Wigmore therefore
offered his own. In times of war, he argued, free speech is largely beside
the point. Once a nation has committed itself to a cause of conflict, "all
rights of the individual, and all internal civic interests, become subor-
dinated to the national rights in the struggle for national life." Nor was
there any reason to worry about stifling the robust debate that was

necessary for making important decisions. Invoking his own experience during the recent hostilities—he had served as a colonel on the judge advocate general's staff—Wigmore assured his readers that military officials would fully consider all competing viewpoints: "I have observed as much or greater clash of extreme and opposed opinions in staff military discussions as in, say, the academic freedom of a law faculty." In any case, the country ordinarily was at peace. And during times of peace, Wigmore was prepared to allow greater latitude for speech. "Here the 'free trade in ideas' may be left to signify unlicensed ventilation of the most extreme views, sane or insane, on any subject whatsoever," with one important qualification: speakers who advocate violence or crime should not be protected by the First Amendment, regardless of how little chance they have of succeeding or how far in the future the danger lies.

Having neatly tied up these loose ends, Wigmore concluded his tirade with one more burst of scorn and disbelief. "'The Constitution is an experiment'!" he wrote in mockery of Holmes's final paragraph. "And 'while that experiment is part of our system'! In the transcendental realms of philosophic and historical discussion by closet jurists, these expressions might pass. But when found publicly recorded in an opinion of the Supreme Guardians of that Constitution, licensing propaganda which in the next case before the court may be directed against that Constitution itself, the language is ominous indeed."

To the officials in the Justice Department still obsessed with the Bolshevist threat, Wigmore's article was like catnip. Francis Caffey, the U.S. attorney for New York, sent a copy to Robert Stewart, the assistant attorney general, who encouraged his underlings to forward it to various federal judges. The secretary of war, Newton D. Baker, also praised the article, informing Wigmore that he agreed with his analysis completely and that the problem was not too much suppression of speech but too much sympathy for radical speakers.

Among the editors of the *New Republic* and the faculty of Harvard Law School, however, Wigmore's article left a bitter taste. "The poor man has not yet come out of his uniform and thinks the war is still on," Frankfurter fumed to Holmes. "All through the war he was hell-bent and humorless beyond words but I had hoped the 'militaristic' virus would wear off. It hasn't."

Holmes took a more philosophical view of the matter, responding that Wigmore's piece "wasn't reasoning but emotion." "He certainly got the military sting good and hard—he was a damned sight more a soldier than I ever was and I shouldn't be surprised to hear him tell me that I didn't understand patriotism as I inferred that he thought I didn't understand the emergencies of war. He seems only less dogmatic than Zane. Absolute beliefs are a rum thing. I always wonder at a man who takes himself seriously all the time."

Certainly no one could accuse Holmes of that. A few weeks after Day Kimball's article appeared in the *Harvard Law Review*, Holmes agreed to hire the young man as his secretary for the following term. As Holmes explained to Frankfurter, he had glanced quickly at the article and got the impression Kimball had bitten off more than he could chew. "Perhaps I shall hear his views one day!" he added. "I hope so."

While Holmes was brushing off the attacks of Wigmore and his future secretary, Laski was dealing with the fallout from the Boston police strike. As promised, a subcommittee of the board of overseers had interviewed him in mid-December at the Harvard Club of Boston. From Laski's standpoint, the meeting had turned out surprisingly well. It was chaired by George Wigglesworth, a local lawyer who was married to Fanny's younger sister Mary (and thus was Holmes's brother-in-law). As Laski recounted the incident later, Wigglesworth "looked at me and said, 'Mr. Laski, do you believe in bloody revolution?' I looked him straight in the eye and said, 'Mr. Wigglesworth, do I look as if I did?' We all laughed and had a good dinner."

The board subsequently voted to take no further action against Laski, concluding that his statements had been "misunderstood and misinterpreted." But that didn't mean he was off the hook entirely. Although Lowell had valiantly defended him in public, privately he informed the young instructor not to expect promotion from the university. For someone as ambitious as Laski, this was a major blow.

Without the rank of professor, he would never have the status and influence he desired outside the academy. And without the protection of tenure, he would never have the security he needed within.

Still absorbing this news, Laski soon received an even bigger blow. On January 16, the *Harvard Lampoon*, a student-run humor magazine, dedicated an entire issue to making fun of him. Styled as an exposé, the issue began by scolding the other publications on campus for failing to express the student body's true feelings about Laski. As a result, it announced, "Lampy feels it incumbent upon him to cloak his Motley for the nonce beneath the black toga of censure, to dip his pen in vitriol, and to put down in black and white what he thinks and what the undergraduate thinks of the Propagandist-in-our-midst." What Lampy thought was not kind. In sixteen pages of poems, plays, cartoons, songs, and articles, the editors savaged Laski as an arrogant, hypocritical self-promoter with eccentric habits and outlandish ideas. A mock Russian constitution anointed Lenin, Trotsky, and Laski the supreme rulers of the world. A faux autobiography reported that Laski was born in Poland at the age of three and completed Oxford in twenty minutes. A Greek chorus indicted him for "misdemeanors so unlawful/Felonies so wildly awful/We could hang him twice for any single deed," and a short story portrayed him as a know-it-all pedant by the name of Professor Moses Smartelickoff. Nothing about Laski escaped ridicule: not his shaggy hair and mustache, not his shapeless bohemian hats, not his penchant for embellishment or his reputation for borrowing money. The illustrations were particularly cruel, exaggerating his scrawny physique and oversized head. On the cover he appeared as a Christ figure wearing only a loincloth and oversized spectacles, his sticklike arms crossed over a sunken chest. Inside he was depicted as an emaciated grim reaper sending respectable capitalists into the fires of hell. The worst of the items were vicious, sophomoric, and anti-Semitic. The best, such as the poem "Alone at Laski," had a dash of Gilbert and Sullivan:

If you happen to inherit
A dominion of some merit,

Which you feel you cannot govern all alone,
Just apply to Mr. Laski,
He's the very man to ask—he
Will advise you how to act upon the throne.

'Twould be greatly to his liking
If the whole world started striking,
With himself established at the strikers' head;
In the parlance of the ghetto,
He would "shake a mean stiletto,"
From the firstski to the laski he's a Red!

The Laski *Lampoon*, as it came to be known, caused a sensation. In one stroke, it reignited all the old passions of the police strike, putting Laski's name back into the news and prompting J. Edgar Hoover to open a file on him. The *Boston Transcript* lauded the magazine, commending its editors for having the courage that the Harvard overseers lacked. The *Boston Herald* denounced the issue as "one of the most scathing attacks ever directed against a college instructor in America." And the *Harvard Crimson* was so deluged with letters of protest against the *Lampoon* that it pleaded with readers to stop sending them.

Ironically, the *Lampoon* itself soon became the subject of a debate over free speech. A group of students and faculty demanded that Lowell punish the editors responsible for the issue, arguing that they had gone beyond the scope of fair comment. To his credit, Laski recognized the hypocrisy of this position and urged Lowell to let the matter drop. Not that Lowell needed any encouragement. Having defended Laski's right to preach militant socialism, he wasn't about to discipline a group of students for parodying a faculty member. He did, however, lecture the president of the *Lampoon* for exercising bad taste and poor judgment. "Humor is a perfectly proper instrument," he wrote, "but not in the form of personal attack on those who differ from us, for the only essential question is the truth, not the personality of him who argues."

Holmes was furious when he received a copy of the Laski *Lampoon*.

"It is disgusting that so serious a scholar and thinker as he should be subjected to the trampling of swine," he wrote to Frankfurter. To Laski he downplayed the attack, describing it as "such a childish and rotten little show as hardly to merit a second thought . . . I don't know whether you are sensitive about such things—(I was for a good while but have got somewhat hardened)—but that serpent seems to me a fangless one—however malignant in intent." Brandeis also offered words of comfort. "I trust that you and Frida are not much concerned about the *Lampoon* episode," he wrote to Laski. "It is really a great compliment and has done good service to the cause of freedom."

For Laski, however, the writing was on the wall. It was one thing to elicit the enmity of Wall Street bankers and reactionary alumni; that was his role as a provocateur. But once a teacher has lost his students, he has lost everything. In Laski's mind, he was no longer welcome at Harvard, no longer welcome in Massachusetts, perhaps no longer welcome anywhere in the country. "I am heartily sick of America," he wrote to the British philosopher Bertrand Russell in February. "I am very eager to get away from this country," to a place "where an ox does not tread upon the tongue."

Once again it was spring. The crocuses bloomed, the tree toads sang, and the boys came out to play marbles on the sidewalks. Taking a break from his work, Holmes drove down to Rock Creek Park to look at the "thousand veils of green and brown and red mists from the just opening buds." "Lord how I love it," he wrote to Nina Gray. "Am I wrong in thinking that you said the spring makes you melancholy? Any beautiful or happy thing can be the source of much melancholy if one takes a turn that way, but it pays to dwell on the other side."

One afternoon in late March, a letter arrived from Laski. Recognizing the handwriting on the envelope, Holmes opened it with his usual anticipation, curious to hear what his young friend was up to now. His excitement soon turned to anguish, however, for when he unfolded the letter this is what he read:

Cambridge, Mass
28.3.20

My dear Justice,

I do not know how to begin this letter. All my abiding love for you comes tumbling to the end of my pen and confuses the thoughts I want to express. The fact is this. I have been offered a professorship at the London School of Economics to begin next October. It offers me £700 a year, an amount of teaching very much less than I now do, colleagueship with the men who are the real masters of my subject, and, above all, England. I have talked it over with Felix, Lowell, Haskins, and my colleagues in general; I have looked at it from the personal angle of Frida & my own people, and the conclusion is that I ought not, personally and intellectually, to refuse it. I have written my acceptance and so when I go in June it will be for good.

You will know what I mean when I say that my love for you and Felix is the one thing that holds me back. It is one of the two or three most precious things I have ever known and to diminish the personal contact that has lit up these last four years so much is not easy. Yet I think it has gone deep enough to make space, I do not say unimportant, but irrelevant. Wherever I am and whatever I do you would be the greatest of my masters and the dearest of my friends. Wherever thought led me you would be the compass by which I set my intellectual direction. Wherever I was, writing to you and hearing from you would be one of the greatest joys I could have. If I end this American adventure will you believe me when I say that I end it only because what you have taught me has made it possible for others to think that I might be useful in what seems a career where I would exercise a larger influence than here. . . . Felix and Lowell both emphasize their belief that the post is, for my work, ideal. I feel that too. But I cannot be content until I know that the seal of your approval is on it.

And I want to say again that the thought of England makes me see how infinitely much I owe to our friendship. Not merely

to the ideas you have given me—though they are the background
of my thought. But above all to a generous affection which, I
think, comes only once or twice in one's life and makes everything
that has ever been bitter or hard seem petty and negligible. I
want while I'm in England to . . . send you week by week comment
and gossip and talk, but above all my love. If I could not do that I
would not, of course, go. For I realize that the bigger thing is to
contribute what I can to your happiness.

Please tell Mrs. Holmes this, for all that I say is for her equally
with you. And give her, as yourself, my dear love.

Ever affectionately yours,
Harold J. Laski

This letter—and the news it conveyed—had been in the works for
some time. As early as 1917, Laski had begun laying the groundwork
for a return to England, writing to his former tutors at Oxford, sending his books and articles to prominent scholars, and striking up a
correspondence with two of the most influential intellectuals in the
country, the social psychologist Graham Wallas and the legal theorist
Viscount Richard Haldane. He had hoped for a position at Oxford or
Cambridge but, realizing that these were long shots, had also set his
sights on the London School of Economics. Founded in 1895 by the
social reformers Beatrice and Sidney Webb, the school was closely tied
to the Fabian Society, a socialist group that believed in promoting economic equality through political means rather than violent revolution.
It was an up-and-coming institution with a liberal, activist faculty;
Laski could hardly have hoped for something better.

Holmes was not completely in the dark about these plans. He knew
that Laski hoped to return to England one day and knew also that
Laski's position at Harvard had become untenable. But that didn't
lessen his sorrow upon hearing the news. For more than three years,
Laski had been his closest friend and confidant, his dear lad, his boy.
And now he was leaving. Not wanting to dissuade him from a promis-
ing opportunity, Holmes agreed with Frankfurter and Lowell that

Laski was making the right decision, for his work, his family, and his future . . .

> But oh, my dear lad, I shall miss you sadly. There is no other man I should miss so much. Your intellectual companionship, your suggestiveness, your encouragement and affection have enriched life to me very greatly and it will be hard not to look forward to seeing you in bodily presence. However, I shall get your letters and that will be much. I shall do my best to hold up my end of the stick—though while the work is on here, as you know, it sometimes is hard to find time or to get free from the cramp to the law—I should say, of the law, in the sense that one's mind after intense preoccupation only slowly recovers its freedom—as the eye only gradually readjusts itself to a new focus—especially with the old. I feel as if I were good for some time yet—but I used to think that the mainspring was broken at 80 and in any event as that hour approaches one is bound to recognize uncertainties even if one does not realize them—as I don't. If we should not meet again you will know that you have added much to the happiness of one fellow-being. Give my love to your wife.
>
>   Affectionately Yours,
>   O.W. Holmes

The last few months of the term were hectic, as usual. After a long delay, McKenna finally circulated his majority opinion in *Schaefer*. The justices had voted to reverse the convictions against the treasurer and president of the *Tageblatt*, figureheads with no real say in the substance of the paper. But they upheld the editors' convictions, citing *Schenck*, *Frohwerk*, *Debs*, and now *Abrams* to support the judgment. In his opinion, McKenna rejected the defendants' claim that the government had failed to prove the falsity of their reports, insisting that the Court was bound by the jury's factual findings. He also dismissed the claim that the articles were innocuous, explaining that under the Espionage Act the government was not required to prove harm. "The tendency of the articles" was enough, he wrote, "and to have required more would have made the law useless."

As in *Abrams*, Holmes and Brandeis dissented. This time, Brandeis wrote the opinion, his first attempt to articulate a theory of the First Amendment. He began where Holmes had left off—with the clear and present danger test. Although McKenna had ignored that standard entirely, Brandeis declared that it, not bad tendency, was the correct test to apply. He also argued that the jury's findings were not inviolable: "In my opinion, no jury acting in calmness could reasonably say that any of the publications set forth in the indictment was of such a character or was made under such circumstances as to create a clear and present danger." As to the charge of altering articles, Brandeis scoffed at the notion that the editors had violated the ban on false reports. "To hold that such harmless additions to or omissions from news items . . . can afford the basis even of a prosecution, will doubtless discourage criticism of the policies of the government," he wrote. "Convictions such as these, besides abridging freedom of speech, threaten freedom of thought and of belief."

A week later Holmes and Brandeis dissented in another Espionage Act case. Argued in November, after the Court decided *Abrams*, this case involved four socialists from Albany who had circulated copies of a pamphlet entitled *The Price We Pay*. Written by an Episcopal clergyman and printed by the national Socialist Party, the pamphlet repeated the standard leftist critiques of the war: that it was being waged to protect J. P. Morgan's loans to England, that victory was impossible, and that the only way out of the mess was to embrace socialism. Initially wary of distributing the pamphlet, the defendants changed their minds after a federal court in Baltimore ruled that it did not violate the Espionage Act. Unfortunately for them, that decision had no authority in New York, and prosecutors there charged them with making false statements and conspiring to cause insubordination in the military. A jury convicted them, and they appealed to the Supreme Court. The majority opinion, written by Justice Pitney, repeated much of what Justice McKenna had said in *Schaefer*. Whether the defendants intended to interfere with the war and whether they posed any risk of doing so were issues of fact for the jury to decide. As long as that decision was supported by some evidence, the Court could not overturn it on appeal even if it might have weighed the facts differently.

Brandeis again wrote the dissent, joined by Holmes. In typical Brandeis fashion, he marched methodically through the evidence, explaining that none of the statements were false, because they were either matters of opinion or hyperbole. He also disputed the claim that the pamphlet had posed a danger of causing insubordination in the military, pointing out that it had been circulated only among civilians and was primarily designed to recruit members for the Socialist Party. "The fundamental right of free men to strive for better conditions," he wrote, "will not be preserved if efforts to secure it by argument to fellow citizens may be construed as criminal incitement to disobey the existing law merely because the argument presented seems to those exercising judicial power to be unfair in its portrayal of existing evils, mistaken in its assumptions, unsound in reasoning or intemperate in language."

Before the term ended, Laski paid one final visit to Holmes. He took the train down from Cambridge in late April and stayed in the capital for three days. Fanny was laid up with a cold, so Holmes could not offer him a place to sleep. But the two friends saw each other as much as possible, taking walks in the afternoon, dining together, and sitting up late to discuss books and Laski's future. Then, at the end of the week, they parted, saying good-bye for what, as far as they knew, might possibly be the last time.

Holmes and Fanny headed back to Beverly Farms that summer. It was quieter without Laski, but Ellen Curtis was there, and Holmes resumed the flirtation with more gusto than before. In consideration of his "age and moral infirmities," Brandeis had given him leave to ignore facts over the vacation, so he returned to his "customary sport with ideas," polishing off a history of the French Revolution, a collection of Aeschylus, and a shelfful of other wonderfully impractical works.

Laski, meanwhile, sailed for England, where he took up his teaching post and immersed himself in politics. As promised, he sent Holmes regular updates about his adventures—his dinners with Lord Haldane and Graham Wallas, his meetings with the prime minister, his visits to Parliament. He also continued to pass along a steady flow of book recommendations, most with a socialist slant. But Holmes, having been pushed as far as he was willing to go, at last rebelled.

"You mention for Beverly Farms, good God! Webb on this and that—and *Clothing Workers of Chicago*," Holmes replied. "If you think that I am going to bother myself again before I die about social improvement or read any of those stinking upward and onwarders—you err. I mean to have some good out of being old."

"I Simply Was Ignorant"

In the summer of 1922, Zechariah Chafee was working on an article about the attitude of state courts toward free speech. It was the latest in a series of free speech projects he had undertaken since writing his first piece for the *New Republic* four years earlier. In April 1920 he had published a blistering critique of the *Abrams* decision in the *Harvard Law Review*. Entitled "A Contemporary State Trial," the article condemned nearly every aspect of the case, from the brutal interrogation tactics of the police to Judge Clayton's hostile treatment of the defendants to the Supreme Court's approval of the excessive sentences. "The whole proceeding, from start to finish, has been a disgrace to our law," Chafee wrote, "and none the less a disgrace because our highest court felt powerless to wipe it out." The only bright spot was Holmes's dissent, with its "magnificent exposition of the philosophic basis" of the First Amendment. Later that same year Chafee published *Freedom of Speech*, a book that combined his prior articles with new chapters on the deportation of radicals and the exclusion of socialists from elective office. Dedicated to Learned Hand, it was the first comprehensive attempt to grapple with the conflict between national security and expressive liberty and is still consulted by legal scholars today.

Chafee's work on free speech eventually pulled him into the cause of civil liberties more generally. At the request of a federal judge in Boston, he and Frankfurter agreed to defend nineteen communists who had been arrested during the Palmer Raids. He also contributed to a report that accused the federal government of widespread violations of the law in its campaign to harass, arrest, and deport suspected radicals. Then, when Congress investigated those accusations, Chafee was one of the lawyers who appeared before a Senate subcommittee to testify.

As a reward for his good deeds, Chafee was labeled a dangerous man, like Laski and Frankfurter before him. J. Edgar Hoover opened a file on him under the heading "Attorney for Radical Organizations." The U.S. attorney's office accused him of misrepresenting the facts in his article on *Abrams*. And a group of prominent Harvard alumni tried to run him out of the law school. Led by a Wall Street lawyer named Austen G. Fox, the group prepared a thirty-two-page report charging Chafee with conduct unbecoming a scholar. Lowell, hoping to avoid yet another public controversy involving a faculty member, referred the charges to a special committee that included Learned Hand's cousin, Augustus, still on the federal bench, and Benjamin Cardozo, a judge on the New York Court of Appeals. The committee met at the Harvard Club of Boston on a sweltering Sunday in May 1921. Chafee, accompanied by Pound and Frankfurter, conceded that he had made a few minor errors in his *Abrams* article. (He had written, for instance, that the trial was Clayton's first Espionage Act case, when in fact it was his third or fourth; he had also referred to the mistress of one of the defendants as his wife.) But he stood behind the substance of the article, insisting that he was "not only honest but right." Lowell defended Chafee as well, pointing out that some of Fox's charges were themselves based on erroneous information and declaring that no faculty member could be disciplined without his consent. That was enough for the committee—barely. It ruled six to five in Chafee's favor, with Cardozo casting the deciding ballot.

Now, one year later, Chafee was hard at work again, researching the free speech decisions of state courts since the end of the war. As he read through the decisions, he noted with satisfaction that a growing number of state courts had embraced the clear and present danger test in interpreting their own constitutional guarantees of free speech. But one thing still puzzled him: where did the expression "clear and present danger" come from? He had not come across it anywhere in his research—not in the English common law sources, not in the debates of the framers, and not in the state law materials he had reviewed. No one else seemed to know the origin of the phrase either. So Chafee decided to ask the one person who would certainly be able to solve the mystery.

June 9, 1922

My Dear Mr. Justice Holmes:

   In going over Freedom of Speech cases in the state courts the last few months, I have been glad to see that your test of clear and present danger is winning acceptance and I hope that it will drive out the old notion of bad tendency. This brings to mind a question that I have long intended to ask you—whether this definition of freedom of speech in the Schenck case was at all suggested to you by any writers on the subject or was the result entirely of your reflections. Since you hit the nail, in my opinion, so squarely on the head, I am wondering whether you had been aiming at it for a long while and whether you had learned of others who had at least succeeded in mashing their fingers somewhere in the neighborhood of the same nail. Any light that you can give me on the background of your opinion in the Schenck case would be extremely welcome, with the understanding of course that I am not seeking to invade the consultation room. . . .

Yours Sincerely,
Zechariah Chafee Jr.

   Holmes had just arrived at Beverly Farms when he received Chafee's letter. His respect and affection for the young professor had only grown since their meeting at Laski's bungalow three years earlier. He had read Chafee's article on *Abrams* in 1920 and described it to Laski as "first rate." He had then watched in distress as Chafee was persecuted for his criticism of that decision. At Brandeis's urging, he had even written Chafee a letter of support just days before his trial at the Harvard Club. Now, upon receiving Chafee's inquiry, he sat down at once to respond:

June 12, 1922

My Dear Professor Chafee:

Your letter arrives here just after myself—and I must make a hurried answer. The expression that you refer to was not helped by any book that I know of. I think it came without doubt after the later cases (and probably you—I do not remember exactly) had taught me that in the earlier Paterson [*sic*] case, if that was the name of it, I had taken Blackstone and Parker of Mass. as well founded, wrongly. I simply was ignorant. But I did think hard on the matter of attempts in my Common Law and a Mass. Case—later in the Swift case (U.S.)—and I thought it out unhelped. I noted that Bishop made a slight modification of his text after I had printed [*The Common Law*] but without reference to me—I speak from ancient memory—and much later I found an English Nisi Prius case in which one of the good judges had expressed this notion in a few words. That early effort no doubt made the formula easy if it is good—as I hope. . . .

If you ever come this way, do let me see you.

Sincerely,
O.W. Holmes

I simply was ignorant. It was the closest Holmes would ever come to admitting that he had been wrong. Even in *Abrams*, he had continued to insist that *Debs* and the other cases were correctly decided. But the man who once defended "the sacred right to kill the other fellow when he disagrees" was not the same man who wrote that "we should be eternally vigilant against attempts to check the expression of opinions that we loathe and believe to be fraught with death." He had changed. Through the intervention of his friends and his own willingness to adapt, he had come to see free speech from a different, more personal perspective. And from that moment forward, he became the champion of the First Amendment we know him as today, writing passionate dissents on behalf of radicals and subversives throughout the rest of his career.

In 1921 he dissented from a decision upholding the postmaster's denial of second-class (or discount) mailing privileges to a socialist newspaper during the war. Although Holmes acknowledged that the government is not obligated to operate a postal service at all, he argued that as long as it does so "the use of the mails is almost as much a part of free speech as the right to use our tongues." In 1925 he objected to the conviction of Benjamin Gitlow, the manager of a socialist newspaper that had advocated overthrow of the government through "revolutionary mass action." A majority of the Court upheld Gitlow's conviction, ruling that the government is not required to wait until a revolution is imminent but may "suppress the threatened danger at its incipiency." Holmes disagreed. "If in the long run the beliefs expressed in proletarian dictatorship are destined to be accepted by the dominant forces of the community the only meaning of free speech is that they should be given their chance and have their way." And in 1929 he dissented in the case of Rosika Schwimmer, a pacifist who had been denied citizenship for refusing to swear that she would take up arms to defend the United States. Although Schwimmer's case did not technically involve the First Amendment, Holmes saw it as one more example of the government's effort to impose uniformity of belief—an effort he now categorically opposed. "If there is any principle of the Constitution that more imperatively calls for attachment than any other it is the principle of free thought—not free thought for those who agree with us but freedom for the thought that we hate."

Holmes's dissents in these and other cases fostered a growing national appreciation for the right of free speech. He was not the only person responsible for this development, of course. Brandeis wrote several eloquent opinions himself, and the contributions of Chafee and other civil libertarians were invaluable. But it was the figure of Holmes, the Civil War veteran, the enlightened aristocrat, the Great Dissenter, who gave the movement its legitimacy and inspiration. And by the early 1940s that movement was no longer speaking in the voice of dissent. A majority of the Supreme Court finally came around, embracing clear and present danger as the governing standard and citing Holmes's dissent in *Abrams* as the foundational document of America's free speech tradition.

Holmes did not live to see that happen. Although he sat "in the seats of the mighty" until ten years past eighty, the strain of the job eventually wore him down. Unable to carry his prodigious load anymore, he retired in January 1932 and was replaced by Benjamin Cardozo, the second Jew to sit on the Supreme Court. Fanny had died in 1929, so Holmes was left alone with the servants and the new secretary who arrived each fall to read to him and accompany him on carriage rides to Arlington Cemetery, where Fanny had been buried. Over the next three years, Holmes plowed through an astonishing number of books (more than 620 in all), as though cramming for a fast-approaching exam. He continued to tackle the heavyweights— Aristotle and Plato, Emerson and Santayana—but more and more the list in his black copybook was sprinkled with the lighter fare of Agatha Christie, P. G. Wodehouse, and his namesake Sherlock Holmes. The last book, entered just days before he died of pneumonia on March 6, 1935, was an odd choice for a committed agnostic: a Thornton Wilder novel with the hopeful title *Heaven's My Destination*.

The other major characters in this story all outlasted Holmes. Brandeis remained a justice until 1939, helping to lead a liberal revival on the Court in response to the New Deal. He died of a heart attack two years later, missing both the worst horrors of World War II and the realization of his Zionist vision with the creation of Israel.

Harold Laski witnessed both. After two decades of rabble-rousing and behind-the-scenes political maneuvering, he was appointed to the executive committee of the Labour Party and served as its chair in

1945. The moment seemed auspicious. With the end of the war in sight and the public demanding social reform, Laski hoped to finally achieve his vision of a socialist state. But his skills as a political leader were not equal to his ambitions, and his term ended in disappointment. Though Labour won the 1945 election and instituted a wave of economic reforms, Laski's own influence waned, and he spent the last years of his life writing a book about American democracy. He died of pneumonia in 1950 at the age of fifty-six, having failed to heed Holmes's warning not to run the machine too hard.

Learned Hand finally got the promotion he felt he had been denied because of his decision in *Masses*. In 1924, he was appointed to the federal appeals court in New York, where he remained for thirty-seven years, eventually becoming chief judge. That was as high as he rose, however. The seat on the Supreme Court that he desperately wanted and that many people felt he deserved eluded him. Once again, he had been refused admission to the most exclusive of clubs. He would always be second-string, his opinions forever subject to review by a higher authority. Perhaps that is why, when the country faced its next major crisis of faith, Hand was unwilling to put his reputation on the line again for the sake of individual rights.

The year was 1950, and the country was once more in the grip of panic. China had fallen to the reds, the Soviet Union had tested its first atomic bomb, and communist North Korea had opened fire on its democratic neighbor to the south. In the midst of these disturbing events, Senator Joseph McCarthy had slithered onto the scene with his infamous lists and ruthless methods, spreading fear and paranoia throughout the land. Congress held hearings, witnesses named names, and hundreds of Hollywood writers, actors, and directors were blacklisted. The Justice Department had also sprung into action. J. Edgar Hoover, now in his third decade as head of the FBI, had teamed up with Representative Richard Nixon to expose Alger Hiss, a former Holmes secretary accused of spying for the Soviets. Meanwhile, in an effort to purge the country of communist infiltrators, prosecutors had dusted off a 1940 law passed in response to the outbreak of World War II. Known as the Smith Act (after its sponsor, Howard W. Smith, of

Virginia), the law made it a crime to advocate overthrow of the government by force, to form an organization for the purpose of advocating overthrow, or even to be a member of such an organization. Although used sparingly at first, the law soon became an important weapon in the Justice Department's campaign against radicals during the cold war. Its biggest test came in 1949 when prosecutors charged Eugene Dennis and ten other leaders of the Communist Party of America with conspiracy to violate the act. In a trial that lasted ten months, prosecutors proved little more than that the defendants had formed an organization to teach the doctrines of Marx and Lenin. There was no evidence they had stockpiled weapons, committed acts of terrorism, plotted the overthrow of the government, or taken any steps whatsoever toward their ultimate goal. Nonetheless, they were admitted communists, which was enough in those days to be branded a criminal. The jury found them guilty, the judge sentenced them to five years in prison, and the case came before Learned Hand on appeal.

Like most other liberals, Hand was troubled by the storm of suspicion and hysteria that had swept across the country. He detested McCarthyism and viewed the events around him as a reprise of the first red scare. One might have expected, therefore, that he would react as he had in 1917, that he would reverse the convictions and write a courageous opinion in defense of free speech. But Hand affirmed the verdict. Even worse, he gutted the clear and present danger standard, which, as he had made clear to Holmes years before, he had never really liked. Clear and present danger could not mean that the government must wait until an overthrow is imminent, he argued. Instead the power to suppress speech depends on the relationship of two factors: the gravity of the threatened danger and the likelihood that it will occur. In each case, Hand argued, a court "must ask whether the gravity of the 'evil,' discounted by its improbability, justifies such invasion of free speech as is necessary to avoid the danger." Although presented as an interpretation of the clear and present danger standard, this was actually closer to the old bad tendency test. Nowhere did Hand mention the requirement that the danger be imminent. Nor did he require that the danger be clear. As long as the harm was grave enough, such as the overthrow of the government, even a slim chance of success in the distant future could justify suppression of speech. Applying this standard, Hand ruled that the Communist Party did pose a clear and present danger. To conclude otherwise, he said, would force the government to "wait until the actual eve of hostilities."

Why did Hand change *his* mind? That is a story for another day, but the short answer is that, in his later years, Hand's commitment to judicial restraint was nearly absolute. He had come to believe that courts should almost never strike down the acts of elected officials and that constitutional rights, instead of being judicially enforceable, are simply admonitory principles to guide the exercise of legislative and executive power. He even went so far as to criticize the Supreme Court's decision in *Brown v. Board of Education*, arguing that the Court had no business enforcing its own vision of equal protection. So regardless of how much he disliked McCarthyism and the persecution of communists, Hand did not think it was his job to stop them. As he explained in letters eerily reminiscent of the way Holmes had defended his *Debs* decision, "Personally, I should never have prosecuted those birds." But that "has nothing to do with my job or what was before me" in *Dennis*.

Hand wasn't the only one whose position on free speech changed in later years. When his decision in *Dennis* reached the Supreme Court, one of the men sitting on that Court was Felix Frankfurter. Frankfurter had been appointed to the bench in 1939, filling the seat vacated by Cardozo, who in turn had replaced Holmes. Prior to his appointment, Frankfurter had become one of the most powerful and controversial liberals in the country. He had represented the anarchists Nicola Sacco and Bartolomeo Vanzetti in their appeal of a murder conviction in 1927 and was one of the primary architects of the New Deal. Once he was on the Court, however, his belief in judicial restraint prevailed over his progressive instincts and he often voted with the Court's conservative bloc. Occupying the seat once held by Holmes, Frankfurter seemed to think he was honoring the legacy of his late friend. But with respect to free speech he nearly destroyed it. For when the Court upheld Hand's decision in *Dennis*, Frankfurter sided with the majority. Explaining his vote in a long and anguished opinion, he argued that the case came down to a question of fact: how dangerous was the American Communist Party? That was a question he thought best answered by the nation's military and diplomatic leaders, not the justices of the Supreme Court.

The Court's decision in *Dennis* marked a setback for the cause of free speech, and over the next several years the government prosecuted nearly 150 members of the Communist Party, many of whom did no more than teach the ideas of Lenin and Stalin or listen to others teach them. But Zechariah Chafee never gave up hope. Unlike Hand and Frankfurter, he kept the faith, spending his twilight years defending free speech. In his last book, *The Blessings of Liberty*, published two years before his death in 1957, he predicted that the current spirit of intolerance would run its course and that the country would one day return to the path Holmes had mapped out.

And eventually it did. In a 1969 case involving a Ku Klux Klan member who advocated violence against the civil rights movement, the Court resuscitated the clear and present danger test, albeit slightly modified. Reversing the defendant's conviction, the Court held that advocacy of violence or unlawful conduct is protected by the First Amendment "except where such advocacy is directed to inciting or producing imminent lawless action and is likely to incite or produce such action." This rule, with its requirement that speech pose a likely and imminent danger before it can be punished, is a direct descendant of Holmes's test and remains the governing standard today.

But Holmes's influence extends beyond a particular test. In nearly every area of First Amendment law, his *Abrams* dissent continues to make its presence felt. It has been invoked in recent decades to protect a vast range of expressive activity, from commercial advertisements and campaign spending to defamation of public figures and the burning of the American flag. Not all of these decisions have been popular. The Supreme Court's 2010 decision upholding the right of corporations to contribute to political campaigns, which is rooted in Holmes's dissent, was widely criticized by scholars and the general public. Nor have all questions about the scope of expressive liberty been resolved. If anything, the First Amendment is more heavily litigated now than it was fifty years ago. But the fact that we continue to fight over the amendment's meaning does not detract from Holmes's accomplishment. For even those disputes are a testament to the centrality of free speech in our legal culture today—a centrality that is due largely to his *Abrams* dissent. As Holmes once said in defense of *The Common Law*, the material thing is that he "gathered the flax, made the thread, spun the cloth, and cut the garment—and started all the inquiries that since have gone over many matters therein."

Holmes's dissent endures on a deeper level as well. His metaphor of the marketplace of ideas and his concept of "clear and present danger" have worked their way into our collective consciousness, becoming part of our language, our view of the world, and our identity as a nation. Without even knowing it, we have internalized his words and come to regard them as our own. Which, come to think of it, is precisely what Holmes would have wanted. In an address to the graduating class at Harvard in 1886, he spoke about "the secret isolated joy of the thinker, who knows that, a hundred years after he is dead and forgotten, men who never heard of him will be moving to the measure of his thought." Were Holmes alive today, that joy would be his.

NOTES

After the completion of this book, the Oliver Wendell Holmes Jr. Papers at Harvard Law School were reorganized, rendering the old box and folder numbers irrelevant. Therefore, citations to the Holmes Papers below include only the microfilm reel numbers, which remain the same. In addition, the bulk of the Holmes collection is now accessible online through the Harvard Law School Library.

PROLOGUE: AN UNEXPECTED VISIT

2 when he wrote a memoir: Acheson, *Morning and Noon*, 119. Acheson does not specify the exact date of the visit, but given that Holmes circulated his dissent on Thursday, November 6, and the justices met all day in conference on Saturday, November 8, it seems clear that it took place on Friday, November 7. It could not have taken place on Sunday, November 9, because Holmes's secretaries did not work on Sundays.

3 The majority of the Court . . . affirmed his conviction: *Debs v. United States*, 249 U.S. 211 (1919).

4 Persecution for the expression . . . required to save the country: *Abrams v. United States*, 250 U.S. 616, 630–31 (1919) (Holmes, J., dissenting).

5 In one of the first Court opinions: *Patterson v. People of State of Colorado ex rel. Attorney Gen. of State of Colorado*, 205 U.S. 454 (1907).

6 In another case: *Fox v. Washington*, 236 U.S. 273 (1915).

6 "a constitutional right to talk politics": *McAuliffe v. City of New Bedford*, 29 N.E. 517, 517 (Mass. 1892).

6   "thick-fingered clowns": OWH to his sister, Amelia, Warrenton, Va., Nov. 1862, in Holmes, *Touched with Fire*, 71.

6   "rests on the death of men": OWH to Sir Frederick Pollock, Washington, D.C., Feb. 1, 1920, in Holmes and Pollock, *Holmes-Pollock Letters*, 2:36. Hereafter cited simply as *Holmes-Pollock*.

6   If a nation needs soldiers: Holmes, *Common Law*, 41.

6   limit the workday of bakers: *Lochner v. New York*, 198 U.S. 45 (1905).

6   "If my fellow citizens want": OWH to Harold Joseph Laski, Washington, D.C., March 4, 1920, in Holmes and Laski, *Holmes-Laski Letters*, 1:249. Hereafter cited simply as *Holmes-Laski*.

8   "The trouble with all explanations"; "amusing and tickling": OWH to Pollock, Beverly Farms, Sept. 24, 1904, in *Holmes-Pollock*, 1:118.

1: TRAIN FEVER

10   "an organized bore": OWH to Pollock, Washington, D.C., Feb. 1, 1920, in *Holmes-Pollock*, 2:36.

10   disliked the business side: Howe, *Proving Years*, 111.

10   "began to grow sober" . . . "academic life is but half life": OWH to Felix Frankfurter, London, 15 July 1913, in Holmes and Frankfurter, *Holmes and Frankfurter, Their Correspondence*, 12. Hereafter cited simply as *Holmes and Frankfurter*.

10   "literary feller"; "brilliant rather than sound": "More Brilliant than Sound: Evening Post Says Judge Holmes Is Able, Not Great—At Least He Is Not a Corporation Lawyer," *Boston Evening Transcript*, Aug. 12, 1902, 3.

12   vied with Holmes and James: Minnie Temple, Henry James's cousin, was a model for Daisy Miller. See Borklund, 76. Minnie Temple was also the model for two other of James's heroines—Isabel Archer and Milly Theale. See LeClair, 36–37.

12   accidental survivor: This phrase is taken from Baker, *Justice*, 147, 156.

12   "Damn a man": OWH to Harold Laski, Washington, D.C., June 9, 1917, in *Holmes-Laski*, 1:90.

12   "a fight of swine": OWH to Laski, Washington, D.C., Nov. 22, 1917, in *Holmes-Laski*, 1:111.

13   "Do I seem too detached": OWH to Baroness Charlotte Moncheur, Washington, D.C., Jan. 22, 1918, Oliver Wendell Holmes Jr. Papers, reel 26.

13   Holmes dismissed the boy's suit: *Erie R. Co. v. Hilt*, 247 U.S. 97 (1918).

13   In the first case . . . regulate child labor?: *Hammer v. Dagenhart*, 247 U.S. 251, 277 (1918) (Holmes, J., dissenting).

13   He did not mention the First Amendment: *Toledo Newspaper Co. v. United States*, 247 U.S. 402, 422 (1918) (Holmes, J., dissenting).

14   "It was sad to see him": Louis Dembitz Brandeis to Alice Goldmark

Brandeis, Washington, D.C., June 15, 1918, in Urofsky and Levy, *Family Letters*, 316.

14   called his condition "train fever": OWH to Pollock, Washington, D.C., June 14, 1918, in *Holmes-Pollock*, 1:266.

15   "Such things make one twitter" . . . "is found everywhere": Ibid., 1: 266–68.

15   "Fanny did once," he confided: Donald Hiss, secretary of Justice Holmes, quoted in Louchheim, *Making of the New Deal*, 42.

15   The journey to New York: Anderson, *Presidents and Pies*, 232–33.

16   When they had first moved to Washington: Novick, *Honorable Justice*, 275.

17   He worshiped the justice: Gunther, *Learned Hand*, 345.

17   Born into a strict, religious family . . . sensitive about his name: Ibid., 4–22.

17   shadow cast by his father . . . he continued to insist: Ibid., 6–22.

17–18   won admission to Harvard . . . influence of James Bradley Thayer: Ibid., 26–52.

18   moving to New York: Ibid., 67–68.

18   an article in the *Harvard Law Review*: "Due Process of Law and the Eight-Hour Day," *Harvard Law Review* 21 (1908): 495.

18   He also befriended . . . helped him secure the spot: Gunther, *Learned Hand*, 127–33.

18   He emerged, too . . . came into contact with Holmes: Ibid., 220–44.

19   Passed in June 1917 . . . the law created a censor: Espionage Act of 1917, ch. 30, tit. I, 40 Stat. 217, 219 (1917).

20   Eastman, in turn, filed a lawsuit: *Masses Pub. Co. v. Patten*, 244 F. 535 (S.D.N.Y. 1917), *rev'd*, 246 F. 24 (2d Cir. 1917).

20   he had written a letter: Gunther, *Learned Hand*, 154.

20   "contradict the normal assumption . . . propriety of its temper": *Masses Pub. Co. v. Patten*, 244 F. 535 at 540.

20   he told his wife: Learned Hand to Frances A. Hand, Cornish, N.H., July 16, 1917, Learned Hand Papers, box 111, folder 13.

21   It was reversed three months later: *Masses Pub. Co. v. Patten*, 246 F. 24 (2d Cir. 1917).

21   "to assimilate agitation": *Masses Pub. Co. v. Patten*, 244 F. at 540.

21   example of Hand's "natural perversity": Hand to Charles C. Burlingham, Oct. 6, 1917, Hand Papers, box 100, folder 26; Gunther, "Learned Hand, and the Origins," 731.

21   "You strike at the sacred right": Referenced by Hand in his letter to OWH, Windsor, Vt., June 22, 1918, Holmes Papers, reel 33.

22   he sent the following letter to Holmes: Ibid.

24   sent back an enthusiastic reply: OWH to Learned Hand, Beverly Farms, June 24, 1918, Holmes Papers, reel 26.

2: A SMART CHAP

28 stretches for a hundred miles: Garland, *Boston's North Shore*, xi–xii. See also Garland, *Boston's Gold Coast*, 14, 148, 187; Hawthorne, *Old Seaport Towns*, 116; Dow, *Old Days*, 42.

28 "Find the Yankee word for Sorrento": James Russell Lowell to Miss Jane Norton, Beverly Farms, Aug. 14, 1854, in *Letters of James Russell Lowell*, 215.

28 "first recollections of country": OWH to Patrick Augustine Sheehan, Beverly Farms, Aug. 14, 1911, in Holmes and Sheehan, *Holmes-Sheehan Correspondence*, 63. Hereafter cited simply as *Holmes-Sheehan*.

29 "Beverly-by-the-Depot": Dow, *Old Days*, 64.

29 "Day of Judgment": OWH to Pollock, Washington, D.C., Dec. 31, 1922, in *Holmes-Pollock*, 2:108; OWH to Lewis Einstein, Beverly Farms, Aug. 10, 1931, in Holmes and Einstein, *Holmes-Einstein Letters*, 328. Hereafter cited simply as *Holmes-Einstein*.

30 weekend visit to Beverly Farms: Baker, *Justice*, 488.

30 When Laski "inadvertently" left: Laski to OWH, New York, N.Y., July 18, 1916, in *Holmes-Laski*, 1:4.

30 Standing at least six foot two: There is some uncertainty about Holmes's exact height. Catherine Drinker Bowen writes that Holmes was over six foot three at the age of eighteen (Bowen, *Yankee from Olympus*, 126). John S. Monagan lists Holmes as "about" six foot two "in his prime" (Monagan, *Great Panjandrum*, 21). Louis Menand describes the justice as standing six foot three (Menand, *Metaphysical Club*, 3). Liva Baker's biographical account says he stood "more than six feet tall" and places the exact height at "six-foot-three" (Baker, *Justice*, 105, 4). It seems that most of these authors agree that Holmes was at least six foot two.

30 "His presence entered a room": Acheson, *Morning and Noon*, 62.

30 Edmund Wilson . . . while others: Kramnick and Sheerman, *Harold Laski*, 195.

31 "At a first glance": Rand, *Fountainhead*, 231.

31 The Olivers arrived in the New World: Baker, *Justice*, 24–25.

31 Laski had arrived in 1914: Newman, *Harold Laski*, 1, 30.

32 "4 years on the bench": OWH to Sheehan, Washington, D.C., Dec. 15, 1912, in *Holmes-Sheehan*, 78.

32 "votes for women" . . . as the culprit: Kramnick and Sheerman, *Harold Laski*, 66–68.

33 "Your comment on Boswell"; "your sentence on Proudhoun"; "this anarchical doctrine": Laski to OWH, Cambridge, Mass., Dec. 1, 1916, in *Holmes-Laski*, 1:39; Laski to OWH, Cambridge, Mass., May 7, 1917, in *Holmes-Laski*, 1:83; Laski to OWH, Cambridge, Mass., Sept. 13, 1916, in *Holmes-Laski*, 1:20.

33   he received "their ideas": Sergeant, "Oliver Wendell Holmes."

33   "most learned men"; "diabolically clever": OWH to Pollock, Washington, D.C., Feb. 18, 1917, in *Holmes-Pollock*, 1:243; OWH to Pollock, Washington, D.C., Nov. 19, 1917, in *Holmes-Pollock*, 1:252.

34   When he was just seventeen: Kramnick and Sheerman, *Harold Laski*, 34–35.

34   his long public career: Newman, *Harold Laski*, x.

34   Both were attracted to eugenics: Kramnick and Sheerman, *Harold Laski*, 34.

34   claimed that Holmes was impotent: Liva Baker's endnotes for page 228 in *Justice* cite a note by Howe in the Holmes Papers. On a note dated April 5, 1961, on unsigned Harvard Law School stationery, Holmes's biographer Mark DeWolfe Howe wrote, "Lunching with Sam Morison and Lewis Einstein at Somerset Club S.M. noted that in that very dining room John T. Morse, Jr., had told him in all seriousness that OWH was sexually impotent. Neither Morison nor Einstein seemed to take any stock in Morse's announcement." Morse was Holmes's first cousin.

34   "This is not the kind of world": Hand to Mark DeWolfe Howe, April 29, 1959, Hand Papers, box 90, folder 31.

35   To his son . . . bad puns and thoughtless barbs: Biddle, *Mr. Justice Holmes*, 44.

35   a slice of carrot: Baker, *Justice*, 144.

35   "Why a Pa's Nip!": Oliver Wendell Holmes Sr. to Dr. Hunt, Boston, Mass., May 25, 1803, in *Life and Letters of Oliver Wendell Holmes*, 25.

35   resented the way the elder Holmes: Biddle, *Mr. Justice Holmes*, 27; Novick, *Honorable Justice*, 14.

35   never forgave his father: Baker, *Justice*, 8.

35   Raised in an Orthodox household . . . with their newborn: Kramnick and Sheerman, *Harold Laski*, 46–47, 78–80, 96.

35   calling Holmes "Grandpa": Diana Laski to "Grandpa" Holmes, London, March 22, 1930, Holmes Papers, reel 35.

35   "my son": OWH to Laski, Washington, D.C., Feb. 27, 1917, in *Holmes-Laski*, 1:64.

35   "My boy will be here Saturday": Laski to Frida Laski, June 2, 1941, quoted in Kramnick and Sheerman, *Harold Laski*, 293.

36   "Here we are at last": OWH to Laski, Beverly Farms, June 25, 1918, in *Holmes-Laski*, 1:158.

36   "Tuesday ten it is": OWH to Laski, June 28, 1918, Holmes Papers, reel 4.

36   "I had a good talk": OWH to Laski, Beverly Farms, June 25, 1918, in *Holmes-Laski*, 1:159.

36   "Progress is born": Laski, *Studies*, 236–37, 274.

37   His own belief in toleration . . . "Carlyle's ultimate question": Laski to

OWH, Rockport, Mass., July 5, 1918, in *Holmes-Laski*, 1:159–60. The quotation attributed to Carlyle—"Can I kill thee or can'st thou kill me?"—appears to be a paraphrase of Carlyle by Walter Bagehot in *Physics and Politics; or, Thoughts on the Application of the Principles of "Natural Selection" and "Inheritance" to Political Society*, 61.

37   pointed it out to him: OWH to Laski, Beverly Farms, July 7, 1918, in *Holmes-Laski*, 1:160–61.

38   "I agree that the logical result": OWH to Einstein, Beverly Farms, July 11, 1918, in *Holmes-Einstein*, 168–69.

38   photographic memory and could read: Kramnick and Sheerman, *Harold Laski*, 18.

39   weather was horrid: J. W. Smith, *Climatological Report: New England Section, July 1918*, U.S. Department of Agriculture, Weather Bureau, vol. 30, no. 7, 51–52.

39   Holmes thought the question too subjective: OWH to Laski, Beverly Farms, July 16, 1918, in *Holmes-Laski*, 1:161.

39   He hated borrowing books: OWH to Laski, Washington, D.C., Feb. 28, 1919, in *Holmes-Laski*, 1:188. (OWH wrote, "How I hate to borrow books.") OWH to Laski, Washington, D.C., Oct. 3, 1920, in *Holmes-Laski* 1:284. (OWH wrote, "as a lent book [it] made me miserable until it was read and returned.")

39   "it is grasped that": Seaton, *Theory of Toleration*, 26–27.

40   "In Boston in those days": Louchheim, "Clerks of the Court on Justice Holmes," ch. 3 of *New Deal*, 22; White, *Justice Oliver Wendell Holmes*, 368.

40   As an undergraduate at Harvard: Howe, *Shaping Years*, 46.

40   "A hundred years ago": Oliver Wendell Holmes Jr., "Books," *Harvard Magazine*, Dec. 1858, 410.

40   "reflection that the majority": Howe, *Shaping Years*, 105.

40   "read it with profit and pleasure": OWH to Laski, Beverly Farms, July 18, 1918, Holmes Papers, reel 4.

40   "Sounds as if": OWH to Laski, Beverly Farms, June 25, 1918, in *Holmes-Laski*, 1:158.

40   "a poor, real scholar": OWH to Einstein, Beverly Farms, July 11, 1918, in *Holmes-Einstein*, 169.

41   "He is remarkable": OWH to Laski, Beverly Farms, Aug. 10, 1918, in *Holmes-Laski*, 1:162.

41   "I was instructed without delight": Ibid.

41   "If you want to know the law": Holmes, "Path of the Law," 457, 459.

41–42   "A lot of learned second raters": OWH to Laski, Beverly Farms, Aug. 24, 1918, Holmes Papers, reel 4, box 4, folder 20.

42   "in a kind of rage": OWH to Pollock, Washington, D.C., Oct. 31, 1918, in *Holmes-Pollock*, 1:271.

42–43   "It is not enough for the knight . . . seems to me silly": Holmes, "Natural Law," 40, 40–43.

43   "The truth is that . . . to be decent": Laski to OWH, Cambridge, Mass., Dec. 8, 1917, in *Holmes-Laski*, 1:116–17.

43   "I do not mind the extent": Laski to OWH, Rockport, Mass., Aug. 27, 1918, in *Holmes-Laski*, 1:163.

44   "Your letter moved me": OWH to Laski, Beverly Farms, Aug. 29, 1918, in *Holmes-Laski*, 1:163.

44   "all the improving works": OWH to Einstein, Beverly Farms, Aug. 16, 1918, in *Holmes-Einstein*, 170.

44   "a good wallow": OWH to John Torrey Morse Jr., Beverly Farms, Sept. 7, 1918, Holmes Papers, reel 26.

44   "with more pleasure than formerly": OWH to Laski, Beverly Farms, Sept. 18, 1918, in *Holmes-Laski*, 1:164.

44   "a rotten and repulsive play" . . . "a bill filler": Ibid.

44   hit by a musket ball . . . badly shot up: OWH to his parents, Sept. 18, 1862, in Holmes, *Touched with Fire*, 64–65.

45   "Hurry up there!": Hallowell, *Reminiscences*, 17.

45   The first doctor who saw Holmes . . . where he was met by his father: Le Duc, "The Man Who Rescued 'The Captain,'" 80.

45   "Boy, nothing": In his *Atlantic Monthly* article "My Hunt after 'The Captain,'" Dr. Holmes claimed his son had responded, "How are you, Dad?" Alexander Woollcott, a reporter, wrote that the younger Holmes actually responded, "Boy, nothing" ("Get Down, You Fool," in *Long, Long Ago*, 3–12. Originally published in the *Atlantic Monthly*, Feb. 1938, 169. See also Woollcott, "The Second Hunt after the Captain," *Atlantic Monthly*, Dec. 1942, 50).

45   old comrades, living and dead: There are many references to these toasts in Holmes's letters to friends. For two examples, see OWH to Sheehan, Beverly Farms, Sept. 21, 1908, in *Holmes-Sheehan*, 37, and OWH to Lady Clare Castletown, Boston, Mass., Sept. 17, 1896, Holmes Papers, reel 20.

45   filled with emotion: OWH to Laski, Beverly Farms, Sept. 18, 1918, in *Holmes-Laski*, 1:165.

45   "just as it seemed beginning": OWH to Einstein, Beverly Farms, Sept. 28, 1918, in *Holmes-Einstein*, 171.

46   Why does time pass more quickly: OWH to Pollock, Beverly Farms, Aug. 27, 1921, in *Holmes-Pollock*, 2:78; OWH to Einstein, Beverly Farms, Sept. 28, 1918, in *Holmes-Einstein*, 171.

46   "Going out over a new road": OWH to Einstein, Beverly Farms, Sept. 28, 1918, in *Holmes-Einstein*, 171.

46   "Your letter comes as we are departing": OWH to Laski, Beverly Farms, Oct. 1, 1918, in *Holmes-Laski*, 1:166.

3: THE HABIT OF INTOLERANCE

47–48   The virus . . . one hundred million: Crosby, *Forgotten Pandemic*.

48   At the peak of the crisis . . . factories to build more: Anderson, *Presidents and Pies*, 244–45; "'Flu' Reaches Crest," *Washington Post*, Oct. 15, 1918.

48   intercepting two railroad cars: Crosby, *Forgotten Pandemic*, 83.

48   heard reports of the epidemic: OWH to Einstein, Beverly Farms, Sept. 28, 1918, in *Holmes-Einstein*, 171; OWH to Laski, Beverly Farms, Oct. 1, 1918, in *Holmes-Laski*, 1:166; OWH to Einstein, Washington, D.C., Oct. 31, 1918, in *Holmes-Einstein*, 173; OWH to Pollock, Washington, D.C., Oct. 31, 1918, in *Holmes-Pollock*, 1:270.

48   One of the oddities: Crosby, *Forgotten Pandemic*, 21.

48   he complained bitterly: OWH to Lady Pollock, Washington, D.C., Feb. 21, 1909, in *Holmes-Pollock*, 1:147.

48   "run the machine too hard": OWH to Laski, Washington, D.C., Dec. 3, 1918, in *Holmes-Laski*, 1:175; OWH to Laski, Washington, D.C., May 12, 1922, in *Holmes-Laski*, 1:426.

48   "divided into two parts": Recounted by Francis Biddle, one of Holmes's secretaries, in *Mr. Justice Holmes*, 7.

49   Unlike modern Supreme Court clerks . . . reflections on life and the law: Louchheim, "Clerks of the Court on Justice Holmes," *New Deal*, 20–46; Messinger, *Judge as Mentor*, 124; White, *Justice Oliver Wendell Holmes*, 313; Belknap et al., "Personal Remembrances," 393.

49   "If baby has the megrims": OWH to Frankfurter, Washington, D.C., Dec. 19, 1915, in *Holmes and Frankfurter*, 40.

49   "some ready-made expression": OWH to Laski, Washington, D.C., Oct. 25, 1918, in *Holmes-Laski*, 1:166–67.

49   "artistically done": OWH to Pollock, Washington, D.C., Oct. 31, 1918, in *Holmes-Pollock*, 1:271.

49   print rooms at the Library of Congress: Ibid.; OWH to Laski, Washington, D.C., Oct. 25, 1918, in *Holmes-Laski*, 1:168.

50   "wallow in potentialities": OWH to Laski, Washington, D.C., Oct. 25, 1918, in *Holmes-Laski*, 1:167.

50   Laski assured him that everything was fine: Laski to OWH, Cambridge, Mass., Nov. 3, 1918, in *Holmes-Laski*, 1:168–69.

50   a suit by the Associated Press: *Int'l News Serv. v. Associated Press*, 248 U.S. 215 (1918).

50   a case involving the Seamen's Act: *Sandberg v. McDonald*, 248 U.S. 185 (1918).

50   a complicated antitrust suit: *Buckeye Powder Co. v. E.I. Dupont de Nemours Powder Co.*, 248 U.S. 55 (1918).

50   "dimensions of a poodle": OWH to Laski, Washington, D.C., Nov. 29, 1918, in *Holmes-Laski*, 1:173.

51 " 'free speech' cases": Laski to OWH, Cambridge, Mass., Nov. 1918, in *Holmes-Laski*, 1:170.

51 Founded just four years . . . violent revolution: Forcey, *Crossroads*.

51–52 The leader of the magazine . . . economic welfare of its citizens: Levy, *Herbert Croly*.

52 embraced by such influential figures: Forcey, *Crossroads*, 123–27; Levy, *Herbert Croly*, 186–89; Phillips, *Felix Frankfurter*, 91.

52 bought adjoining town houses . . . assembled a staff: Forcey, *Crossroads*, 184.

52 The first two editors he hired . . . *A Preface to Politics*: Ibid., 178–83; Levy, *Herbert Croly*, 189–96, 209–14.

52–53 Consistent with their pragmatist . . . supported the decision wholeheartedly: Levy, *Herbert Croly*, 226–33.

53 Conceding that some censorship was necessary: Editorial Notes, *New Republic*, March 3, 1917, 119; Editorial Notes, *New Republic*, July 21, 1917, 316; Feldman, "Free Speech," 205; Graber, *Transforming Free Speech*, 83; Levy, *Herbert Croly*, 251.

53 continued to send mixed signals: Editorial Notes, *New Republic*, June 2, 1917, 119; "Public Opinion in War Time," *New Republic*, Sept. 22, 1917, 204; Editorial Notes, *New Republic*, Sept. 29, 1917, 228; Editorial Notes, *New Republic*, Oct. 6, 1917, 255.

53 Dewey voiced frustration: Dewey, "Future of Pacifism."

53 launched a campaign against the Industrial Workers: Freeberg, *Democracy's Prisoner*, 63.

53 private vigilante groups carried out: Ibid., 58–61.

53 Congress passed the Sedition Act: Sedition Act of 1918, ch. 75, 40 Stat. 553, repealed by Act of March 3, 1921, ch. 136, 41 Stat. 1359.

53–54 Nearly two thousand indictments . . . ten, and fifteen years: Kohn, *American Political Prisoners*, 9–11; Chafee, *Freedom of Speech*, 1.

54 Magazines and newspapers were targeted: Chafee, *Freedom of Speech*, 106–7, 115; Forcey, *Crossroads*, 281–82.

54 closely allied with his administration: Forcey, *Crossroads*, 265–66.

54 Croly appealed to Wilson privately: Ibid., 281.

54 But although Wilson reassured him: Freeberg, *Democracy's Prisoner*, 58–59, 119.

54 demanded that it take a firmer stand: Ragan, "Justice Oliver Wendell Holmes."

54 Congress passed the Sedition Act of 1798: Alien and Sedition Acts of 1798, ch. 74, § 2, 1 Stat. 596 (expired 1801).

55 First Amendment simply codified the common law: Stone, *Perilous Times*, 39–41.

55 Defending a Virginia resolution . . . was necessarily invalid: Virginia General Assembly, House of Delegates, *The Virginia Report of 1799–1800*.

55   Federalists prevailed in the courts... convicted under it: Stone, *Perilous Times*, 68–73.

55   1833 Supreme Court ruling: *Barron v. City of Baltimore*, 32 U.S. 243 (1833).

55   "Please spare me the trouble": Abraham Lincoln to John M. Schofield, Washington, D.C., July 13, 1863, in Basler, *Collected Works of Abraham Lincoln*, 326.

55   controversy raged over the Comstock Act: Rabban, *Free Speech*, 27–31.

56   confrontations known as the free speech fights: Ibid., 70.

56   "to prevent all such *previous restraints*": *Patterson v. People of State of Colorado ex rel. Attorney Gen. of State of Colorado*, 205 U.S. 454 (1907).

57   free speech "consists in laying": Blackstone, *Commentaries on the Laws of England*, 151.

57   Croly went looking... Free Speech League in the early 1900s: Graber, *Transforming Free Speech*, 50–56; Rabban, *Free Speech*, 52–53.

57–58 helped manage his father's iron foundry... understanding of free speech: Smith, *Zechariah Chafee, Jr.*, 2–3, 16–18.

58   One ruling in particular caught his attention: Ibid., 28.

58   "persuade real salesgirls to follow": Zechariah Chafee Jr., "Thirty-Five Years," 2.

58   "My sympathies and all my associations": Chafee to Upton Sinclair, Oct. 5, 1922, Zechariah Chafee Papers, box 14, folder 27, enclosing "Mr. Lowell and the Harvard Club Meeting about Professor Chafee," 3.

58   he suggested that Croly ask him... "view of a professional lawyer": Herbert Croly to Zechariah Chafee, New York City, Sept. 24, 1918, Chafee Papers, box 1, folder 9.

59   many state courts had embraced Blackstone: *Commonwealth v. Blanding*, 20 Mass. 304, 308 (Mass. 1825); *Republica v. Oswald*, 1 Dall. 319, 325 (Pa. July 1788); *Dailey v. Superior Court of City & County of San Francisco*, 112 Cal. 94, 100 (Cal. 1896).

59–60 "is possible only through"... "weigh very heavily in the scale": Chafee, "Freedom of Speech," 67.

60   "The pacifists and Socialists are wrong now": Ibid., 68.

60   "We have made a mistake under the pressure": Ibid., 69.

4: CATSPAWNED

61   based his opinion on a ruling: *Patterson*, 205 U.S. 454, 462, citing *Commonwealth v. Blanding*, 20 Mass. 304, 308 (Mass. 1825).

61   wrote him a long letter filled with praise: OWH to Herbert Croly, Washington, D.C., Nov. 22, 1914, autograph file H, Houghton Library, Harvard College Library, Harvard University.

61 "a monstrous clever lad": OWH to Pollock, Washington, D.C., Dec. 29, 1915, in *Holmes-Pollock*, 1:229.

61 magazine's literary editor, as a genius: Phillips, *Felix Frankfurter*, 92.

61 He also paid regular visits: Snyder, "House That Built Holmes," 661; O'Connell and Dart, "House of Truth," 79, 86, 88; Phillips, *Felix Frankfurter*, 110–12; Steel, *Walter Lippmann*, 120–21.

62 group of twenty-seven socialists: *Baltzer v. United States*, 248 U.S. 593 (1918); Transcript of Record at 1–7, Baltzer v. United States, 248 U.S. 593 (1918) (No. 320).

62 "will spell sure defeat": Brief for the United States at 4, Baltzer v. United States, 248 U.S. 593 (1918) (No. 320).

63 The Mennonites had already met: *South Dakota State Historical Society* 38 (1977): 447–48.

64 "Christ, what dignity!": Biddle, *Mr. Justice Holmes*, 112.

64 a former lieutenant . . . and tired eyes: Highsaw, *Edward Douglass White*, 16, 43; Umbreit, *Our Eleven Chief Justices*, 392.

64 They walked home from court together: Novick, *Honorable Justice*, 255, 266.

64 White brought him a red rose: Acheson, "Reminiscences of a Supreme Court Law Clerk," 4.

64 Convicted of receiving stolen postage stamps: *Kirby v. United States*, 174 U.S. 47 (1899).

64 returned to the Court three times: *Sioux Remedy Co. v. Cope*, 235 U.S. 197 (1914); *Strub, ex parte*, 234 U.S. 752 (1914); *Bartell v. United States*, 227 U.S. 427 (1913).

65 Originally from Iowa . . . chopped it down: Fuller, "Lawyer Gained Fame," 121–24; Kirby, "German Socialist Farmers," 245–47; Joseph P. Kirby (Joe Kirby's great-grandson) in discussion with the author, Oct. 2010.

65 He argued that the selection . . . "not amenable to the law": Brief in Error to the District Court of the United States for the District of South Dakota, Baltzer v. United States, 248 U.S. 593 (1918) (No. 320).

66 Holmes was the only one: Bowen, *Yankee from Olympus*, 406–7.

66 A graduate of Harvard College . . . believed strongly in free speech: "Remarks of Charles A. Horsky at the Dedication of John Lord O'Brian Hall," Commemorative Issue, *Buffalo Law Review* (April 8, 1974), 1–3, 5–7.

66 he argued that it did not violate . . . a formal petition: Brief for the United States, Baltzer v. United States, 248 U.S. 593 (1918) (No. 320).

67 windowless room on the ground floor: Biddle, *Mr. Justice Holmes*, 112; Novick, *Honorable Justice*, 246; Baker, *Justice*, 328.

67 In earlier years . . . nine members of the Court: Biddle, *Mr. Justice Holmes*, 113.

67   bickering and grandstanding . . . everyone was tired and tense: Pratt, *Supreme Court under Edward Douglass White*, 60–61; Chauncey Belknap, unpublished diary, entry Jan. 4, 1916.

67   "We waste two thirds of the day": OWH to Einstein, Washington, D.C., Jan. 6, 1908, in *Holmes-Einstein*, 32.

68   They had known each other for forty years: Urofsky, *Louis D. Brandeis*, 565.

68   formed a partnership with Samuel Warren: Ibid., 50–57; Murphy, *Brandeis-Frankfurter Connection*, 19.

68   Holmes drank champagne and beer: Louis D. Brandeis to Alfred Brandeis, Boston, Mass., July 31, 1879, in Urofsky and Levy, *Family Letters*, 23.

68   helped raise money for the professorship: Urofsky, *Louis D. Brandeis*, 79.

68   built a successful commercial practice . . . earning his first million: Ibid., 73–74.

68   threw himself into progressive causes: Ibid., 89–91, ch. 6, "Traction and Utilities," 130–54, and ch. 8, "Taking on Morgan," 181–200.

68   Brandeis opposed largeness of any kind: Ibid., 346–47.

68   in his 1934 book: Brandeis, *Curse of Bigness*.

69   known as the People's Attorney: Urofsky, *Louis D. Brandeis*, 95.

69   Raised a Republican . . . officially became a Democrat: Ibid., 84–85.

69   played a key role in Wilson's victory: Ibid., 344, 384.

69   one of his most trusted advisers: Murphy, *Brandeis-Frankfurter Connection*, 26–27.

69   for both attorney general and secretary of commerce: Urofsky, *Louis D. Brandeis*, 372–74.

69   nominated him to the Supreme Court: Murphy, *Brandeis-Frankfurter Connection*, 28–30.

69   graduated first in his class at Harvard: Ibid., 19.

70   quickly became Holmes's closest companion: Urofsky, *Louis D. Brandeis*, 565–66; White, *Justice Oliver Wendell Holmes*, 319–22.

70   "thoroughly Anglo-Saxon": OWH to Nina Gray, Washington, D.C., March 5, 1921, Holmes Papers, reel 23.

70   Even Fanny snubbed Brandeis: Novick, *Honorable Justice*, 316.

70   "A whirlwind struck me in the middle": OWH to Laski, Washington, D.C., Dec. 3, 1918, in *Holmes-Laski*, 1:176. Although Holmes did not mention *Baltzer* by name in his letter to Laski, it seems clear that it was the subject of his conversation with Brandeis. Other than *Baltzer*, there were only two other cases in which Holmes wrote a dissent in the months after Brandeis's visit. In one, *Ruddy v. Rossi*, 248 U.S. 104 (1918), Brandeis joined the majority, not Holmes's dissent. In the other, *International News Service v. Associated Press*, 248 U.S. 215 (1918), Brandeis wrote his own dissent, making it unlikely that he would solicit a sepa-

rate dissent from Holmes. Moreover, the latter case involved a dispute between wire services about the use of each other's articles—hardly a "burning theme." In a letter to Nina Gray several years later, Holmes referred obliquely to his dissent in *Baltzer* and suggested that he reached his view of the case "independent" of Brandeis. But he acknowledged that Brandeis had sometimes "turned the scale on the question whether I should write" and did not rule out the possibility that Brandeis had done just that in *Baltzer*. OWH to Nina Gray, Washington, D.C., March 5, 1921, Holmes Papers, reel 23.

70–71 but would "shut up": Baker, *Justice*, 500; OWH to Pollock, Washington, D.C., Nov. 6, 1919, in *Holmes-Pollock*, 2:29.

71 personal dislike of friction: Acheson, *Morning and Noon*, 71.

71 dashed off a dissent in a few hours: *Baltzer v. United States* (Holmes, J., dissenting) (unpublished opinion), memorandum distributed to the justices, Dec. 3, 1918, Holmes Papers, reel 70.

72 Justice Pitney was not persuaded: Justice Pitney's note regarding *Baltzer* on back sheet of return to OWH, *U.S. Supreme Court, October Term, 1919*. Justice Holmes's personal copy, with annotations, Holmes Papers, reel 70.

72 Brandeis, naturally, was on board: Brandeis note regarding *Baltzer* on back of sheet return to OWH, *U.S. Supreme Court, October Term, 1919*. Justice Holmes's personal copy, with annotations, Holmes Papers, reel 70.

73 "Please state me as joining": Chief Justice White note regarding *Baltzer* on back sheet of return to OWH, Holmes Papers, reel 70. Sheldon Novick has construed the first two words of White's note as reading "Please stall." However, Novick concedes that the second word is "not entirely clear" and he does not attempt to decipher the remainder of the sentence (Novick, "Unrevised Holmes," 332). I have arrived at my own interpretation based on a detailed examination of the original note and a comparison of it with other notes from White to Holmes.

73 government unexpectedly confessed error: *Baltzer v. United States*, 248 U.S. 593 (1918).

73 confession was based on technical errors: "Orders New Trial in Espionage Cases," *Washington Post*, Dec. 17, 1918.

73 In a private memo . . . "embarrassing in other cases": Solicitor General Alex C. King to Secretary of the Treasury Carter Glass, memorandum, March 10, 1919, National Archives and Records Administration, record group 60, stack 230, 10/24/2, box 767, file 9–19–278.

74 article on alleged leaks at the Court: Theodore M. Knappen, "Guarding the Secrets of the Supreme Court," *New York Tribune*, Dec. 28, 1919.

74 in regular contact with many high-ranking officials: Murphy, *Brandeis-Frankfurter Connection*, 50–51.

74–75   an assignment that many critics thought inappropriate: "Says Brandeis Is Studying War on Turk and Bulgar," *New York Tribune*, June 11, 1918.

75   friend of Attorney General Thomas Watts Gregory: Murphy, *Brandeis-Frankfurter Connection*, 48–49.

75   two men had dined together the night before: Louis D. Brandeis to Alice Goldmark Brandeis, Washington, D.C., Dec. 3, 1918, in Urofsky and Levy, *Letters of Louis D. Brandeis*, 369.

75   Davis visited Brandeis at his house: Brandeis to Alice Goldmark Brandeis, Washington, D.C., Dec. 4, 1918, in Urofsky and Levy, *Family Letters*, 328.

75   a young man named Robert Szold: Urofsky and Levy, *Letters of Louis D. Brandeis*, 375n1.

75   written the government's brief in *Baltzer*: Alfred Bettman to John Lord O'Brian, memorandum, Oct. 1, 1918, National Archives and Records Administration, record group 60, stack 230, 10/24/2, box 767, file 9-19-278.

75   communicated that year about Zionist activities: Brandeis to Chaim Weizmann, Washington, D.C., Jan. 16, 1919, in Urofsky and Levy, *Letters of Louis D. Brandeis*, 375n1. In the letter to Weizmann, Brandeis refers to Szold as a man of "the finest character." In a footnote, the editors explain that Szold had recently given up his post as assistant solicitor general and joined the Zionist movement at Brandeis's request.

75   paid lieutenant in Washington . . . course of important New Deal legislation: Murphy, *Brandeis-Frankfurter Connection*, 113–23, 54, 106–7.

75   Court issued a one-line order: *Baltzer v. United States*, 248 U.S. 593 (1918).

75   Justice Department then instructed the U.S. attorney: John Lord O'Brian to Robert P. Stewart, Feb. 25, 1919, National Archives and Records Administration, record group 60, stack 230, 10/24/2, box 767, file 9-19-278.

76   "After opinion written by": Note in Holmes's index of his opinion for the term, *U.S. Supreme Court, October Term, 1919.* Justice Holmes's personal copy, with annotations, Holmes Papers, reel 70.

76   Both his dissent and that note: Credit for discovering Holmes's dissent in *Baltzer* belongs to Sheldon Novick. Novick, "Unrevised Holmes," 304.

5: THE OLD EWE AND THE HALF-BAKES

77   capital would never again . . . growing business district: Anderson, *Presidents and Pies*, 225, 235–41; "437,414 People Live Here," *Washington Post*, Feb. 23, 1920, 6; "City Building Is Brisk," *Daily Journal of Commerce*, June 30, 1917, 1; "The New Year," *Washington Post*, Jan. 1, 1919, 6; "Prosperous City," *Washington Post*, Jan. 26, 1919, R2.

77   "The horrible nightmare": OWH to Laski, Washington, D.C., Nov. 6, 1918, in *Holmes-Laski*, 1:169.

78   "off my beat"... "I said, Produce the documents": OWH to Einstein,
        Washington, D.C., Jan. 5, 1919, in *Holmes-Einstein*, 179–80.

78   time to visit his favorite print shop: OWH to Laski, Washington,
        D.C., Dec. 11, 1919, in *Holmes-Laski*, 1:227; OWH to Pollock, Wash-
        ington, D.C., Dec. 14, 1919, in *Holmes-Pollock*, 2:32; OWH to Ethel
        Scott, Washington, D.C., March 8, 1919, Holmes Papers, reel 26.

78   print by Adriaen van Ostade... made him want to cry: OWH to Pol-
        lock, Washington, D.C., Nov. 5, 1923, in *Holmes-Pollock*, 2:123; OWH
        to Morris Raphael Cohen, Washington, D.C., Feb. 3, 1919, in Holmes
        and Cohen, "Holmes-Cohen Correspondence," 14.

78   "It has the line of piety": OWH to Laski, Washington, D.C., Jan. 25,
        1919, in *Holmes-Laski*, 1:180.

79   "John M. Zane has been walking": OWH to Laski, Washington, D.C.,
        Jan. 25, 1919, in *Holmes-Laski*, 1:180.

79   "I suspect he means a different thing": OWH to Pollock, Washington,
        D.C., Jan. 24, 1919, in *Holmes-Pollock*, 2:3.

80   "just as the clavicle in the cat": Holmes, *Common Law*, 34.

80   He had a superstition: OWH to Mrs. Charles S. Hamlin, Oct. 12, 1930,
        Holmes Papers, quoted in Howe, *Proving Years*, 8n18. OWH wrote, "If
        a man was to do anything he must do it before 40."

80   Holmes beat the deadline, barely: White, *Justice Oliver Wendell Holmes*,
        148–49.

81   devoted seven pages to the work: Holland, "Holmes's Common Law,"
        331–38.

81   "tediously discursive and aimless air": Holland, "Holmes's Common
        Law," 465. In *Proving Years*, Howe explains that the article was written
        by Holland although it was not signed by him (249).

81   "the reasoning in some cases": "Holmes's Common Law," 338.

81   "most original work of legal speculation": Dicey, review of *The Com-
        mon Law*, by Holmes, originally published anonymously in *The Specta-
        tor, Literary Supplement* 55, 745.

81   writing in the *Saturday Review*: Pollock, "Holmes on the Common
        Law," 759.

81   "I don't know whether": OWH to Laski, Washington, D.C., Feb. 1, 1919,
        in *Holmes-Laski*, 1:184.

81   "It is not merely": Laski to OWH, Cambridge, Mass., Jan. 29, 1919, in
        Holmes-Laski, 1:181.

82   "A man who calls everyone": OWH to Laski, Washington, D.C., Feb. 1,
        1919, in *Holmes-Laski*, 1:183.

82   two fervent and starry-eyed officers: "Dr. Baer and Schenck Win Brief
        Respite," *Evening Public Ledger*, March 21, 1918, 2; "Four Socialist Chiefs
        Surrender," *Evening Public Ledger*, Sept. 17, 1917, 2; "Socialists Guilty
        of Opposing Draft," *Philadelphia Inquirer*, Dec. 21, 1917, 22; Transcript

of Record at 12–19, Schenck v. United States, 249 U.S. 47 (1919) (No. 1017).

82   In her failed run: "Fewer Pots and Pans Platform of Woman Congress Nominee," *Evening Public Ledger*, Sept. 19, 1916, 8; "First Penna. Woman to Run for Congress," *Philadelphia Inquirer*, April 18, 1916, 2; "Philadelphia's Vote Officially Counted," *Philadelphia Inquirer*, Nov. 26, 1919, 6.

82   had overseen the publication . . . "United States to retain": Transcript of Record at 17–18, Schenck v. United States, 249 U.S. 47 (1919) (No. 1017); "Socialists Guilty of Opposing Draft"; *Schenck v. United States*, 249 U.S. 47 (1919).

83   Some of the flyers were sent: Transcript of Record at 31–37, Schenck v. United States, 249 U.S. 47 (1919) (No. 1017).

83   They were charged: "Socialists Guilty of Opposing Draft."

83–84   Abraham Sugarman, a sickly twenty-two-year-old . . . sentenced to three years in prison: *Sugarman v. United States*, 249 U.S. 182 (1919); Transcript of Record, Sugarman v. United States, 249 U.S. 182 (1919) (No. 345).

84–85   filed by Jacob Frohwerk . . . Gleeser, who pleaded guilty: "Two Missouri Editors Held," *New York Times*, Jan. 27, 1918; Transcript of Record, Frohwerk v. United States, 249 U.S. 204 (1919) (No. 685); "Frohwerk Case Up Today: Trial under the Espionage Act to Open Before Youmans," *Kansas City Times*, June 25, 1918, 11; "Convicted in 3 Minutes: Verdict on Frohwerk Case Set Record for Haste," *Kansas City Times*, June 29, 1918, 1; "German Editor Sentenced: Gleeser of Missouri Staats-Zeitung Goes to Jail for Five Years," *New York Times*, April 30, 1918.

85–86   Born in Terre Haute . . . talked about across the country: Ginger, *Bending Cross*, 6; Salvatore, *Eugene V. Debs*, 8–9; Freeberg, *Democracy's Prisoner*, 11–22.

86   Debs campaigned vigorously . . . suspected German sympathizers: Ibid., 25–30, 44.

86–87   verge of physical collapse . . . nothing that could be construed: Ibid., 62–68; Ginger, *Bending Cross*, 234, 353–59.

87   "I must be exceedingly careful, prudent": Transcript of Record at 177, Debs v. United States, 249 U.S. 211 (1919) (No. 714).

87   "Oh, just think": Ibid., 181.

88   "They have always taught": Ibid., 184.

88   "those class-conscious proletarians . . . light of the coming day": Ibid., 186.

88   "How good the touch of the hand": Ibid., 185.

89   The speech was covered by the local press . . . eager to oblige: Miller, "The Man I Sent to Prison," *Progressive*, October 1963, 34; Brief for Plaintiff in Error at 49, 50, Debs v. United States, 249 U.S. 211 (1919) (No. 714).

89   landed on the desk of John Lord O'Brian: Edwin S. Wertz to John Lord

O'Brian, Cleveland, Ohio, June 17, 1918, John Lord O'Brian Papers, box 18, folders 5–7, Law Special Collections 05; Salvatore, *Eugene V. Debs*, 294.

89   "the Department does not feel strongly convinced": John Lord O'Brian to Edwin S. Wertz, June 20, 1918, O'Brian Papers, box 18, folders 5–7, Law Special Collections 05.

89   Wertz called several witnesses: Transcript of Record at 166–77, Debs v. United States, 249 U.S. 211 (1919) (No. 714).

90   "Gentlemen, I abhor war ... I am prepared for the verdict": Ibid., 239–40, 248.

90–91   "Now, with regard to some" ... "charged with murder": Ibid., 249–64.

91   The entire courtroom was mortified: Eastman, 20.

6: "HE SHOOTS SO QUICKLY"

92   First, the parties in Frohwerk's case: Brief for the Plaintiff in Error to the District Court of the United States for the Western District of Missouri at 94–97, Frohwerk v. United States, 249 U.S. 204 (1919) (No. 685).

92   Then Frohwerk's attorney ... to file a proper brief: Brief on Behalf of Plaintiff in Error to the District Court of the United States, for the Western Division, of the Western District of Missouri (1918) (No. 308).

92–93   the end of the month ... morning of January 6: "The Daily Legal Record," *Washington Post*, Dec. 23, 1918; Jan. 7, 1919, 4.

93   "Washington is full of famous men": Bowen, *Yankee from Olympus*, 362.

93   But the relationship cooled ... who was likeable, decisive, and shrewd: OWH to Pollock, Washington, D.C., Feb. 9, 1921, in *Holmes-Pollock*, 2:63–64; OWH to Einstein, Washington, D.C., April 1, 1928, in *Holmes-Einstein*, 279.

93   the founding generation had rejected the Blackstonian view: Brief for Plaintiffs in Error to the District Court of the United States for the Eastern District of Pennsylvania at 5–6, Schenck v. United States, 249 U.S. 47 (1919) (Nos. 437 and 438); Amicus Curiae Brief of Gilbert E. Roe at 23–26, Debs v. United States, 249 U.S. 211 (1919) (No. 714).

93   right to criticize the government: Brief for Plaintiffs in Error to the District Court of the United States for the Eastern District of Pennsylvania at 6–7, Schenck v. United States, 249 U.S. 47 (1919) (Nos. 437 and 438); Brief for Plaintiff in Error at 63, Debs v. United States, 249 U.S. 211 (1919) (No. 714); Amicus Curiae Brief of Gilbert E. Roe at 46–48, Debs v. United States, 249 U.S. 211 (1919) (No. 714); Supplemental and Reply Brief for Plaintiff in Error, Frohwerk v. United States, 249 U.S. 204 (1919) (No. 685).

94   Sedition Act of 1798 had been condemned: Brief for Plaintiffs in Error to the District Court of the United States for the Eastern District of Pennsylvania at 6, Schenck v. United States, 249 U.S. 47 (1919) (Nos.

437 and 438); Brief for Plaintiff in Error at 62, Debs v. United States, 249
U.S. 211 (1919) (No. 714); Brief for Gilbert E. Roe as Amicus Curiae
Supporting Plaintiff in Error at 32–36, Debs v. United States, 249 U.S.
211 (1919) (No. 714).

94 The Constitution gave Congress . . . lower courts at the time: Brief for
the United States, Frohwerk v. United States, 249 U.S. 204 (1919) (No.
685).

95 justices decided they lacked jurisdiction: *Sugarman v. United States*,
249 U.S. 182 (1919).

95 But McKenna was a poor writer: Urofsky, "Brandeis-Frankfurter Conversations," 326–27. These conversations between Brandeis and Frankfurter took place during the Court's summer recesses. Frankfurter
often visited Brandeis and then wrote down what they discussed on
blue law school exam books. On August 11, 1923, Frankfurter wrote,
"the only way of dealing with him [McKenna] is to appoint guardians
for him. . . . He knows he (McK) doesn't count, his suggestions are [not]
taken, so every once in a while he sends up a balloon just to show that
he is there. He breaks loose occasionally—he did in Atlanta case (No.
260) but I was able to control myself and say nothing. . . . Every once in
a while McK really does mischief—more often than appears. His opinions are often suppressed—they are held up & held up & gets mad &
throws up the opinion and it's given to someone else."

95 So when White sent him: Although *Schenck* was argued on January 9
and 10, two weeks before *Frohwerk* and *Debs*, there are several reasons
to conclude that all three cases were assigned to Holmes as a group in
early February while the Court was in recess. First, Holmes almost
always wrote his opinions as soon as they were assigned to him and
handed them down at the first opportunity—usually within two weeks.
Therefore, if *Schenck* had been assigned to him at the conference on
Saturday, January 11, the opinion likely would have been issued long
before March 3, like the other cases he was assigned from the first
weeks of January. Second, Holmes's opinion in *Schenck* relied on an
argument made by U.S. Attorney Edwin Wertz during his closing
argument in Debs's trial. This suggests that Holmes did not write his
opinion in *Schenck* until after he had read the record in *Debs*, which he
was not likely to have done before *Debs* was assigned to him. Finally,
after Holmes finished his other assignments from the January calendar,
he stated in a letter to Morris Cohen on February 11 that he was expect-
ing an assignment of new cases soon. And based on letters to Learned
Hand and Harold Laski, it was shortly after this that Holmes read
Mill's *On Liberty* and Hand's opinion in *Masses*, both of which were
relevant to the issues in *Schenck*, *Frohwerk*, and *Debs*.

  Holmes did receive one other belated assignment from the January calendar. During the week of February 24, he indicated in letters that he had received an additional case from Chief Justice White. However, he referred to the assignment as a "case," not "cases," which makes it unlikely that he was referring to *Schenck*, *Frohwerk*, and *Debs*. Furthermore, he said that the case was one "that I hoped the Chief would give me." This suggests that Holmes was referring not to any of the Espionage Act cases, which he had no great interest in and later said he "hated" having to write, but instead to *Panama Railway Company v. Bosse*. That case involved the liability of an employer for the negligence of his employees, an issue Holmes was deeply interested in and had explored at length in *The Common Law*.

95 He prepared, as always: Baker, *Justice*, 382–83; Lloyd H. Landau to Mr. Derby, Washington, D.C., June 7, 1935, Holmes Papers, reel 42. Landau was OWH's law secretary for the 1918–19 term.

95 "Nothing conduces to brevity": Bowen, *Yankee from Olympus*, 324.

96 "This is an indictment": *Schenck v. United States*, 249 U.S. 47 (1919).

97 The defense attorneys cited Learned Hand's position: Brief for Plaintiff in Error at 63–71, Debs v. United States, 249 U.S. 211 (1919) (No. 714).

98 "powerless to punish any incitement to lawlessness": Brief for the United States, Schenck v. United States, 249 U.S. 47 (1919) (Nos. 437 and 438).

98 "I read your Masses decision": OWH to Hand, Washington, D.C., Feb. 25, 1919, Hand Papers, box 103B, folders 25–26.

98 he even hung a portrait of Mill: Laski to OWH, Cambridge, Mass., Feb. 22, 1918, in *Holmes-Laski*, 1:138.

98 Holmes was well acquainted with Mill: OWH, diary entries, May 28, 1866, June 1, 1866, and June 11, 1866, Holmes Papers, reel 16, cited in Baker, *Justice*, 180.

98 he returned to one book in particular: OWH to Laski, Washington, D.C., Feb. 28, 1919, in *Holmes-Laski*, 1:187.

99 "Yet it is as evident in itself": Mill, *On Liberty*, 78.

99 "If even the Newtonian philosophy": Ibid., 81.

99–100 "even opinions lose" . . . "form of a placard": Ibid., 119.

101 "As the aim of the law is not to punish": *Com. v. Kennedy*, 48 N.E. 770, 772 (Mass. 1897).

101 if a person lights a match: Holmes, *Common Law*, 62.

101 "It is a question of proximity": *Swift & Co. v. United States*, 196 U.S. 375, 402 (1905).

101 "The question in every case": *Schenck v. United States*, 249 U.S. 47, 52 (1919).

101 "bad tendency"—meaning there was *some* chance: Rabban, *Free Speech*, 132–46.

102 His opinion in *Frohwerk* conceded: *Frohwerk v. United States*, 249 U.S. 204, 208–9 (1919).

103   used that phrase casually: Konefsky, *Legacy*, 201; Rabban, *Free Speech*, 280–85.

103   "But if a part or the manifest intent": *Debs v. United States*, 249 U.S. 211, 212–13 (1919).

103   "We should add that the jury": Ibid., 216.

103   "sufficiently consider the need of others": Urofsky, "Brandeis-Frankfurter Conversations," 335.

104   "Yea verily": William R. Day note regarding *Schenck* on back sheet of return to OWH, *U.S. Supreme Court Opinions Delivered by Justice Holmes, October Term 1918.* Justice Holmes's personal copy, with annotations, Holmes Papers, reel 70.

104   "Direct as you usually are": Joseph McKenna note regarding *Schenck* on back sheet of return to OWH, *U.S. Supreme Court Opinions Delivered by Justice Holmes, October Term 1918.* Justice Holmes's personal copy, with annotations, Holmes Papers, reel 70.

104   "Admirably well put": Edward Douglass White note regarding *Schenck* on back sheet of return to OWH, *U.S. Supreme Court Opinions Delivered by Justice Holmes, October Term 1918.* Justice Holmes's personal copy, with annotations, Holmes Papers, reel 70.

104   "I think you have happily": Willis Van Devanter note regarding *Debs* on back sheet of return to OWH, *U.S. Supreme Court Opinions Delivered by Justice Holmes, October Term 1918.* Justice Holmes's personal copy, with annotations, Holmes Papers, reel 70.

104   "He doesn't give a fellow": Louis D. Brandeis to Frankfurter, Aug. 8, 1923, in "Brandeis-Frankfurter Conversations," 324.

7: DEFENDING SOPHISTRIES

105   Their styles of delivery were as different: Chauncey Belknap, unpublished diary, entry Nov. 29, 1915. Belknap was Holmes's secretary during the 1915–16 term.

105   Brandeis, the People's Attorney: Ralph Block, "There Sits Justice," *New York Tribune*, April 5, 1918, 10.

105   White, the chief justice: Belknap, unpublished diary, entry Nov. 29, 1915.

106   far more interested in the Panama case: Writing to Laski on February 28, 1919, in *Holmes-Laski*, 1:186, Holmes described a recent opinion that "wrapped itself around me like a snake in a deadly struggle to present the obviously proper in the forms of logic—the real substance being: Damn your eyes—that's the way 'it's going to be.'" Although some writers have assumed that Holmes was describing his opinion in *Schenck*, it is more likely that he was describing the opinion in *Panama Railroad Co. v. Bosse*, 249 U.S. 41. The reason is that Holmes also said the case was one he hoped Chief Justice White would give him. And

while Holmes at this point had no particular interest in the Espionage Act cases, he was very interested in the issue of employer liability that was at the heart of *Panama Railroad*.

106   "the foothills of 80": OWH to Esther B. Owen, Washington, D.C., March 13, 1919, Holmes Papers, reel 26.

106   Fanny arranged a surprise party . . . admiration of youthful eyes: OWH to Einstein, Washington, D.C., March 10, 1919, in *Holmes-Einstein*, 124; Baker, *Justice*, 486–87.

106   paid a visit to the print shop: OWH to Ethel Scott, Washington, D.C., March 8, 1919, Holmes Papers, reel 26.

107   "March Eighth is the anniversary": Hand to OWH, telegram, New York, N.Y., March 7, 1919, Holmes Papers, reel 33.

107   "never seen the spirit of man": Morris Raphael Cohen to OWH, New York, N.Y., March 7, 1919, in Holmes and Cohen, "Holmes-Cohen Correspondence," 16.

107   He had put that very question: OWH to Alice Stopford Green, Washington, D.C., March 26, 1919, Holmes Papers, reel 32.

107   "The book arrived this morning": OWH to Laski, Washington, D.C., March 7, 1919, in *Holmes-Laski*, 1:189.

107   He was in excellent health: OWH to Ethel Scott, Washington, D.C., March 8, 1919, Holmes Papers, reel 26.

108   sent her the following lines of verse: OWH to Esther B. Owen, Washington, D.C., March 13, 1919, Holmes Papers, reel 26.

108   "Nothing has occurred since the beginning": "At the Rope's End," *Washington Post*, April 1, 1919, 6.

108   "How, therefore, could he": "The Case of Debs," *New York Times*, March 12, 1919, 10.

108   "who try to shelter themselves": "The Case of Debs," *New York Tribune*, March 11, 1919, 10.

108   Gilbert Roe, a prominent civil rights lawyer: Freeberg, *Democracy's Prisoner*, 132.

108   "a perversion of the Constitution": "A Dangerous Encroachment upon the Freedom of Speech," editorial, *San Francisco Examiner*, March 29, 1919.

108   In New York, a thousand people attended: "Says Debs Decision Imperils Freedom," *Washington Times*, April 18, 1919, 11.

108   in Toledo riots broke out: "Riot to Hear Debs," *Washington Post*, March 31, 1919, 1; "Debs Supporters Riot in Toledo," *New York Times*, March 31, 1919, 4.

108   "I am not concerned": "Jails Debs Ten Years: Goes to Picture Theatre," *Washington Post*, March 11, 1919.

109   petitioned the president for a pardon: "President Asked to Pardon Debs," *Washington Times*, March 25, 1919, 5.

109   cabled his advisers in Washington: Freeberg, *Democracy's Prisoner*, 134–35.

109   government denied the pleas for clemency: "Palmer Rejects Petitions for Debs," *New York Times*, April 8, 1919, 8; "Debs Leaving Soon," *Washington Post*, April 9, 1919, 6.

109   "bold invasion of the cardinal principles": Twain Michelsen to OWH, Santa Cruz, Calif., April 3, 1919, Holmes Papers, reel 45.

109   "provided and guaranteed to every citizen": William S. Hoffman to OWH, Bridgeport, Conn., March 26, 1919, Holmes Papers, reel 45.

109   "When law becomes an obstacle": President of the American Industrial Co. to OWH, Chicago, Ill., April 1, 1919, Holmes Papers, reel 45.

109   "Just now I am receiving": OWH to Einstein, Washington, D.C., April 5, 1919, in *Holmes-Einstein*, 184.

110   In letter after letter: OWH to Einstein, Washington, D.C., April 5, 1919, in *Holmes-Einstein*, 184–85; OWH to Laski, Washington, D.C., March 16, 1919, in *Holmes-Laski*, 1:190; OWH to Pollock, Washington, D.C., April 5, 1919, in *Holmes-Pollock*, 2:7; OWH to Green, Washington, D.C., March 26, 1919, Holmes Papers, reel 32; OWH to Baroness Charlotte Moncheur, Washington, D.C., April 4, 1919, Holmes Papers, reel 26.

110   "as the inevitable result": OWH to Pollock, Washington, D.C, April 5, 1919, in *Holmes-Pollock*, 2:7.

110   "There was a lot of jaw": Ibid.

110   "But as I said": OWH to Green, Washington, D.C., March 26, 1919, Holmes Papers, reel 32.

110   "I hope the President will pardon him": OWH to Pollock, Washington, D.C., April 27, 1919, in *Holmes-Pollock*, 2:11.

110   "I read your three opinions": Laski to OWH, Cambridge, Mass., March 18, 1919, in *Holmes-Laski*, 1:191.

111   "Words are not only the keys of persuasion": *Masses Pub. Co. v. Patten*, 244 F. 535, 540 (S.D.N.Y. 1917), *rev'd*, 246 F. 24 (2d Cir. 1917).

111   "you give to Tomdickandharry": Hand to Chafee, New York, N.Y., Jan. 2, 1921, Chafee Papers, box 4, folder 20.

112   "Dear Mr. Justice": Hand to OWH, New York, N.Y., April 1, 1919, Holmes Papers, reel 33.

113   "Dear Judge Hand": OWH to Hand, Washington, D.C., April 3, 1919, Hand Papers, box 103B, folders 25–26.

114   "I kept up my hopes": Hand to Chafee, New York, N.Y., Dec. 3, 1920, Chafee Papers, box 4, folder 20.

8: DANGEROUS MEN

115   "a bee toiling in sticky buds": OWH to William James, April 1919, in Biddle, *Mr. Justice Holmes*, 45–46.

115   "to look at all the wild things": OWH to Green, Washington, D.C., March 26, 1919, Holmes Papers, reel 32.

115   "the fragrance of eternity": Holmes, *Writings of Oliver Wendell Holmes*, 5:437.

115–16   It was late when they returned . . . "pass the scissors, Wendell": Biddle, *Mr. Justice Holmes*, 149–51.

116   A few mornings later . . . "Why the Armistice": OWH to Moncheur, Washington, D.C., April 4, 1919, Holmes Papers, reel 26.

116   kaiser's agents in disguise: Murray, *Red Scare*, 34.

116   A Senate committee investigating the loyalty: Hagedorn, *Savage Peace*, 53–59; "Senate Orders Reds Here Investigated," *New York Times*, Feb. 5, 1919, 1.

117   conditions under Soviet rule: Murray, *Red Scare*, 94–98; "Red Agitators from This City Potent in Russia," *New York Times*, Feb. 13, 1919, 1; "Senators Tell What Bolshevism in America Means," *New York Times*, June 15, 1919, 4; "Tell of Red Plans to Rule America," *New York Times*, Feb. 14, 1919, 4; "Tells Senators of Mass Terror by Bolshevik," *New York Times*, Feb. 12, 1919, 1.

117   preached in the Jewish ghetto: Murray, *Red Scare*, 148–49; "Dr. Simons Stands by Senate Words," *New York Times*, Feb. 17, 1919, 4; "Praise Patriotism of East Side Jews," *New York Times*, Feb. 17, 1919, 4.

117   meeting of Russian sympathizers: "Bolsheviks Are Busy in the United States," *New York Times*, Feb. 9, 1919; "Senate Orders Reds Here Investigated," *New York Times*, Feb. 5, 1919, 1.

117   troubling incidents rocked the country: Hagedorn, *Savage Peace*, 51–52.

117   fourteen Spanish immigrants . . . looking for work: Ibid., 121–26.

117   stagnant wages and spiraling inflation: Ibid., 276–77.

118   The first showdown took place: Hagedorn, *Savage Peace*, 59; "Seattle to Face Army unless Strike Ends Today," *New York Times*, Feb. 8, 1919, 1; "Troops on Guard in Seattle Strike," *New York Times*, Feb. 7, 1919, 1.

118   388 strikes, and by the end of the year: Hagedorn, *Savage Peace*, 277.

118   Events overseas also fed the hysteria: Murray, *Red Scare*, 15–16.

118   circulated nearly five million copies: Ibid., 46.

118–19   American Communist Party . . . scarcely any bigger: Ibid., 53, 31.

119       $500,000 for an investigation: Ibid., 81.

119   enactment of a peacetime Espionage Act: Hagedorn, *Savage Peace*, 159; "Drastic Red Bill Ready for Senate," *New York Times*, June 12, 1919, 17; "Senators Tell What Bolshevism in America Means."

119   And the Overman Committee released: Hagedorn, *Savage Peace*, 55–57.

119   a complaint was filed against him: Kramnick and Sheerman, *Harold Laski*, 128.

119   a "poisonous influence": Edwin H. Hall to Paul Tuckerman, Nov. 20, 1919, Lowell Papers, Harvard University Library, quoted in Kramnick and Sheerman, *Harold Laski*, 128.

120   Laski offered to resign his position: Kramnick and Sheerman, *Harold Laski*, 130.

120   he took part in a strike: Ibid., 120.

120   founding the Boston Trade Union College: Ibid.; Stoddard, "Labor Goes to College," 218–20; "Signalmen Get Increase to 72 Cents an Hour: Trade Union College Term Opens Tomorrow," *Boston Daily Globe*, Jan. 4, 1920, 4.

120   "represent in any dominant and exclusive": Laski, *Authority*, 81.

120   "to divide industrial power from political control": Ibid., 91.

120   "To admit the trade union": Ibid.

121   Laski was not yet a Marxist: Kramnick and Sheerman, *Harold Laski*, 125–26.

121   "The only real security": Laski, *Authority*, 55–56.

121   Born in Vienna in 1882 . . . long line of rabbis: Baker, *Felix Frankfurter*, 16, 18, 20.

121   Unable to speak a word of English: Phillips, *Felix Frankfurter*, 8.

121   went from office to office . . . Frankfurter didn't stay long: Ibid., 35–38.

122   including Learned Hand, who introduced him: Ibid., 88.

122   Stimson's right-hand man: Ibid., 41–42.

122   in 1911 when Stimson moved to Washington: Ibid., 56.

122   Carrying a letter of introduction: Ibid., 58; *Holmes and Frankfurter*, xiii.

122   charmed and flattered the older man: Baker, *Justice*, 454–55.

122   He also introduced the justice . . . the house got its name: Phillips, *Felix Frankfurter*, 105–12.

122   "Wherever Frankfurter is": Josephson, "Profiles: Felix Frankfurter," 25.

122–23 As law officer for the Bureau of Insular Affairs . . . Federal Power Commission: Phillips, *Felix Frankfurter*, 56, 62, 73–74.

123   Frankfurter remained in the War Department: Ibid., 74–75.

123   stuck in a bureaucratic dead end: Hirsch, *Enigma*, 39.

123   Harvard Law School asked him to return: Phillips, "The Call to Harvard," ch. 9 of *Felix Frankfurter*, 77–87; Hirsch, *Enigma*, 38.

123   He assisted Brandeis on a series of cases: Phillips, *Felix Frankfurter*, 94–98.

123   took over the cases: Hirsch, *Enigma*, 46.

123   He worked closely with the editors: Phillips, *Felix Frankfurter*, 93; Baker, *Felix Frankfurter*, 107.

123   endorsing Wilson in 1916: Lash, "A Brahmin of the Law: A Biographical Essay," in Frankfurter, *Diaries*, 19; Hirsch, *Enigma*, 51.

123   a network of allies: Lash, "A Brahmin of the Law," 20–24.

123   telegram from Secretary of War: Phillips, *Felix Frankfurter*, 114.

123   The immediate question...extended beyond the Northeast: Baker, *Felix Frankfurter*, 59–63; Phillips, *Felix Frankfurter*, 121.

124   Frankfurter proposed that the president: Frankfurter to N. D. Baker, Sept. 4, 1917, quoted in Baker, *Felix Frankfurter*, 63.

124   convened a high-profile commission: Phillips, *Felix Frankfurter*, 115–28.

124   Wilson, became ill midway through: Ibid., 121.

124   incident known as the Bisbee Deportation: Ibid., 135–37; Baker, *Felix Frankfurter*, 66–67.

125   actions of local officials "wholly illegal": "Report of President's Mediation Commission," *Monthly Review of the U.S. Bureau of Labor Statistics*, Jan. 1918 (Washington, D.C.: GPO, 1918), 16.

125   the case of Tom Mooney: Phillips, *Felix Frankfurter*, 130–35; Parrish, *His Times*, 97–101.

125   case was a miscarriage of justice: "Report on the Mooney Dynamiting Cases in San Francisco," *Official Bulletin*, Jan. 28, 1918.

125   he proposed that Wilson urge: Phillips, *Felix Frankfurter*, 132.

126   Jack Greenway had spearheaded: Ibid., 136.

126   "as thoroughly misleading a document": Theodore Roosevelt to Frankfurter, Dec. 19, 1917, in Bishop, *Theodore Roosevelt*, 464.

126   accused Frankfurter of "excusing men": Bishop, *Theodore Roosevelt*, 465.

126   chairman of the War Labor Policies Board: Parrish, *His Times*, 107.

126   imposing progressive labor standards: Ibid., 85.

126   chairman of U.S. Steel: Phillips, *Felix Frankfurter*, 139–42; Parrish, *His Times*, 113.

126   launched a major fund-raising campaign: Parrish, *His Times*, 186.

126   remove Frankfurter (still on leave): Laski to OWH, April 20, 1919, in *Holmes-Laski*, 1:196; Louis D. Brandeis to Alice Goldmark Brandeis, New York, N.Y., June 13, 1919, in Urofsky and Levy, *Letters*, 398; Phillips, *Felix Frankfurter*, 169–70.

126   one of Frankfurter's former students: Parrish, *His Times*, 120.

127   Pound warned Frankfurter: Roscoe Pound to Frankfurter, April 28, 1919, May 17, 1919. Felix Frankfurter Papers, 1846–66, box 90, reel 55, Roscoe Pound, 1914–63.

127   But Frankfurter was in Paris: Baker, *Felix Frankfurter*, 83.

127   So Pound explained the situation to Brandeis: Louis D. Brandeis to Alice Goldmark Brandeis, New York, N.Y., June 14, 1919, in Urofsky and Levy, *Letters*, 400; Phillips, *Felix Frankfurter*, 170.

127   "the crowd now has substantially": OWH to Einstein, Washington, D.C., Oct. 28, 1912, in *Holmes-Einstein*, 74.

127   "the upward and onwarders": OWH to Laski, Washington, D.C., June 1, 1922, in *Holmes-Laski*, 1:430.

127   "Every once in a while": OWH to Laski, Washington, D.C., April 4, 1919, in *Holmes-Laski*, 1:193.

127   "Hale is abominable": Laski to OWH, Cambridge, Mass., April 20, 1919, in *Holmes-Laski*, 1:196.

128   Aside from Laski . . . under pressure to step down: Kramnick and Sheerman, *Harold Laski*, 130; Newman, *Harold Laski*, 62.

128   Lowell had circulated a petition: Yeomans, *Abbot Lawrence Lowell*, 327.

128   cap the number of Jewish students: Ibid., 209–15.

128   "It never occurs to me": OWH to Pollock, Washington, D.C., April 5, 1919, in *Holmes-Pollock*, 2:8.

128   "whether loveableness is a characteristic": OWH to Laski, Washington, D.C., Jan. 12, 1921, in *Holmes-Laski*, 1:304.

128   "I didn't know it": OWH to Laski, Washington, D.C., May 1, 1919, in *Holmes-Laski*, 1:200.

129   "I understand your hesitation": Laski to OWH, Cambridge, Mass., May 11, 1919, in *Holmes-Laski*, 1:201.

129   "They ask for suggestions": OWH to Laski, Washington, D.C., May 13, 1919, in *Holmes-Laski*, 1:202.

129   "Only one word": Laski to OWH, Cambridge, Mass., May 15, 1919, in *Holmes-Laski*, 1:204.

129   "Your letter invites suggestion": OWH to Laski, quoting his letter to F. W. Grinnell, Washington, D.C., May 18, 1919, in *Holmes-Laski*, 1:204.

130   "That is a most generous letter": Laski to OWH, Cambridge, Mass., May 20, 1919, in *Holmes-Laski*, 1:205.

130   "worth realms of resolutions": Roscoe Pound to OWH, Cambridge, Mass., May 29, 1919, Holmes Papers, reel 36.

130   He discussed the matter with Brandeis: OWH to Laski, Washington, D.C., June 1, 1919, in *Holmes-Laski*, 1:210.

130   If the school should lose Pound: Ibid., 210–11.

131   "very strong feeling that Pound": OWH to Abbott Lawrence Lowell, June 2, 1919, in *Holmes-Laski*, 1:211n2.

131   "I have the notion that Pound": OWH to Laski, Beverly Farms, June 16, 1919, Holmes Papers, reel 4. Lowell's response to Holmes has not been found. My description of its substance is based on Holmes's letter to Laski and the fact that Holmes gave Laski permission to show Lowell's response to Pound.

9: "THEY KNOW NOT WHAT THEY DO"

132   April 30, a clerk: "36 Were Marked as Victims by Bomb Conspirators," *New York Times*, May 1, 1919.

132   exploded at the apartment of Thomas Hardwick: "Net Out for Terrorists in Plot Thought Nation-wide; 16 Bombs for Notables Held in New York," *Washington Post*, May 1, 1919.

132   at the main post office on Eighth Avenue: Ibid.

132–33   addressed to some of the most prominent: "36 Were Marked as Victims."

133   authorities discovered an additional eighteen: "22 More Bombs Found in Mail; Sixteen Here," *New York Tribune*, May 1, 1919.

133   officials launched a massive investigation: "Find More Bombs Sent in the Mails; One to Overman," *New York Times*, May 2, 1919, 1; "Find Strong Clue in the Bomb Plot," *New York Times*, May 6, 1919, 28.

133   suspicion immediately fell on the Bolshevists: "The Bomb Plotters," *Washington Post*, May 2, 1919.

133   the perpetrators were never found: Murray, *Red Scare*, 73.

133   "I am writing you a brief note": Einstein to OWH, Florence, Italy, May 5, 1919, in *Holmes-Einstein*, 185–86.

133   "I haven't thought much about it": OWH to Einstein, May 22, 1919, in *Holmes-Einstein*, 186.

134   "Eugene Debs has gone": Editorial Notes, *New Republic*, April 19, 1919, 362.

134–35   "There was nothing to show actual obstruction" . . . "so manifestly inappropriate": Freund, "Debs Case," 13, 14.

135   Freund was one of the most influential: Firmage, *Ernst Freund*, 3, 10; Oscar Kraines, *World and Ideas of Ernst Freund*, 148, 191, 2–3, 5.

136   My dear Mr. Croly: OWH to Herbert Croly, Washington, D.C., enclosed in a letter to Harold Laski on May 13, 1919, in *Holmes-Laski*, 1:202–4.

138   "I am eager to hear if you read Freund": Laski to OWH, Cambridge, Mass., May 11, 1919, in *Holmes-Laski*, 1:201–2.

138   "Yesterday I wrote the within": OWH to Laski, Washington, D.C., May 13, 1919, in *Holmes-Laski*, 1:202.

138   "Your article in last week's 'New Republic'": Hand to Freund, May 7, 1919, Hand Papers, box 21, folder 1.

138   "I own I was chagrined that Justice Holmes": Ibid.

139   "and has done it in such a kind": OWH to Laski, Washington, D.C., June 1, 1919, in *Holmes-Laski*, 1:210.

139   Holmes and Brandeis walked together: OWH to Frankfurter, Washington, D.C., Jan. 26, 1924, in *Holmes and Frankfurter*, 168; OWH to Laski, Washington, D.C., April 20, 1919, in *Holmes-Laski*, 1:198.

139   "You talk about improving your mind": OWH to Pollock, Washington, D.C., May 26, 1919, in *Holmes-Pollock*, 2:13.

139   *ex facto jus oritur*: Brandeis to Edward MacInall, Washington, D.C., July 20, 1917, in Urofsky and Levy, *Letters of Louis D. Brandeis*, 299.

139   appeared before the Supreme Court: Brief for Defendant in Error, Muller v. Oregon, 208 U.S. 412 (1908) (No. 107); Urofsky, *Louis D. Brandeis*, 212–22.

140   "Now I think the opinion is persuasive": Paul Freund, "Justice Brandeis:

A Law Clerk's Remembrance," *American Jewish Archives* 68 (1977), 11, quoted in Urofsky, *Louis D. Brandeis*, 476.

140   "For the rational study of the law": Holmes, "Path of the Law," 469.

140   "If I wanted to be epigrammatic": OWH to Frankfurter, Washington, D.C., Dec. 3, 1925, in *Holmes and Frankfurter*, 194.

140   "this and that, that a gentleman should have read": OWH to Pollock, Beverly Farms, June 17, 1919, in *Holmes-Pollock*, 2:14.

140–41 "too old to acquire knowledge" . . . "anything he couldn't acquire": Urofsky, "Brandeis-Frankfurter Conversations," 335.

141   wrote to Laski in search of sympathy: OWH to Laski, Washington, D.C., May 18, 1919, in *Holmes-Laski*, 1:204–5.

141   he fired off an unusually critical reply: Laski to OWH, Cambridge, Mass., May 20, 1919, in *Holmes-Laski*, 1:205–6.

142   "What you say to explain my opinions": OWH to Laski, Washington, D.C., May 24, 1919, in *Holmes-Laski*, 1:207.

142   "The temptation is strong": OWH to Laski, Washington, D.C., June 16, 1919, in *Holmes-Laski*, 1:212.

10: THE RED SUMMER

143   May 1, a traditional day for celebration of labor: "Kirchwey Sees Trouble Ahead from Idleness," *New York Tribune*, May 3, 1919, 22.

143   In Boston, patrolmen used clubs: "4 Shot, 1 Stabbed, Many Beat in Boston Riots," *New York Tribune*, May 2, 1919, 2.

143   In New York, hundreds of returned soldiers: "New York Police Repel Raid by Sailors and Soldiers on Radicals," *Washington Post*, May 2, 1919, 1; "Scores Hurt throughout City in Riots," *New York Tribune*, May 2, 1919, 1.

143   The worst violence occurred in Cleveland: "1 Dead, Many Hurt in Cleveland Riot," *New York Times*, May 2, 1919, 1; "Dies in May Day Riot," *Washington Post*, May 2, 1919, 1; "Tanks Used in Cleveland Riot; 1 Dead, 11 Shot," *New York Tribune*, May 2, 1919, 1.

144   bombs exploded in eight different cities: "Recalls April Plot to Kill through Mails," *New York Times*, June 3, 1919, 2; "Clews to 'Red' Who Dynamited Palmer House Are Discovered; Wide War Begun on Radicals," *Washington Post*, June 4, 1919, 1.

144   doorstep of his Washington home: "Special to the New York Times," *New York Times*, June 3, 1919, 1.

144–45 feverish days of July . . . put a stop to the manhunt: Hagedorn, *Savage Peace*, 302–3.

145   twenty-eight lynchings of black men: Ibid., 253.

145–46 The trouble began . . . blacks were homeless: Ibid., 312–15; "2 Killed, 50 Hurt in Furious Race Riots in Chicago," *New York Times*, July 28, 1919,

1; "Street Battles at Night: Five Negroes Are Killed in One Fight—Rioting Subsides at Midnight," *New York Times*, July 29, 1919, 1.

146 he woke up to find a police officer: OWH to Pollock, Beverly Farms, June 17, 1919, in *Holmes-Pollock*, 2:15.

146 their mail was being screened: OWH to Laski, Beverly Farms, Aug. 19, 1919, Holmes Papers, reel 4.

146 Fanny had fallen ill: OWH to Pollock, Beverly Farms, June 27, 1919, in *Holmes-Pollock*, 2:17; OWH to Einstein, Beverly Farms, Sept. 19, 1919, in *Holmes-Einstein*, 189; Baker, *Justice*, 534.

146 Holmes worried she might have the flu: OWH to Leslie Scott, Beverly Farms, July 23, 1919, Holmes Papers, reel 61; OWH to Kentaro Kaneko, Beverly Farms, June 21, 1919, Holmes Papers, reel 61.

146 Shortly after they were married: White, *Justice Oliver Wendell Holmes*, 105. In n. 101, White cites a letter from Dr. Oliver Wendell Holmes Sr. to Thornton Hunt, July 16, 1872, Thornton Hunt Papers, Keats House, London. In the letter, Holmes wrote that his daughter-in-law had rheumatic fever.

147 She had another spell: OWH to Lady Pollock, July 20, 1897, in *Holmes-Pollock*, 1:75.

147 oldest child of a respected Cambridge family: Baker, *Justice*, 220; White, *Justice Oliver Wendell Holmes*, 104.

147 distinguished herself as a skillful embroiderer: Howe, *Proving Years*, 254–55.

147 they were exhibited in museums: Laidlaw, "Painting with Silken Threads," 49–55.

147 And she developed a strong sensitivity: Bowen, *Yankee from Olympus*, 334; Monagan, *Grand Panjandrum*, 54.

147 She played practical jokes: Bowen, *Yankee from Olympus*, 402; OWH to Thomas Barbour, April 20, 1920, Holmes Papers, reel 28.

147 she had become a recluse: Novick, *Honorable Justice*, 154–55; White, *Justice Oliver Wendell Holmes*, 105.

147 She kept her gray hair netted: Bowen, *Yankee from Olympus*, 340.

147 "she really did look like a monkey": Mrs. James B. Ayer, interview with Mark DeWolfe Howe, Holmes Papers, reel 40, quoted in White, *Justice Oliver Wendell Holmes*, 105.

148 "like an abandoned farm in Maine": Bowen, *Yankee from Olympus*, 349.

148 always been something of a flirt: Baker, *Justice*, 182.

148 "I admire and love ladies' society": OWH to Miss Lucy Hale, May 24, 1858, Holmes Papers, reel 40, quoted in White, *Justice Oliver Wendell Holmes*, 30.

148 Not until he was thirty-one: White, *Justice Oliver Wendell Holmes*, 103.

148 "for many years my most intimate friend.": OWH to Mrs. Howard Kennedy, March 11, 1872, quoted in White, *Justice Oliver Wendell Holmes*,

92. This letter is also quoted in Anna Howell Kennedy Findlay, "Where the Captain Was Found," *Maryland Historical Magazine* 109 (1938): 121.

148   He called regularly on several young wives: Baker, *Justice*, 312.

148–49   began a romantic relationship ... invitation to lunch: White, *Justice Oliver Wendell Holmes*, 230–31.

149   another lunch, a dinner, and a visit: Novick, *Honorable Justice*, 209; White, *Justice Oliver Wendell Holmes*, 231.

149   Lady Castletown invited Holmes to Doneraile: Baker, *Justice*, 314; White, *Justice Oliver Wendell Holmes*, 231; Novick, *Honorable Justice*, 209–10.

149   he and Lady Castletown were inseparable: White, *Justice Oliver Wendell Holmes*, 231; OWH to Lady Clare Castletown, Worcester, Mass., Sept. 30, 1896, Holmes Papers, reel 20.

149   "It is the stopping so sudden that hurts": OWH to Lady Castletown, Queenstown, Ireland, Aug. 22, 1896, Holmes Papers, reel 20.

149   smoking cigars on deck and talking: OWH to Lady Castletown, *Etruria*, Aug. 23, 1896, Holmes Papers, reel 20.

149   his house on Beacon Street ... unwilling to make himself: OWH to Lady Castletown, Boston, Mass., Sept. 5, 1896, Holmes Papers, reel 20.

150   "to know every minutest movement": OWH to Lady Castletown, Boston, Mass., Nov. 21, 1896, Holmes Papers, reel 20.

150   "I wish you would just pulsate": OWH to Lady Castletown, Boston, Mass., March 3, 1898, Holmes Papers, reel 20.

150   "I still carry in my pocket": OWH to Lady Castletown, Boston, Mass., Sept. 7, 1896, Holmes Papers, reel 20.

150   "Is he still in statu quo?": OWH to Lady Castletown, Boston, Mass., May 7, 1897, Holmes Papers, reel 20.

150   "Oh it is time that I heard": OWH to Lady Castletown, Boston, Mass., Sept. 30, 1896, Holmes Papers, reel 20.

150   "*Please* don't let it be so long again": OWH to Lady Castletown, Boston, Mass., Nov. 9, 1896, Holmes Papers, reel 20.

150   "The thing to believe and take comfort in,": OWH to Lady Castletown, Boston, Mass., Sept. 5, 1896, Holmes Papers, reel 20.

150   instructing Lady Castletown to write to him: OWH to Lady Castletown, Queenstown, Ireland, Aug. 22, 1896, Holmes Papers, reel 20.

150   He returned to England two summers later: Baker, *Justice*, 325.

150   Fanny was still ill: Ibid., 322–24.

150   "Do you swear that I should see": OWH to Lady Castletown, Boston, Mass., Jan. 18, 1898, Holmes Papers, reel 20.

151   "very little doubt": OWH to Lady Castletown, Boston, Mass., Feb. 17, 1898, Holmes Papers, reel 20.

151   prospects were "clouded": OWH to Lady Castletown, Boston, Mass., March 28, 1898, Holmes Papers, reel 20.

151   In April, they were "dim" . . . "Just settled sail Umbria June twenty five": OWH to Lady Castletown, Boston, Mass., April 29, 1898, June 1, 1898, June 9, 1898, July 18, 1898, Holmes Papers, reel 20.

151   he dined with Lord Castletown: White, *Justice Oliver Wendell Holmes*, 240.

151   Then it was on to Ireland: Ibid.

151   embarrassing case of shingles: Baker, *Justice*, 325.

151   "And now do you think": OWH to Lady Castletown, Beverly Farms, Sept. 5, 1898, Holmes Papers, reel 20.

151   "Whatever you say or don't say": OWH to Lady Castletown, Beverly Farms, Sept. 16, 1898, Holmes Papers, reel 20.

151   there was another man in her life: White, *Justice Oliver Wendell Holmes*, 233.

152   "It is *impossible* to really keep in touch,": OWH to Lady Castletown, May 19, 1899, Holmes Papers, reel 20. Holmes's letter quoted Lady Castletown's letter.

152   "Oh my dear it is possible to be unchanged": Ibid.

152   she had fallen from a horse: White, *Justice Oliver Wendell Holmes*, 243.

152   Lord Castletown sailed for South Africa: Ibid.

152   to see Lady Castletown once again: Ibid.; Baker, *Justice*, 333.

152   Holmes paid three more visits . . . half blind: White, *Justice Oliver Wendell Holmes*, 244–47.

153   "I was in the house": OWH to Laski, Beverly Farms, June 22, 1919, Holmes Papers, reel 4.

153   "Why shouldn't I call on you": OWH to Laski, June 24, 1919, Holmes Papers, reel 4.

153   "my impression is that an intelligent modern": OWH to Laski, Beverly Farms, July 21, 1919, Holmes Papers, reel 4.

153   "What influences are you going to count": OWH to Laski, Beverly Farms, Aug. 14, 1919, Holmes Papers, reel 4.

154   He read over fifty books: Holmes, "Black Book" List of Readings, 1881–1935, Holmes Papers, reel 61.

154   In May, he gave Holmes: Laski to OWH, Cambridge, Mass., May 20, 1919, in *Holmes-Laski*, 1:206.

154   *The History of English Rationalism*: Laski to OWH, Cambridge, Mass., May 30, 1919, in *Holmes-Laski*, 1:209; OWH to Laski, Beverly Farms, July 7, 1919, Holmes Papers, reel 4; OWH to Laski, Beverly Farms, July 21, 1919, Holmes Papers, reel 4.

154   *The History of English Democratic Ideas*: OWH to Laski, Beverly Farms, Aug. 19, 1919, Holmes Papers, reel 4.

154   "You are a bad boy": OWH to Laski, Beverly Farms, July 17, 1919, Holmes Papers, reel 4.

154   "had had considerable influence": Chafee, "Freedom of Speech," 938.

154   "use" of speech but not its "abuse": Ibid., 941.

155   "Justice Holmes in his" . . . "limits of constitutional protection": Ibid., 943–44.

155   he favored the test proposed by Learned Hand: Ibid., 962–63.

155   the bad tendency test: Ibid., 949–50.

155   "the interest in public safety": Ibid., 960.

156   "The question in every case": *Schenck v. United States*, 249 U.S. 47, 52 (1919).

156   "natural tendency and reasonably probable effect": *Debs v. United States*, 249 U.S. 211, 216 (1919).

156   "were clear cases of incitement": Chafee, "Freedom of Speech," 963.

156–57   "it is hard to see how" . . . "of overt acts": Ibid., 967–68.

157   "You have, I dare say, done well": Learned Hand to Zechariah Chafee Jr., New York, N.Y., Jan. 2, 1921, Hand Papers, box 15, folder 26.

157   "It is regrettable": Chafee, "Freedom of Speech," 968.

157   "many things that might be said": *Schenck*, 249 U.S. at 52, quoted in Chafee, "Freedom of Speech," 967.

157   "sanction any restriction of speech": Ibid., 969.

157   "some valuable suggestions pointing": Ibid., 945.

157   "habitual felicity" of Holmes's phrasemaking: Ibid., 955.

158   He sent a copy to Holmes: Laski to Zechariah Chafee Jr., July 23, 1919, Chafee Papers, box 14, folder 15.

158   Laski wrote to inform him of the plan: Ibid.

159   "I was delighted with Chafee": OWH to Laski, Beverly Farms, July 27, 1919, Holmes Papers, reel 4.

159   "ablest discussion of the First Amendment": Charles Amidon to Chafee, Fargo, N.D., Aug. 29, 1919, Chafee Papers, box 4, folder 1.

159   "inclined to allow a very wide latitude": Chafee to Amidon, Sept. 30, 1919, Chafee Papers, box 4, folder 1.

159–60   He slept late most mornings: OWH to Laski, Beverly Farms, June 24, 1919, Holmes Papers, reel 4; OWH to Laski, Beverly Farms, July 17, 1919, Holmes Papers, reel 4; OWH to Laski, Beverly Farms, Sept. 15, 1919, Holmes Papers, reel 4.

160   "not very enlivening,": OWH to Nina Gray, Beverly Farms, Sept. 2, 1919, Holmes Papers, reel 26.

160   "I got one leg on the fly paper": OWH to Ellen A. Curtis, Beverly Farms, Sept. 3, 1919, Holmes Papers, reel 26.

160   *Essays on Freethinking and Plainspeaking*: OWH to Laski, Beverly Farms, Sept. 23, 1919, Holmes Papers, reel 4.

160   They met in 1863 while Stephen was visiting: *Holmes-Pollock*, 1:xxv; Baker, *Justice*, 182.

160   Then, when Holmes traveled to Europe: OWH to Laski, Dec. 3, 1918, in *Holmes-Laski*, 1:175n2; Baker, *Justice*, 182–83.

160   *English Literature and Society*: Holmes, "Black Book" List of Readings,
        1881–1935, Holmes Papers, reel 61.

161   "waste their power in an attempt" . . . "happiness of our race depend":
        Stephen, *Essays*, 45, 409.

161   *The Decline of Liberty in England*: OWH to Pollock, Beverly Farms,
        Sept. 19, 1919, in *Holmes-Pollock*, 2:25; OWH to Laski, Beverly Farms,
        Sept. 17, 1919, Holmes Papers, reel 4.

161   "to the wishes of the Executive" . . . "collectivist point of view": Haynes,
        Decline of Liberty, 205, 213–14.

161   "The whole collectivist tendency": OWH to Pollock, Beverly Farms,
        Sept. 19, 1919, in *Holmes-Pollock*, 2:25.

162   On the third weekend of September: OWH to Laski, Beverly Farms,
        Sept. 17, 1919, Holmes Papers, reel 4; OWH to Laski, Beverly Farms,
        Sept. 22, 1919, Holmes Papers, reel 4.

162   He had been in Europe: Baker, *Felix Frankfurter*, 83.

162   "listened dumb and admiring like a little boy.": OWH to Laski, Beverly
        Farms, Sept. 22, 1919, Holmes Papers, reel 4.

162   "Your letter brings joy to my heart,": OWH to Frankfurter, Beverly
        Farms, Sept. 25, 1919, in *Holmes and Frankfurter*, 73.

11: "WORKERS—WAKE UP!"

164   Fanny was still weak: OWH to Einstein, Beverly Farms, Sept. 19, 1919,
        in *Holmes-Einstein*, 189.

164   "My apprehensive mind has contrived": OWH to Baroness Moncheur,
        Beverly Farms, Sept. 28, 1919, Holmes Papers, reel 26.

164   Holmes paid a call on Nina Gray: OWH to Nina Gray, Beverly Farms,
        Sept. 27, 1919, Holmes Papers, reel 23.

164   forced to check into a hotel: OWH to Gray, Beverly Farms, Sept. 2, 1919,
        Holmes Papers, reel 26; OWH to Einstein, Beverly Farms, Sept. 19,
        1919, in *Holmes-Einstein*, 189.

164   He was joined by his new secretary: OWH to Laski, Beverly Farms, July
        27, 1919, Holmes Papers, reel 4.

164   "passionately anxious to come,": Laski to OWH, Cambridge, Mass.,
        April 14, 1919, Holmes Papers, reel 4.

165   "though I grieve": OWH to Laski, Washington, D.C., April 20, 1919,
        Holmes Papers, reel 4.

165   an editor on the *Law Review*: "Memorial Resolution for Stanley Mor-
        rison (1892–1955)," *Stanford Historical Society Faculty Memorials*.
        Accessed Nov. 12, 2012. http://histsoc.stanford.edu/alpha_list.shtml
        #mm.

165   Brandeis stopped by in the midst: OWH to Laski, Washington, D.C.,
        Oct. 5, 1919, in *Holmes-Laski*, 1:212.

165 "I don't feel the usual glow": Ibid.

165 "I hope that is not your feeling,": Laski to OWH, Cambridge, Mass., Oct. 8, 1919, in *Holmes-Laski*, 1:213.

165 compilation of his speeches in 1891: OWH to Laski, Sept. 1, 1919, Holmes Papers, reel 4.

165 bring together Holmes's most important contributions: Holmes, *Collected Legal Papers*.

166 "I leave it all to you.": OWH to Laski, Oct. 26, 1919, in *Holmes-Laski*, 1:217.

166 The government's antitrust suit against U.S. Steel: *United States v. U.S. Steel Corp.*, 251 U.S. 417 (1920).

166 a boundary dispute between: *State of Minnesota v. State of Wisconsin*, 252 U.S. 273 (1920).

166 a challenge to the War-Time Prohibition Act: *Hamilton v. Kentucky Distilleries Co.*, 251 U.S. 146 (1919).

166 The first of these: *Schaefer v. United States*, 251 U.S. 466 (1919).

166 Founded in 1877: Transcript of Record at 129, Schaefer v. United States, 251 U.S. 466 (1919) (No. 804).

166 known primarily as a "society" paper: Ibid., 145; Waldenrath, "German Language Newspress in Pennsylvania," 30–31.

167 Instead they copied articles: Brief for Defendants in Error to the District Court of the United States for the Eastern District of Pennsylvania at 14, Schaefer v. United States, 251 U.S. 466 (1919) (No. 804); Transcript of Record at 185, Schaefer v. United States, 251 U.S. 466 (1919) (No. 804).

167 charged the editors with making false reports: Transcript of Record at 9–10, Schaefer v. United States, 251 U.S. 466 (1919) (No. 804).

167 Rather, they claimed that by altering: Brief for the United States in Error to the District Court of the United States for the Eastern District of Pennsylvania at 10–11, Schaefer v. United States, 251 U.S. 466 (1919) (No. 804).

167 "From this it can be concluded": Transcript of Record at 34, Schaefer v. United States, 251 U.S. 466 (1919) (No. 804).

167 "increasingly bad economic conditions": Transcript of Record at 31, Schaefer v. United States, 251 U.S. 466 (1919) (No. 804).

167–68 "Many Suicides in Pershing's Army" . . . "Sarrail's Troops Beaten": Ibid., 32, 27.

168 a story about Robert La Follette: *Schaefer*, 251 U.S. at 481; Transcript of Record at 23–24, Schaefer v. United States, 251 U.S. 466 (1919) (No. 804).

168 According to the testimony of one of the editors: Transcript of Record at 295, Schaefer v. United States, 251 U.S. 466 (1919) (No. 804).

168 charged the defendants with obstructing recruiting: Ibid., 34.

168 an editorial on July 4 . . . "for the benefit of England": Ibid., 35–36, 38.

168–69   Just weeks earlier, officials had rounded up: Polenberg, *Fighting Faiths*, 84.

169   A new drive for war bonds: "New Loan Drive to Start Sept. 28," *New York Times*, August 1, 1918, 1; Polenberg, *Fighting Faiths*, 82–86.

169   it dispatched Owen Roberts: "Tageblatt Trial Set," *Evening Public Ledger*, June 8, 1918, 1.

169   After a three-day trial: "5 Years in Jail for Editors in Tageblatt Case," *New York Times*, Dec. 18, 1919.

169   the second case before the Court: *Abrams v. United States*, 250 U.S. 616 (1919).

169   from twenty-one to thirty-three: Polenberg, *Fighting Faiths*, 126, 285.

169   All five had arrived: *Abrams*, 250 U.S. at 617.

169   Their leader was Jacob Abrams . . . 1905 Russian Revolution: Polenberg, *Fighting Faiths*, 23.

169   serving time in Siberia: "Bolshevist Witness Curbed by Court," *New York Times*, Oct. 22, 1918, 10; Chafee, "Contemporary State Trial," 760.

169   moved to the United States . . . a furrier named Samuel Lipman: Polenberg, *Fighting Faiths*, 11–27. Unlike the other members of the group, Lipman was actually a socialist, not an anarchist. However, he later testified that he was an anarchist to facilitate his deportation to Russia (since anarchists, but not socialists, were deportable under the law). Ibid., 13, 327.

169   young woman named Mollie Steimer: Ibid., 126.

170   "a slip of a girl,": Goldman, *Living My Life*, 705.

170   opposed the United States' involvement: Polenberg, *Fighting Faiths*, 22.

170   Czechs made their own agreement: Ibid., 40–41.

171   Wilson ordered five thousand troops: Ibid., 41.

171   rented a six-room apartment . . . print and circulate two leaflets: Ibid., 42–43.

171   "The Hypocrisy of the United States" . . . "WORKERS—WAKE UP!": Transcript of Record at 16–19, Abrams v. United States, 250 U.S. 616 (1919) (No. 316).

173   Working in the basement store: Ibid., 169–70.

174   gathered at the intersection of Crosby and Houston . . . 104th Street after work: Transcript of Record at 23–27, Abrams v. United States, 250 U.S. 616 (1919) (No. 316).

174   The scene in East Harlem that night: Polenberg, *Fighting Faiths*, 47.

174   Rosansky stood out front: Transcript of Record at 47–52, Abrams v. United States, 250 U.S. 616 (1919) (No. 316).

175   They began with Lachowsky . . . other members of the group: Ibid., 72–75.

175   Tunney had a reputation: Polenberg, *Fighting Faiths*, 59–60.

175   According to Lachowsky: Ibid., 62.

175   They used similar tactics: Ibid., 62–65.

176 For the federal prosecutor in New York . . . weapons and ammunition: Brief on Behalf of the United States in Error to the District Court of the United States for the Southern District of New York at 2–7, Abrams v. United States, 250 U.S. 616 (1919) (No. 316).

176 As John Lord O'Brian, head: Polenberg, *Fighting Faiths*, 73.

176–77 Clayton was no stranger . . . deportation for radicals and subversives: Polenberg, "Progressivism and Anarchism," 397.

177 "I have no sympathy with any naturalized citizen": "Grand Jury Told America Is First," *New York Times*, Jan. 7, 1916, 5.

177 his brother, a colonel in the army: Polenberg, "Progressivism and Anarchism," 402–3.

177 "Freedom of speech is one thing": "Free Speech Does Not Protect Disloyalty," *New York Times*, Sept. 13, 1918, 15.

177 The prosecution was led by John M. Ryan: Transcript of Record at 20–106, Abrams v. United States, 250 U.S. 616 (1919) (No. 316).

178 The defense lawyer, Harry Weinberger: Ibid., 110–25.

178 The day before the trial began: "Four Bolshevik Prisoners Will Say Police Beat Them," *New York Tribune*, Oct. 16, 1918, 18.

179 The anarchists then took the stand: Transcript of Record at 162–225, Abrams v. United States, 250 U.S. 616 (1919) (No. 316).

179 took over the examination himself: Ibid., 170–96.

179 "Well, I wish these people": Trial Transcript at 434–36, Abrams v. United States, 35, quoted in Polenberg, *Fighting Faiths*, 121.

179 Steimer, who refused to stand up: Polenberg, *Fighting Faiths*, 127.

179–80 "And when the love grows cold": Trial Transcript at 700–03, Abrams v. United States, quoted in Polenberg, *Fighting Faiths*, 130.

180 Weinberger shifting his focus: Leonard Abbott, Political Prisoners Defense and Relief Committee, *Sentenced to Twenty Years Prison* (New York, 1918), 21–29, cited in Polenberg, *Fighting Faiths*, 132–34.

180 "a man that is afraid of the truth": Polenberg, *Fighting Faiths*, 133.

180 "I do not want any mercy" . . . "That being the case": "Long Prison Terms for the Bolsheviki," *New York Times*, Oct. 26, 1918, 18.

180 launched into a two-hour diatribe: Trial Transcript, 832–35, cited in Polenberg, *Fighting Faiths*, 141–42.

180 sentenced Abrams, Lipman . . . in the state penitentiary: Transcript of Record at 242–44, Abrams v. United States, 250 U.S. 616 (1919) (No. 316); "Find 5 Russians Guilty," *New York Times*, Oct. 24, 1918, 11; "Long Prison Terms for the Bolsheviki."

180 After the sentencing, Weinberger declared: Polenberg, *Fighting Faiths*, 148.

181 "vouch for the honesty": Harry Weinberger to Attorney General G. Carroll Todd, Memorandum, November 5, 1918, quoted in Polenberg, *Fighting Faiths*, 150.

181   On November 11, 1918: Ibid., 150; "The Daily Legal Record," *Washington Post*, Nov. 12, 1918, 10.

181   had little trouble raising the funds: Polenberg, *Fighting Faiths*, 151.

181   one of 164 people . . . $500 bail: Ibid., 184–85.

181   In mid-October, while attending the trial: Hagedorn, *Savage Peace*, 373.

181   copies of a flyer entitled "Arm Yourselves": "Molly Steimer, Red Agitator, Is Arrested," *New York Tribune*, Oct. 19, 1919, 1.

181   she promptly began a hunger strike: Polenberg, *Fighting Faiths*, 194.

181   justices combined *Abrams* and *Schaefer*: "The Daily Record," *Washington Post*, Oct. 22, 1919, 17.

12: A PLEA FOR HELP

182   Sticking his neck out in support: Kramnick and Sheerman, *Harold Laski*, 134.

182–83 It had all started . . . joining outside groups: "Arms Go to Boston," *Washington Post*, Sept. 16, 1919, 1; "Discharges 19 Park Police," *New York Times*, Sept. 21, 1919; "Strike Secrecy Caused Boston Riot, Curtis Says," *New York Tribune*, Dec. 24, 1919, 7; Murray, *Red Scare*, 123–25; Slater, "Labor and the Boston Police Strike."

183   he called for volunteers to patrol the streets . . . "right here in Boston": Kramnick and Sheerman, *Harold Laski*, 132.

183   Peters appointed a committee to mediate: Ibid.; Murray, *Red Scare*, 124.

183   But Commissioner Curtis rejected it: Murray, *Red Scare*, 124.

183   Gangs of hooligans roamed: Ibid., 126–28.

183   Riots broke out: "Disorder in Boston," *New York Times*, Sept. 11, 1918, 14; "Fatal Riot in Boston," *Washington Post*, Sept. 11, 1919, 1.

183   A ragtag band of volunteers: "Serious Strike Position in America," *Manchester Guardian*, Sept. 12, 1918, 7; "Call for Volunteer Force Answered by 250 Students," *Harvard Crimson*, Sept. 19, 1919.

183   Massachusetts State Guard: "Fatal Riot in Boston"; "Serious Strike Position in America," *Manchester Guardian*, Sept. 12, 1918, 7.

184   The officers had hoped to receive support: Murray, *Red Scare*, 128–29.

184   Newspapers branded the policemen as radicals: Ibid., 133–34.

184   "a crime against civilization.": "Boston Now Faces General Strike to Aid Police; Four More Are Killed; Damage Estimated at $300,000; Wilson Says Strike Is a Crime against Civilization," *New York Times*, Sept. 12, 1919, 1; "Victory for Law and Order," *New York Times*, Nov. 6, 1919, 12; "Wilson Denounces Police Strike That Left Boston a Prey to Thugs," *New York Times*, Sept. 12, 1919, 1.

184   Senator Henry L. Myers of Montana: "Senator Myers Deplores Police Unions; Predicts Move Here for Soviet Rule," *New York Times*, Sept. 12, 1919, 1.

184   its members voted down a proposal: Murray, *Red Scare*, 128–29.

184   AFL president Samuel Gompers urged the police: Ibid., 130.

184   "there is no right to strike": Washburn, *Calvin Coolidge*, 87.

184   Indeed, he dedicated the final chapter: Laski, "Administrative Syndicalism in France," ch. 5 of *Authority*, 321–87.

185   "The class struggle is no less": Ibid., 337.

185   the editors at the *New Republic* thought: "The Police Strike," *New Republic*, Sept. 24, 1919, 217–18.

185   referred approvingly to earlier police strikes: Laski, *Authority*, 339–40.

185   Every man has the right to affiliate: "Laski Scores Commissioner's Action in Walkout Crisis," *Harvard Crimson*, Oct. 10, 1919.

185   nothing more than a "boudoir Bolshevist": "Comment on Mr. Laski," *Harvard Crimson*, Oct. 17, 1919.

186   "the striking of soldiers": Norman H. White, "A Dangerous Comparison," *Harvard Crimson*, Oct. 14, 1919.

186   alumni wrote to President Lowell: Kramnick and Sheerman, 134–35.

186   On October 15, Laski was invited: Ibid., 134.

186   "We are told the police are deserters": "Women Take a Hand in the Police Strike," *Boston Daily Globe*, Oct. 16, 1919, 1.

186   Hall accused Laski of glorifying Bolshevism: Hall's letter to the *Boston Herald*, dated Oct. 9, 1919, was reprinted in the *Harvard Alumni Bulletin* under the heading "The Boston Police Strike" (Oct. 23, 1919, 106).

186   "It is not too much to ask": *Boston Evening Transcript*, Oct. 16, 1919, quoted in "Attack on Academic Freedom," *Harvard Crimson*, Oct. 17, 1919.

186–87 $15 million fund-raising . . . "principles of academic freedom": Kramnick and Sheerman, *Harold Laski*, 135–38.

187   "Why not clean house": Ted Morgan, *FDR: A Biography* (New York: Simon and Schuster, 1985), 214–15, quoted in Kramnick and Sheerman, *Harold Laski*, 138.

187   The arguments lasted two days: Baker, *Justice*, 536.

187–88   argued that the government had failed: Brief for Defendants in Error to the District Court of the United States for the Eastern District of Pennsylvania at 14–20, Schaefer v. United States, 251 U.S. 466 (1919) (No. 804).

188   "was that the articles which were published": Ibid., 14.

188   Weinberger offered a more general theory: Brief for Plaintiffs in Error to District Court of the United States for the Southern District of New York at 42–50, Abrams v. United States, 250 U.S. 616 (1919) (No. 316).

188   "break out into overt acts against peace": Ibid., 46.

188   no intent to hinder the war against Germany: Ibid., 6–8, 15–16, 24.

188   "Russia had been surrounded": Ibid., 29–30.

188   "The argument here looks good": Harry Weinberger to Jerome Weiss, Weinberger MSS, box 1, quoted in Polenberg, *Fighting Faiths*, 198.

188   He and his assistant, Alfred Bettman: Ibid., 230.

189   two of the most progressive lawyers: Ibid., 30.

189   written to Zechariah Chafee congratulating him: Alfred Bettman to Zechariah Chafee Jr., Cincinnati, Ohio, Sept. 20, 1919, Chafee Papers, box 14, folder 3.

189   "typical supporters of the proletarian republic": Robert P. Stewart to A. Mitchell Palmer, memorandum, Sept. 27, 1919, quoted in Polenberg, *Fighting Faiths*, 231–32.

189   Stewart argued that it didn't matter: Brief for the United States in Error to the District Court of the United States for the Eastern District of Pennsylvania at 10–11, Schaefer v. United States, 251 U.S. 466 (1919) (No. 804).

190   false "statements" and false "reports": Ibid., 18.

190   "Whether the false 'report' is true": Ibid., 19.

190   "they must, if they wish to avoid": Ibid.

190   "it follows necessarily" that they were "equally constitutional": Brief on Behalf of the United States in Error to the District Court of the United States for the Southern District of New York at 17, Abrams v. United States, 250 U.S. 616 (1919) (No. 316).

190   intended to "fix the liberty of the press": Ibid., 19.

191   "We are entirely willing to take the judgment": Ibid., 37.

191   In his *New Republic* article, Freund: Freund, "Debs Case," 14.

191   Holmes shared his thoughts with the rest: OWH to Pollock, Washington, D.C., Oct. 26, 1919, in *Holmes-Pollock*, 2:28. In this letter, written the day after the Saturday conference at which *Abrams* was discussed, Holmes wrote, "I see various conflicts of opinion ahead," then added, "I hope that we have heard the last, or nearly the last, of the Espionage Act cases. Some of our subordinate Judges seem to me to have been hysterical during the war. It is one of the ironies that I, who probably take the extremist view in favor of free speech (in which, in the abstract I have no very enthusiastic belief, though I hope I would die for it), that I should have been selected for blowing up. I don't understand the Government pressing those cases and trust cases against corporations for doing what it still is doing and what is likely to be sanctioned by legislation— but that is not my business."

192   Holmes and Fanny had been invited to dine: OWH to Pollock, Washington, D.C., Oct. 26, 1919, Holmes Papers, reel 10. The reference to dinner at the ambassador's was deleted from the published version of this letter.

192   "Where are you going to draw the line?": OWH to Pollock, Washington, D.C., Oct. 26, 1919, in *Holmes-Pollock*, 2:28.

192   "On sovereignty in general" . . . "often loose and sometimes erroneous": Pollock to OWH, Rye, U.K. Sept. 20, 1919, in *Holmes-Pollock*, 2:25.

193   "I believe that this country like yours": OWH to Pollock, Washington, D.C., Oct. 26, 1919, in *Holmes-Pollock*, 2:28.

193   Sixty years earlier, as a student editor: Baker, *Justice*, 87–89.

193   "books of an agitating tendency": Holmes, "Books," *Harvard Magazine*, Dec. 1858, 408.

193–94   Frankfurter had paid a visit . . . "has courage & speaks sense": Frankfurter to Marion Denman, Oct. 23, 1919, Frankfurter Papers, Aug.–Nov. 1919, box 9, reel 4.

194   It was a shame that Holmes: Laski's letter to Holmes has not been found. This description of it is based on Holmes's response to Laski and a similar response to Frankfurter a week later. OWH to Laski, Oct. 26, 1919, in *Holmes-Laski*, 1:217–18; OWH to Frankfurter, Washington, D.C., Nov. 1, 1919, in *Holmes and Frankfurter*, 74.

194   revealed just how far Holmes had come: OWH to Laski, Oct. 26, 1919, in *Holmes-Laski*, 1:217–18.

195   "If a man is on a plank in the deep sea" . . . "it does the same thing": Holmes, *Common Law*, 42.

195   "the felt necessities of the time,": Ibid., 1.

196   "cold talk if you have been": OWH to Laski, Oct. 26, 1919, in *Holmes-Laski*, 1:217–18.

196   reassured him that everything would work out: Laski to OWH, Cambridge, Mass., Oct. 28, 1919, in *Holmes-Laski*, 1:218.

196   consensus was that Laski's behavior warranted: Kramnick and Sheerman, *Harold Laski*, 138.

13: *"QUASI IN FURORE"*

198   Holmes liked to prepare his dissents: OWH to Laski, Washington, D.C., Feb. 10, 1920, in *Holmes-Laski*, 1:240.

198   his familiar spot at the upright desk: Bowen, *Yankee from Olympus*, 380.

198   They were "abusive" . . . "usual tall talk": *Abrams v. United States*, 250 U.S. 616, 625 (Holmes, J., dissenting).

199   "it is evident from the beginning": Ibid., 628–29.

199   As prosecutors had pointed out . . . intervention in Russia: Brief on Behalf of the United States at 26, Abrams v. United States, 250 U.S. 616 (1919) (No. 316).

200   "perfectly consistent with the harm": Holmes, *Common Law*, 49.

200   "I am aware of course": *Abrams*, 250 U.S. at 626–27.

200–201   "A patriot might argue" . . . "Debs were rightly decided": Ibid.

201   "But as against dangers peculiar": Ibid., 628.

202   three times in one sentence alone: Ibid., 630.

202   precisely what he and Brandeis would argue: *Whitney v. California*, 274 U.S. 357 (1927) (Brandeis, J., concurring); *Gitlow v. New York*, 268 U.S. 652, 672 (1925) (Holmes, J., dissenting); *Pierce v. United States*, 252 U.S. 239, 253 (1929) (Brandeis, J., dissenting); *Schaefer v. United States*, 251 U.S. 466, 482 (1920) (Brandeis, J., dissenting).

202   "Now nobody can suppose": *Abrams*, 250 U.S. at 628.

202–3   criticizing Judge Clayton's handling: Ibid., 629–30.

203   *"quasi in furore"*—as if possessed: OWH to Frankfurter, Washington,
          D.C., Nov. 1, 1919, in *Holmes and Frankfurter*, 74.

204   If persecution for the expression of opinions: *Abrams*, 250 U.S. at 630.

204   "Tolerance," in his words: Hand to OWH, Windsor, Vt., June 22, 1918,
          Holmes Papers, reel 33.

204–5   "complete liberty of contradicting" . . . "prove them unfounded": Mill,
          On Liberty, 79, 81.

205   As he had told his secretary: Biddle, *Mr. Justice Holmes*, 149.

205   "And though all the winds of doctrine": Milton, *Areopagitica*, 40–41.

205   "Yet in the clash of ideas": Laski, *Authority*, 279–80.

206   He had read *The Wealth of Nations*: OWH to Pollock, Beverly Farms, July
          28, 1911, in *Holmes-Pollock*, 1:183. Holmes wrote, "I do not get much
          nourishment except when the writers become sociological (I remember
          getting much pleasure from Adam Smith)—because there he gives his
          general views of life."

206   loaned to him by: Laski to OWH, Warwick Gardens, July 17, 1921, in
          Holmes-Laski, 1:351. In this letter, Laski refers to Francis Hirst and
          adds, "you may remember that I lent you his life of Adam Smith."

206   *"The Wealth of Nations* is a forest" . . . "siege of Troy": Hirst, *Adam
          Smith*, 193, 204.

206   "free trade in ideas": *Abrams*, 250 U.S. at 630.

206   profound, and unforgettable sentence: Ibid.

207   "upon an economic theory which": *Lochner v. New York*, 198 U.S. 45,
          75–76 (1905) (Holmes, J., dissenting).

207   "'The point of contact'": OWH to Frankfurter, Washington, D.C., Dec.
          19, 1915, in *Holmes and Frankfurter*, 40.

208   as a matter of accepted fact: *Abrams*, 250 U.S. at 630.

208   relied on it as support: Ibid., 630–31.

209   "so that the axe may fall": OWH to Albert J. Beveridge, July 11, 1926,
          Holmes Papers, reel 27.

209   "as if they had been written": OWH to Pollock, Beverly Farms, Aug. 13,
          1906, in *Holmes-Pollock*, 1:130.

209   a rare public acknowledgment: *Abrams*, 250 U.S. at 631.

14: ADULATION

211   it would be ready to distribute: OWH to Nina Gray, Nov. 5, 1919,
          Holmes Papers, reel 23.

211   Frankfurter had inquired: This letter from Frankfurter has not been
          found. My description of it is based on Holmes's reply as well as his
          reply to a similar letter from Laski a week earlier.

211   he sent the following reply: OWH to Frankfurter, Washington, D.C., Nov. 1, 1919, in *Holmes and Frankfurter*, 74. In a note to the Holmes-Frankfurter letters, the editors, Robert M. Mennel and Christine L. Compston, indicate that Holmes had been asked to deliver the Phi Beta Kappa oration at Harvard, implying that it is this request, rather than the request to write an article on tolerance, that Holmes is denying in his letter to Frankfurter. See *Holmes and Frankfurter*, 74n1. However, Holmes makes clear in this letter that Frankfurter and Laski had asked him to write "an article," not to give an oration. Moreover, in his letter to Laski a week earlier, Holmes wrote that in addition to being too busy to grant Laski's request, he had also "just declined once more on the same ground to deliver the Phi Beta Kappa oration." See OWH to Laski, Oct. 26, 1919, in *Holmes-Laski*, 1:217–18. It is therefore clear that in his letter to Frankfurter he was referring not to that oration but to the article on tolerance. Further supporting this conclusion is his remark to Frankfurter that he is "full of a tentative statement . . . on kindred themes to your subject." His *Abrams* dissent, of course, was directly related to the theme of tolerance.

212   engaged to Marion Denman: Baker, *Felix Frankfurter*, 40.

212   His father had died: Frankfurter to OWH, New York, N.Y., March 6, 1916, in *Holmes and Frankfurter*, 47n1.

212   "Tell her! Tell her!" . . . again in silence: Mendelson, *Felix Frankfurter*, 39, 40.

212   Justice Clarke circulated the majority opinion: OWH to Pollock, Washington, D.C., Nov. 6, 1919, in *Holmes-Pollock*, 2:29.

212   "sufficiently discussed and is definitely negatived" . . . "war program of the United States": *Abrams*, 250 U.S. at 618, 621.

213   "Today I am stirred": OWH to Pollock, Washington, D.C., Nov. 6, 1919, in *Holmes-Pollock*, 2:29.

213   On Friday, November 7: Acheson, *Morning and Noon*, 119.

213   "I think there was a case": Pitney to OWH, *U. S. Supreme Court Opinions Delivered by Justice Holmes, October Term 1919*. Justice Holmes's personal copy, with annotations, Holmes Papers, reel 70.

213   The Boston police force had been disbanded: "Arms Go to Boston," *Washington Post*, Sept. 16, 1919, 1; Hagedorn, *Savage Peace*, 353.

213   steelworkers had gone on strike: "Serious Strike Position in America," *Manchester Guardian*, Sept. 12, 1919, 7.

213   Senate was locked in a bitter fight: Hagedorn, *Savage Peace*, 404–5.

213   speak with one voice: Acheson, *Morning and Noon*, 119.

214   to see the cherry blossoms: OWH to Frankfurter, Washington, D.C., April 25, 1920, in *Holmes and Frankfurter*, 89.

214   in a case out of Louisville: *Buchanan v. Warley*, 245 U.S. 60 (1917).

214   initially opposed the Court's decision: Freund and Katz, *History of the*

Supreme Court, 804–6. Holmes's undelivered dissent in *Buchanan v. Warley* is reprinted in an insert following p. 592. The original is located in the Art Collection at Harvard Law School.

214   Holmes felt he had a duty: OWH to Pollock, Washington, D.C., Nov. 6, 1919, in *Holmes-Pollock*, 2:29; OWH to Gray, Washington, D.C., Dec. 10, 1919, Holmes Papers, reel 26.

214   "full of a tentative statement": OWH to Frankfurter, Washington, D.C., Nov. 1, 1919, in *Holmes and Frankfurter*, 74.

214   "I join you heartily & gratefully": Brandeis to OWH, *U.S. Supreme Court Opinions Delivered by Justice Holmes, October Term 1919*. Justice Holmes's personal copy, with annotations, Holmes Papers, reel 70.

214   That evening at 8:45: "200 Caught in New York," *New York Times*, Nov. 8, 1919, 1; "IWW and Russian People's House Raided: Men Are Clubbed without Mercy," "53 Held for Exile," *New York Call*, Nov. 8, 1919, 1, 5.

215   150 people in Newark . . . 30 in Philadelphia: "Red Raids in Other Cities," *New York Times*, Nov. 8, 1919, 2; "200 Caught in New York"; "Seize 500 Alien Reds," *Washington Post*, Nov. 9, 1919, 1.

215   A graduate of George Washington Law School: Powers, *Secrecy and Power*, 38.

215   joined the Justice Department . . . anniversary of the Russian Revolution: Ibid., 64–69, 39, 68, 77.

216   thirty-nine were ultimately charged: "Seize 500 Alien Reds."

216   transport 249 aliens back to Russia: Powers, *Secrecy and Power*, 86.

216   In New York, a committee: "73 Red Centres Raided Here by Lusk Committee," *New York Times*, Nov. 8, 1919, 1.

216   "Too long the government": "Raiding the Reds," *Washington Post*, Nov. 9, 1919, E4.

217   Persecution for the expression of opinions: *Abrams*, 250 U.S. at 630–31.

219   "In the midst of a feverish week": Laski to OWH, Cambridge, Mass., Nov. 12, 1919, in *Holmes-Laski*, 1:220.

219   "And now I may tell you the gratitude": Frankfurter to OWH, Cambridge, Mass., Nov. 12, 1919, in *Holmes and Frankfurter*, 75.

220   "Am I allowed to thank you": Walter Lippmann to OWH, Nov. 13, 1919, Holmes Papers, reel 35, frame 0337.

220   "I have just seen the complete text": Herbert Croly to OWH, Nov. 13, 1919, Holmes Papers, reel 30, frame 0357.

220   "Opportunity to read your opinion": Roscoe Pound to OWH, Nov. 26, 1919, Holmes Papers, reel 36, frame 0747.

221   "I told you what a glorious opinion": Laski to OWH, New Haven, Conn., Nov. 14, 1919, in *Holmes-Laski*, 1:222.

221   "I still read and rejoice": Frankfurter to OWH, Cambridge, Mass., Nov. 26, 1919, in *Holmes and Frankfurter*, 76.

221   "I was greatly pleased": Hand to OWH, Nov. 25, 1919, Holmes Papers,
           reel 33, frame 0077.

223   "Your letter gives me the greatest pleasure": OWH to Hand, Nov. 26,
           1919, Hand Papers, box 103B, folders 25–26.

223   "I have supposed that": OWH to Frankfurter, Washington, D.C., Nov.
           30, 1919, in *Holmes and Frankfurter*, 76.

15: "ALONE AT LASKI"

224   Harvard Liberal Club held a meeting. . . . but all three declined: Chafee
           to Hand, Cambridge, Mass., Dec. 2, 1919, Hand Papers, box 15, folder
           26; Chafee to Hand, Cambridge, Mass., Dec. 5, 1919, Hand Papers, box
           15, folder 26; Hand to Chafee, New York, N.Y., Jan. 8, 1920, Hand
           Papers, box 15, folder 26.

224   "For obvious reasons I should not care": Holmes, *His Book Notices and
           Uncollected Letters*, 137.

224   "Only you could have written": Laski to OWH, Cambridge, Mass., Jan.
           14, 1920, in *Holmes-Laski*, 1:178.

224–25   In March, he persuaded Frankfurter . . . "amnesty at this time": Polen-
           berg, *Fighting Faiths*, 273; Smith, *Zechariah Chafee*, 40.

225   Wilson rejected the petition: Polenberg, *Fighting Faiths*, 329–43.

225   Writing in the *Yale Law Journal*: Corwin, "Freedom of Speech and
           Press," 54.

225   Day Kimball, a student editor: Kimball, "Espionage Act and the Lim-
           its," 446.

255   "a positive menace to society" . . . "'poor and puny anonymities'": Ger-
           man, "An Unfortunate Dissent," 77–78, 80.

226   "If you do know of such a piece": OWH to Frankfurter, Washington,
           D.C., April 12, 1920, in *Holmes and Frankfurter*, 85.

226   "our greatest American or English": John H. Wigmore to OWH, April
           29, 1894, John H. Wigmore Papers, Northwestern Univ. Law School
           Library, quoted in Polenberg, *Fighting Faiths*, 249n22.

226–29   "There is here nothing further" . . . "language is ominous indeed":
           Wigmore, "Abrams v. U.S.," 543–61.

229   To the officials in the Justice Department . . . sympathy for radical
           speakers: Polenberg, *Fighting Faiths*, 255–56.

229   "The poor man has not yet": Frankfurter to OWH, Cambridge, Mass.,
           April 19, 1920, in *Holmes and Frankfurter*, 86.

230   "wasn't reasoning but emotion": OWH to Frankfurter, Washington,
           D.C., April 25, 1920, in *Holmes and Frankfurter*, 88.

230   Holmes agreed to hire the young man: OWH to Frankfurter, Washing-
           ton, D.C., Feb. 11, 1920, in *Holmes and Frankfurter*, 81–82.

230   As Laski recounted the incident later: Martin, *Harold Laski*, 33.

230 The board subsequently voted: Kramnick and Sheerman, *Harold Laski*, 139.

232 prompting J. Edgar Hoover to open a file: Ibid., 148–49.

232 The *Boston Transcript* lauded the magazine: *Boston Transcript*, Jan. 26, 1920.

232 "one of the most scathing attacks": *Boston Herald*, Jan. 28, 1920.

232 pleaded with readers to stop sending them: "Communications," *Harvard Crimson*, Jan. 29, 1920.

232 A group of students and faculty . . . "of him who argues": Kramnick and Sheerman, *Harold Laski*, 141, citing A. Lawrence Lowell to Edward A. Bacon, Feb. 5, 1920, A. Lawrence Lowell Papers, Harvard University.

233 "It is disgusting that so serious a scholar": OWH to Frankfurter, Washington, D.C., Feb. 11, 1920, in *Holmes and Frankfurter*, 82.

233 "such a childish and rotten little show": OWH to Laski, Washington, D.C., Feb., 10, 1920, in *Holmes-Laski*, 1:184.

233 "I trust that you and Frida": Brandeis to Laski, in Urofsky and Levy, *Letters of Louis D. Brandeis*, 450.

233 "I am heartily sick of America": Laski to Bertrand Russell, Cambridge, Mass., Feb. 18, 1920, in *Autobiography of Bertrand Russell*, 160.

233 "thousand veils of green and brown": OWH to Nina Gray, Washington, D.C., March 28, 1920, Holmes Papers, reel 26.

234 "My dear Justice": Laski to OWH, Cambridge, Mass., March 28, 1920, in *Holmes-Laski*, 1:255–56.

235 Laski had begun laying the groundwork: Kramnick and Sheerman, *Harold Laski*, 142–46.

236 "But oh, my dear lad": OWH to Laski, Washington, D.C., March 31, 1920, in *Holmes-Laski*, 1:256.

236 The justices had voted to reverse: *Schaefer v. United States*, 251 U.S. 466, 471, 482 (1920).

236–37 bound by the jury's factual findings . . . "made the law useless": Ibid., 476, 479.

237 Brandeis declared that it, not bad tendency: *Schaefer*, 251 U.S. at 482 (Brandeis, J., dissenting).

237 "In my opinion no jury": Ibid., 483.

237 "To hold that such harmless": Ibid., 493–94.

237 this case involved four socialists: *Pierce v. United States*, 252 U.S. 239 (1920).

238 As long as that decision was supported by some evidence: Ibid., 249–51.

238 "The fundamental right of free men": Ibid., 273.

238 Before the term ended: Laski to OWH, Cambridge, Mass., April 2, 1920, in *Holmes-Laski*, 1:257; OWH to Laski, Washington, D.C., April

6, 1920, in *Holmes-Laski*, 1:258; Laski to OWH, Cambridge, Mass., May 7, 1920, in *Holmes-Laski*, 1:260.

238   Holmes resumed the flirtation: OWH to Ellen Curtis, Washington, D.C., June 12, 1920, Holmes Papers, reel 26; OWH to Curtis, Beverly Farms, June 20, 1920, Holmes Papers, reel 26; OWH to Curtis, Beverly Farms, July 12, 1920, Holmes Papers, reel 26.

238   In consideration of his "age and moral infirmities": OWH to Laski, Washington, D.C., June 11, 1920, in *Holmes-Laski*, 1:268.

238   polishing off a history: Holmes, "Black Book" List of Readings, 1881–1935, Holmes Papers, reel 61.

239   "You mention for Beverly Farms": OWH to Laski, Washington, D.C., June 1, 1922, in *Holmes-Laski*, 1:430.

EPILOGUE: "I SIMPLY WAS IGNORANT"

240   "The whole proceeding, from start to finish" . . . "the philosophic basis": Chafee, "Contemporary State Trial," 774, 769.

241   At the request of a federal judge . . . before a Senate subcommittee to testify: Smith, *Zechariah Chafee*, 45–50.

241   Chafee was labeled a dangerous man . . . disciplined without his consent: Ibid., 36–57; Polenberg, *Fighting Faiths*, 272–84.

241   That was enough for the committee: Smith, *Zechariah Chafee*, 55.

242   "My Dear Mr. Justice Holmes": Chafee to OWH, Cambridge, Mass., June 9, 1922, Chafee Papers, box 14, folder 12.

242–43 He had read Chafee's article: OWH to Laski, Washington, D.C., Dec. 17, 1920, in *Holmes-Laski*, 1:297.

243   At Brandeis's urging: Holmes to Chafee, Washington, D.C., May 19, 1921, Chafee Papers, box 4, folder 21; Brandeis to Frankfurter, Washington, D.C., May 20, 1921, in Urofsky and Levy, *Letters of Louis D. Brandeis*, 559.

243   "My Dear Professor Chafee": OWH to Chafee, Beverly Farms, June 12, 1922, Chafee Papers, box 14, folder 12.

243   It was the closest: Feldman, "Free Speech," 194, 238. Nor did Holmes ever admit that he had changed his mind on the issue of free speech as a result of the events of 1918 and 1919. In a letter to Nina Gray in 1921, he defended himself against the charge that Brandeis had influenced his views on a range of issues by claiming that he had "turned" toward a liberal position on free speech "long before" Brandeis joined the Court in 1916. OWH to Nina Gray, Washington, D.C., March 5, 1921, Holmes Papers, reel 23. In light of the events chronicled in this book, that claim is not credible.

244   Through the intervention of his friends: Gengarelly, "Abrams Case," 11–12.

244   champion of the First Amendment: There were only two cases after
           Abrams in which Holmes voted to uphold a conviction based on
           speech. The first was *Gilbert v. Minnesota*, 254 U.S. 325 (1920), in which
           the defendant was convicted under a state law nearly identical to the
           federal Espionage Act. However, it was not clear in *Gilbert* that the
           defendant had properly raised the issue of free speech in the trial court.
           Memorandum from Dean Acheson to Louis D. Brandeis, Nov. 19, 1920,
           Brandeis Papers, box 5, folder 12. In addition, the prosecution was
           brought by a state, not the federal government, and Holmes was appar-
           ently reluctant to extend the protections of the First Amendment
           against the states. Urofsky, "Brandeis-Frankfurter Conversations," 320.
           The second case was *Whitney v. California*, 274 U.S. 357 (1927), in which
           Holmes joined a concurrence written by Brandeis. Although Brandeis
           eloquently defended the right of free speech, he concurred in upholding
           the defendant's conviction on procedural grounds.

244   In 1921 he dissented: *United States ex rel. Milwaukee Social Democrat
           Pub. Co., v. Burleson*, 255 U.S. 407 (1921) (Holmes, J., dissenting).

244   "the use of the mails": Ibid., 437.

244   A majority of the Court upheld: *Gitlow v. New York*, 268 U.S. 652, 669
           (1925) (Holmes, J., dissenting).

244   "If in the long run": Ibid., 673.

244   "If there is any principle": *United States v. Schwimmer*, 279 U.S. 644
           (1929) (Holmes, J., dissenting).

244   Brandeis wrote several eloquent opinions: *Whitney v. California*, 274
           U.S. 357 (1927) (Brandeis, J., concurring); *United States ex rel. Milwau-
           kee Social Democrat Pub. Co., v. Burleson*, 255 U.S. 407 (1921) (Brandeis,
           J., dissenting); *Gilbert v. Minnesota*, 254 U.S. 325 (1920) (Brandeis, J.,
           dissenting).

245   Supreme Court finally came around: *Bridges v. California*: 314 U.S. 252
           (1941); *Thomas v. Collins*, 323 U.S. 516, 530 (1945).

245   Holmes plowed through . . . *Heaven's My Destination*: Holmes, "Black
           Book" List of Readings, 1881–1935, Holmes Papers, reel 61.

245–46   appointed to the executive committee . . . book about American democ-
           racy: Kramnick and Sheerman, *Harold Laski*, 477–515, 567–77.

246   appointed to the federal appeals court: Gunther, *Learned Hand*, 275.

246   once more in the grip of panic: Stone, *Perilous Times*, 323–95.

246   Known as the Smith Act: Alien Registration Act, Pub. L No. 670, 54
           Stat. 670, 671 (1940) (codified as amended at 18 U.S.C.A. § 2385).

247   Its first test came in 1949: *Dennis v. United States*, 341 U.S. 494 (1951).

247   Like most other liberals, Hand was troubled: Gunther, *Learned Hand*,
           578–92.

247   But Hand affirmed the verdict: *United States v. Dennis*, 183 F.2d 201
           (1950).

247   a court "must ask whether the gravity": Ibid., 212.

248   "wait until the actual eve": Ibid., 213.

248   Hand's commitment to judicial restraint: Gunther, *Learned Hand*, 652–59.

248   "Personally, I should never have": Hand to Frankfurter, June 8, 1951, quoted in Gunther, *Learned Hand*, 603.

248   "has nothing to do with": Hand to Berenson, June 11, 1951, quoted in Gunther, *Learned Hand*, 603.

248   He had represented the anarchists: Baker, *Felix Frankfurter*, 117–30, 145–210.

248   Once he was on the Court: Ibid., 222–34.

248   Frankfurter sided with the majority: *Dennis v. United States*, 341 U.S. 494 (1951) (Frankfurter, J., concurring).

249   prosecuted nearly 150 members: Stone, *Perilous Times*, 411.

249   he kept the faith: Smith, *Zechariah Chafee*, 242–71.

249   In a 1969 case: *Brandenburg v. Ohio*, 395 U.S. 444 (1969).

249   "except where such advocacy": Ibid., 447.

249   from commercial advertisements: *Consolidated Edison Co. of New York Inc., v. Public Service Commission of New York*, 447 U.S. 530, 534 (1980); *Bigelow v. Virgina*, 421 U.S. 809, 826 (1975).

249   campaign spending: *McConnell v. Federal Election Commission*, 540 U.S. 93, 265–66 (2003) (Thomas, J., dissenting), *overruled by Citizens United v. Federal Election Commission*, 558 U.S. 310 (2010); *First Nat. Bank of Boston v. Bellotti*, 435 U.S. 765, 791n.31 (1978).

249   defamation of public figures: *Hustler Magazine, Inc., v. Falwell*, 485 U.S. 46, 51 (1988); *Monitor Patriot Co. v. Roy*, 401 U.S. 265, 275 (1971); *Garrison v. Louisiana*, 379 U.S. 64, 82–83 (1964) (Douglas, J., concurring); *New York Times v. Sullivan*, 376 U.S. 254, 276 (1964).

249   burning of the American flag: *Texas v. Johnson*, 491 U.S. 397, 418–19 (1989).

249   upholding the right of corporations: *Citizens United v. Federal Election Commission*, 558 U.S. 310 (2010).

250   "gathered the flax, made the thread": OWH to Laski, Washington, D.C, Feb. 1, 1919, in *Holmes-Laski*, 1:184.

250   "the secret isolated joy": Holmes, "Profession of the Law," *Collected Works*, 3:473.

BIBLIOGRAPHY

MANUSCRIPT COLLECTIONS

Louis Dembitz Brandeis Papers, Harvard Law School Library
Zechariah Chafee Papers, Harvard Law School Library
Felix Frankfurter Papers, Library of Congress, Manuscript Division
Learned Hand Papers, Harvard Law School Library
Oliver Wendell Holmes Jr. Papers, Harvard Law School Library
National Archives and Records Administration, College Park, Md.
John Lord O'Brian Papers, Charles B. Sears Law Library, State University of
    New York at Buffalo

BOOKS AND ARTICLES

Acheson, Dean. *Morning and Noon*. Boston: Houghton Mifflin, 1965.
———. "Reminiscences of a Supreme Court Law Clerk." *Pittsburgh Legal Journal*, Jan. 29, 1955, 3–9.
Alschuler, Albert W. *Law Without Values: The Life, Work, and Legacy of Justice Holmes*. Chicago: University of Chicago Press, 2000.
Anderson, Isabel. *Presidents and Pies: Life in Washington, 1897–1919*. Boston: Houghton Mifflin, 1920.
Bagehot, Walter. *Physics and Politics; or, Thoughts on the Application of the Principles of "Natural Selection" and "Inheritance" to Political Society*. New York: D. Appleton, 1904. First published in 1896.

Baker, Liva. *Felix Frankfurter*. New York: Coward-McCann, 1969.

———. *The Justice from Beacon Hill: The Life and Times of Oliver Wendell Holmes*. New York: HarperCollins, 1991.

Basler, Roy P., ed. *Collected Works of Abraham Lincoln*. With the assistance of Marion Dolores Pratt and Lloyd A. Dunlap. Vol. 6: 1862–63. New Brunswick: Rutgers University Press, 1953.

Belknap, Chauncey. Unpublished diary. Collection of Patterson, Belknap, Webb and Tyler, New York, N.Y.

Belknap, Chauncey, Laurence Curtis, et al. "Personal Remembrances of Mr. Justice Holmes by His Former Law Clerks." *University of Florida Law Review* 28 (1976): 392–98.

Biddle, Francis. *Mr. Justice Holmes*. New York: Charles Scribner's Sons, 1942.

Bishop, Joseph Bucklin. *Theodore Roosevelt and His Time: Shown in His Own Letters*. Vol. 2. New York: Charles Scribner's Sons, 1920.

Blackstone, William. *Commentaries on the Laws of England*. Vol 4. Oxford: Clarendon Press, 1765–69.

Blasi, Vincent. "Holmes and the Marketplace of Ideas." *Supreme Court Review* (2004): 1–46.

———. "Learned Hand and the Self-Government Theory of the First Amendment: Masses Publishing Co. v. Patten." *University of Colorado Law Review* 61 (1990): 1–37.

———. "Reading Holmes through the Lens of Schauer: The Abrams Dissent." *Notre Dame Law Review* 72 (1997): 1343–60.

———. "Shouting 'Fire!' in a Theater and Vilifying Corn Dealers." *Capital University Law Review* 39 (2011): 535–69.

Bobertz, Bradley C. "The Brandeis Gambit: The Making of America's 'First Freedom,' 1909–1931." *William and Mary Law Review* 40 (1999): 557–651.

Bogen, David S. "The Free Speech Metamorphosis of Mr. Justice Holmes." *Hofstra Law Review* 11 (1982): 97–189.

Boorstin, Daniel J. "The Elusiveness of Mr. Justice Holmes." *New England Quarterly* 14 (1941): 478–87.

Borklund, Elmer. "Portrait of the Artist as a Young Man." Review of *Henry James: The Untried Years, 1840–1870*, by Leon Edel. *Chicago Review* 7 (Fall–Winter 1953): 72–79.

Bowen, Catherine Drinker. *Yankee from Olympus: Justice Holmes and His Family*. Boston: Little, Brown, 1944.

Brandeis, Louis Dembitz. *The Curse of Bigness: Miscellaneous Papers of Louis D. Brandeis*. New York: Viking, 1934.

Burton, Steven J., ed. *"The Path of the Law" and Its Influence: The Legacy of Oliver Wendell Holmes, Jr.* Cambridge: Cambridge University Press, 2000.

Chafee, Zechariah, Jr. "A Contemporary State Trial: The United States versus Jacob Abrams Et Al." *Harvard Law Review* 33 (1920): 9–14. Republished as ch. 3 in Chafee, *Freedom of Speech*.

———. "Freedom of Speech." *New Republic*, Nov. 16, 1918, 66–69.

———. *Freedom of Speech*. New York: Harcourt, Brace and Howe, 1920.

———. "Freedom of Speech in War Time." *Harvard Law Review* 32 (1919): 932–73.

———. "Thirty-Five Years with Freedom of Speech." *Kansas Law Review* 1 (1952–53): 1–36.

Collins, Ronald K. L., ed. *The Fundamental Holmes: A Free Speech Chronicle and Reader*. Cambridge: Cambridge University Press, 2010.

Corwin, Edwin S. "Freedom of Speech and Press under the First Amendment: A Résumé." *Yale Law Journal* 30 (1920): 48–55.

Cover, Robert M. "The Left, the Right, and the First Amendment: 1918–1928." *Maryland Law Review* 40 (1981): 349–88.

Croly, Herbert. *The Promise of American Life*. New York: Macmillan, 1914.

Crosby, Alfred W. *America's Forgotten Pandemic: The Influenza of 1918*. 2nd ed. Cambridge: Cambridge University Press, 1989.

Dewey, John. "The Future of Pacifism." *New Republic*, July 28, 1917, 358–60.

Dicey, Albert V. Review of *The Common Law*, by Oliver Wendell Holmes Jr. Originally published anonymously in *The Spectator, Literary Supplement* 55 (June 3, 1882): 745. Reprinted in Saul Touster, "Holmes a Hundred Years Ago: *The Common Law* and Legal Theory," *Hofstra Law Review* 10 (1982): 673–717.

Dow, Mary Larcom. *Old Days at Beverly Farms*. Beverly: North Shore Printing, 1921.

Eastman, Max. "The Trial of Eugene Debs." *Liberator*, Nov. 1918, 5–12.

Feldman, Stephen M. "Free Speech, World War I, and Republican Democracy: The Internal and External Holmes." *First Amendment Law Review* 6 (2008): 192–251.

Firmage, Edwin Brown. *Ernst Freund, Pioneer: The Contributions of Ernst Freund to Administrative Law*. Chicago: University of Chicago Press, 1963.

Forcey, Charles. *The Crossroads of Liberalism: Croly, Weyl, Lippman, and the Progressive Era, 1900–1925*. New York: Oxford University Press, 1961.

Frankfurter, Felix. *From the Diaries of Felix Frankfurter*. Ed. Joseph P. Lash. New York: Norton, 1975.

——. *Mr. Justice Holmes and the Supreme Court.* Cambridge: Harvard University Press, 1938.

Freeberg, Ernest. *Democracy's Prisoner: Eugene V. Debs, the Great War, and the Right to Dissent.* Cambridge: Harvard University Press, 2008.

Freund, Ernest. "The Debs Case and Freedom of Speech." *New Republic*, May 3, 1919, 13–15.

Freund, Paul A., and Stanley N. Katz, eds. *History of the Supreme Court of the United States: The Oliver Wendell Holmes Demise.* Vol. 9: *1910–1921.* Part 1 written by Alexander M. Bickel and part 2 by Benno C. Schmidt Jr. New York: Macmillan, 1984.

Fuller, Larry. "Lawyer Gained Fame for Bonds and Brawls." *South Dakota 99: Illustrated Profiles of 99 People Who Significantly Contributed to South Dakota's History.* Ed. Argus Leader. Sioux Falls: Ex Machina, 1989.

Garland, Joseph E. *Boston's Gold Coast: The North Shore, 1890–1929.* Boston: Little, Brown, 1981.

——. *Boston's North Shore: A Social History of Summers among the Noteworthy, Fashionable, Rich, Eccentric, and Ordinary on Boston's Gold Coast, 1823–1890.* Boston: Little, Brown, 1978.

Gengarelly, Anthony W. "The Abrams Case: Social Aspects of a Judicial Controversy." *Boston Bar Journal* 25 (1981): 9, 19.

Gény, François. *Science et technique en droit privé positif.* Paris: Recueil Sirey, 1921.

German, C. W. "An Unfortunate Dissent." *University of Missouri Bar Bulletin* 21 (1920): 75–80.

Gilmore, Grant. "Some Reflections on Oliver Wendell Holmes, Jr." *Green Bag* 2 (1999): 379.

Ginger, Ray. *The Bending Cross: A Biography of Eugene Victor Debs.* Chicago: Haymarket Books, 2007. First published in 1947.

Goldman, Emma. *Living My Life.* Vol. 2: *1869–1940.* New York: Dover, 1970.

Gordon, Robert W. "Holmes' Common Law as Legal and Social Science." *Hofstra Law Review* 10 (1982): 719–46.

——, ed. *The Legacy of Oliver Wendell Holmes, Jr.* Stanford: Stanford University Press, 1992.

Graber, Mark A. *Transforming Free Speech: The Ambiguous Legacy of Civil Libertarianism.* Berkeley: University of California Press, 1991.

Gunther, Gerald. *Learned Hand: The Man and the Judge.* New York: Knopf, 1994.

——. "Learned Hand and the Origins of Modern First Amendment Doctrine: Some Fragments of History." *Stanford Law Review* 27 (1975): 719–73.

Hagedorn, Ann. *Savage Peace: Hope and Fear in America, 1919*. New York: Simon and Schuster, 2007.

Hallowell, Norwood Penrose. *Reminiscences: Written for My Children by Request of Their Mother*. Nöddebo, West Medford: printed by author, 1897.

Hamilton, Walton H. "On Dating Mr. Justice Holmes." *University of Chicago Law Review* 9 (1941): 1–29.

Hawthorne, Hildegarde. *Old Seaport Towns of New England*. New York: Dodd, 1916.

Haynes, E. S. P. *The Decline of Liberty in England*. London: Grant Richards, 1916.

Highsaw, Robert B. *Edward Douglass White: Defender of the Conservative Faith*. Baton Rouge: Louisiana State University Press, 1981.

Hirsch, H. N. *The Enigma of Felix Frankfurter*. New York: Basic Books, 1981.

Hirst, Francis Wrigley. *Adam Smith*. New York: Macmillan, 1904.

Holland, Henry Ware. "Holmes's Common Law." *Nation*, June 30, 1881, 464–66.

Holmes, Oliver Wendell. *The Writings of Oliver Wendell Holmes*. Vol. 5: *Elsie Venner: A Romance of Destiny*. Cambridge: Riverside Press, 1891.

Holmes, Oliver Wendell. "My Hunt after the Captain." *Atlantic Monthly*, Dec. 1862.

Holmes, Oliver Wendell, Jr. *Collected Legal Papers*. New York: Harcourt, Brace and Howe, 1920.

———. *The Collected Works of Justice Holmes: Complete Public Writing and Selected Judicial Opinions of Oliver Wendell Holmes*. Ed. Sheldon M. Novick. 3 vols. Chicago: University of Chicago Press, 1995.

———. *The Common Law*. Cambridge: Belknap Press of Harvard University Press, 2009. First published in 1881.

———. *His Book Notices and Uncollected Letters and Papers*. Ed. Harry C. Shriver. New York: Central Book, 1936.

———. *Justice Holmes Ex Cathedra*. Comp. Edward J. Bander. Buffalo: William S. Hein, 1991.

———. *Justice Holmes to Doctor Wu: An Intimate Correspondence, 1921–1932*. New York: Central Book, n.d., ca. 1947.

———. "Natural Law." *Harvard Law Review* 32 (1918): 40–44.

———. "The Path of the Law." *Harvard Law Review* 10 (1897): 457–78.

———. "Privilege, Malice, and Intent." *Harvard Law Review* 8 (1894): 1–14.

———. *Speeches by Oliver Wendell Holmes*. Boston: Little, Brown, 1896.

———. *Touched with Fire: Civil War Letters and Diary of Oliver Wendell Holmes,*

Jr., 1861–1864. Ed. Mark DeWolfe Howe. Cambridge: Harvard University Press, 1946.

Holmes, Oliver Wendell, Jr., and Morris Cohen. "Holmes-Cohen Correspondence." Ed. with a foreword Felix S. Cohen. *Journal of the History of Ideas* 9 (Jan. 1948): 3–52.

Holmes, Oliver Wendell, Jr., and Lewis Einstein. *The Holmes-Einstein Letters: Correspondence of Mr. Justice Holmes and Lewis Einstein, 1903–1935*. Ed. James Bishop Peabody. New York: St. Martin's Press, 1964.

Holmes, Oliver Wendell, Jr., and Felix Frankfurter. *Holmes and Frankfurter: Their Correspondence, 1912–1934*. Ed. Robert M. Mennel and Christine L. Compston. Hanover: University Press of New England, 1996.

Holmes, Oliver Wendell, Jr., and Harold J. Laski. *Holmes-Laski Letters: The Correspondence of Mr. Justice Holmes and Harold J. Laski, 1916–1935*. Ed. Mark DeWolfe Howe. 2 vols. Cambridge: Harvard University Press, 1953.

Holmes, Oliver Wendell, Jr., and Frederick Pollock. *Holmes-Pollock Letters: The Correspondence of Mr. Justice Holmes and Sir Frederick Pollock, 1874–1932*. Ed. Mark DeWolfe Howe. 2nd ed. 2 vols. Cambridge: Belknap Press of Harvard University Press, 1961.

Holmes, Oliver Wendell, Jr., and Patrick Augustus Sheehan. *Holmes-Sheehan Correspondence: Letters of Justice Oliver Wendell Holmes, Jr. and Canon Patrick Augustine Sheehan*. Ed. David H. Burton. Rev. ed. New York: Fordham University Press, 1993.

"Holmes's Common Law," *American Law Review* 15 (1881): 331–38.

Horne, Philip. "Writing and Rewriting in Henry James." *Journal of American Studies* 23 (Dec. 1989): 357–74.

Howe, Mark DeWolfe. *Justice Oliver Wendell Holmes: The Proving Years, 1870–1882*. Cambridge: Belknap Press of Harvard University Press, 1963.

———. *Justice Oliver Wendell Holmes: The Shaping Years, 1841–1870*. Cambridge: Belknap Press of Harvard University Press, 1957.

Hughes, Charles Evans. *The Autobiographical Notes of Charles Evans Hughes*. Ed. David J. Danelski and Joseph S. Tulchin. Cambridge: Harvard University Press, 1973.

Josephson, Matthew. "Profiles: Felix Frankfurter." *New Yorker*, Nov. 30, 1940, 24–32.

Kalven, Harry, Jr. "Professor Ernst Freund and Debs v. United States." *University of Chicago Law Review* 40 (1973): 235–47.

Kellogg, Frederic R. *Oliver Wendell Holmes, Jr., Legal Theory and Judicial Restraint*. Cambridge: Cambridge University Press, 2007.

Kimball, Day. "The Espionage Act and the Limits of Legal Toleration." Editorial. *Harvard Law Review* 33 (1920): 442–49.

Kirby, Joe P. "The Case of the German Socialist Farmers: Joe Kirby Challenges the Espionage Act of 1917." *South Dakota History* 42 (Fall 2012): 237.

Kohn, Stephen M. *American Political Prisoners: Prosecutions under the Espionage and Sedition Acts*. Westport: Praeger, 1994.

Konefsky, Samuel J. *The Legacy of Holmes and Brandeis: A Study in the Influence of Ideas*. New York: Macmillan, 1956.

Kraines, Oscar. *The World and Ideas of Ernst Freund: The Search for General Principles of Legislation and Administrative Law*. Tuscaloosa: University of Alabama Press, 1974.

Kramnick, Isaac, and Barry Sheerman. *Harold Laski: A Life on the Left*. New York: Allen Lane/Penguin, 1993.

Laidlaw, Christine W. "Painting with Silken Threads: Fanny Dixwell Holmes and Japanism in Nineteenth-Century Boston." *Studies in the Decorative Arts* 10 (Spring–Summer 2003): 42–68.

Laski, Harold J. *Authority in the Modern State*. New Haven: Yale University Press, 1919.

———. *Studies in the Problem of Sovereignty*. New Haven: Yale University Press, 1917.

LeClair, Robert C. "Henry James and Minnie Temple." *American Literature* 21 (March 1949): 35–48.

Le Duc, Alice Sumner. "The Man Who Rescued 'The Captain.'" *Atlantic Monthly*, Aug. 1947, 80–86.

Levy, David W. *Herbert Croly of the New Republic: The Life and Thought of an American Progressive*. Princeton: Princeton University Press, 1985.

Louchheim, Katie, ed. *The Making of the New Deal: The Insiders Speak*. Cambridge: Harvard University Press, 1983.

Lowell, James Russell. *Letters of James Russell Lowell*. Ed. Charles Eliot Norton. Vol. 1: *1819–1868*. New York: Harper and Brothers, 1893.

Martin, Kingsley. *Harold Laski (1893–1950): A Biographical Memoir*. New York: Viking, 1953.

Menand, Louis. *The Metaphysical Club*. New York: Farrar, Straus and Giroux, 2002.

Mendelson, Wallace, ed. *Felix Frankfurter: A Tribute*. New York: Reynal, 1964.

Messinger, I. Scott. "The Judge as Mentor: Oliver Wendell Holmes, Jr., and His Law Clerks." *Yale Journal of Law and the Humanities* 11 (1999): 119–52.

Mill, John Stuart. *On Liberty.* New York: Penguin Books, 1985. First published in 1859.

Miller, Clyde R. "The Man I Sent to Prison." *Progressive*, Oct. 1963, 33–35.

Milton, John. *Areopagitica: A Speech of Mr. John Milton for the Liberty of Unlicensed Printing, to the Parliament of England.* Santa Barbara: Bandanna Books, 1922. First printed in London in 1644.

Monagan, John S. *The Great Panjandrum: Mellow Years of Justice Holmes.* Lanham: University Press of America, 1988.

Morse, John Torrey, Jr. *Life and Letters of Oliver Wendell Holmes.* Boston: Houghton Mifflin, 1896.

Murphy, Bruce Allen. *The Brandeis-Frankfurter Connection: The Secret Political Activities of Two Supreme Court Justices.* New York: Oxford University Press, 1982.

Murray, Robert K. *Red Scare: A Study in National Hysteria, 1919–1920.* Minneapolis: University of Minnesota Press, 1955.

Newman, Michael. *Harold Laski: A Political Biography.* London: Macmillan, 1993.

Novick, Sheldon M. *Honorable Justice: The Life of Oliver Wendell Holmes.* Boston: Little, Brown, 1989.

———. "The Unrevised Holmes and Freedom of Expression." *Supreme Court Review* (1991): 303–90.

O'Connell, Jeffrey, and Nancy Dart. "The House of Truth: Home of the Young Frankfurter and Lippmann." *Catholic University Law Review* 35 (1985): 79–95.

Parrish, Michael E. *Felix Frankfurter and His Times: The Reform Years.* New York: Free Press, 1982.

Phillips, Harlan B., ed. *Felix Frankfurter Reminisces.* New York: Reynal, 1960.

Pohlman, H. L. *Justice Oliver Wendell Holmes: Free Speech and the Living Constitution.* New York: New York University Press, 1991.

Polenberg, Richard. *Fighting Faiths: The Abrams Case, the Supreme Court, and Free Speech.* New York: Viking, 1987.

———. "Progressivism and Anarchism: Judge Henry Clayton and the Abrams Trial." *Law and History Review* 3 (1985): 397–408.

Pollock, Frederick. "Holmes on the Common Law." Review of *The Common Law,* by Oliver Wendell Holmes Jr. *Saturday Review,* June 11, 1881, 758–59.

Posner, Richard A. "Foreword: Holmes." *Brooklyn Law Review* 63 (1997): 7–17.

Powers, Richard Gid. *Secrecy and Power: The Life of J. Edgar Hoover.* New York: Free Press, 1987.

Pratt, Walter F., Jr. *The Supreme Court under Edward Douglass White, 1910–1921*. Columbia: University of South Carolina Press, 1999.

Rabban, David M. *Free Speech in Its Forgotten Years*. Cambridge: Cambridge University Press, 1997.

Ragan, Fred D. "Justice Oliver Wendell Holmes, Jr., Zechariah Chafee, Jr., and the Clear and Present Danger Test for Free Speech: The First Year, 1919." *Journal of American History* 58 (June 1971): 24–45.

Rand, Ayn. *The Fountainhead*. New York: Plume, 1994. First published in 1943.

"Report on the Mooney Dynamiting Cases in San Francisco." *Official Bulletin*, Jan. 28, 1918, 14–15.

Rogat, Yosal. "The Judge as Spectator." *University of Chicago Law Review* 31 (1964): 213–56.

———. "Mr. Justice Holmes: A Dissenting Opinion." *Stanford Law Review* 15 (1962): 3–44; 15 (1963): 254–308.

Rogat, Yosal, and James M. O'Fallon. "Mr. Justice Holmes: A Dissenting Opinion—The Speech Cases." *Stanford Law Review* 36 (1984): 1349–406.

Russell, Bertrand. *The Autobiography of Bertrand Russell*: Vol. 3: *1914–1944*. Reprint, Boston: Little, Brown, 1968.

Salvatore, Nick. *Eugene V. Debs: Citizen and Socialist*. 2nd ed. Urbana: University of Illinois Press, 2007.

Seaton, Alexander Adam. *The Theory of Toleration under the Later Stuarts*. Cambridge: Cambridge University Press, 1911.

Sergeant, Elizabeth Shepley. "Oliver Wendell Holmes." *New Republic*, Dec. 8, 1926, 61.

Shriver, Harry. *What Gusto: Stories and Anecdotes about Justice Oliver Wendell Holmes*. Potomac: Fox Hills Press, 1970.

Slater, Joseph. "Labor and the Boston Police Strike of 1919." *Encyclopedia of Strikes in American History*. Ed. Aaron Brenner, Benjamin Day, and Immanuel Ness. New York: Myron E. Sharpe, 2009, 241–51.

Smith, Donald L. *Zechariah Chafee, Jr.: Defender of Liberty and Law*. Cambridge: Harvard University Press, 1986.

Snyder, Brad. "The House That Built Holmes." *Law and History Review* 30 (2012): 661–721.

Steel, Ronald. *Walter Lippmann and the American Century*. Boston: Little, Brown, 1980.

Stephen, Sir Leslie. *Essays on Freethinking and Plainspeaking*. London: Smith Elder, 1907.

Stoddard, William Leavitt. "Labor Goes to College." *Independent*, May 10, 1919.

Stone, Geoffrey R. "Judge Learned Hand and the Espionage Act of 1917: A Mystery Unraveled." *University of Chicago Law Review* 70 (2003): 335–58.

———. *Perilous Times: Free Speech in Wartime from the Sedition Act of 1798 to the War on Terrorism.* New York: Norton, 2004.

Touster, Saul. "Holmes a Hundred Years Ago: *The Common Law* and Legal Theory." *Hofstra Law Review* 10 (1982): 673–717.

Umbreit, Kenneth Bernard. *Our Eleven Justices: A History of the Supreme Court in Terms of Their Personalities.* New York: Harper and Brothers, 1938.

Urofsky, Melvin I. "The Brandeis-Frankfurter Conversations." *Supreme Court Review* (1985): 299–399.

———. *Louis D. Brandeis: A Life.* New York: Pantheon, 2009.

Urofsky, Melvin I., and David W. Levy, eds. *The Family Letters of Louis D. Brandeis.* Vol. 4. Norman: University of Oklahoma Press, 2002.

———, eds. *Letters of Louis D. Brandeis.* Vol. 4: *1916–1921: Mr. Justice Brandeis.* Albany: State University of New York Press, 1975.

Virginia General Assembly, House of Delegates. *The Virginia Report of 1799–1800: Touching the Alien and Sedition Acts Together with the Virginia Resolutions of December 21, 1798.* 1850. New York: Da Capo Press, 1970.

Waldenrath, Alexander. "The German Language Newspress in Pennsylvania during World War I." *Pennsylvania History* 42 (Jan. 1975): 25–41.

Washburn, Robert M. *Calvin Coolidge: His First Biography.* Boston: Small, Maynard, 1923.

Weinberg, Louise. "Holmes' Failure." *Michigan Law Review* 96 (1997): 691–723.

West, Rebecca. "Holmes-Laski Letters." Review of *Holmes-Laski Letters*, ed. Mark DeWolfe Howe. *Harvard Law Review* 67 (1953): 361–67.

White, G. Edward. *Justice Oliver Wendell Holmes: Law and the Inner Self.* New York: Oxford University Press, 1993.

———. "Justice Holmes and the Modernization of Free Speech Jurisprudence: The Human Dimension." *California Law Review* 80 (1992): 391–467.

Wigmore, John H. "Abrams v. U.S.: Freedom of Speech and Freedom of Thuggery in War-Time and Peace-Time." *Illinois Law Review* 14 (1920): 539–61.

Wilson, Edmund. *Patriotic Gore: Studies in the Literature of the American Civil War.* New York: Norton, 1994.

Woollcott, Alexander. *Long, Long Ago.* New York: Viking, 1943.

Yeomans, Henry Aaron. *Abbott Lawrence Lowell: 1856–1943.* Cambridge: Harvard University Press, 1948.

Zane, John M. "A Legal Heresy." *Illinois Law Review* 13 (1918): 431–62.

ACKNOWLEDGMENTS

Writing this book would not have been possible without a first-rate librarian to guide me through the labyrinth of archives and databases where history resides. I therefore begin by acknowledging the tremendous assistance of Maja Basioli, who spent the past several years providing me with ready access to books, articles, and manuscript collections while also tracking down all sorts of esoteric information, from old weather reports and train schedules to the bloom dates for various flowers in Washington, D.C. Her diligence and resourcefulness have added more to this book than she likely realizes. And Maja's help would not have been possible without the support of the entire staff of the Rodino Library at Seton Hall Law School, who managed my large file of interlibrary loan requests, took good care of my research assistants, and provided gentle reminders when borrowed items were long overdue. Thanks to all of you for making my job so much easier.

Of course, no library can function without the help of numerous other libraries and archives, and so I am also indebted to the staffs of the following institutions for providing valuable assistance and materials: the Beverly Public Library, the Boston Public Library, the Case Western Reserve University Archives, the City University of New York

Libraries, the Free Library of Philadelphia, the Georgia State University Library, the Harvard Law School Library, the Hull History Centre, the International Institute of Social History, the Library of Congress Manuscript Division and Prints and Photograph Division, the Louisiana State University Library, the Massachusetts Historical Society, The National Archives and Records Administration, the National Railway Historical Society, the Newark Public Library, the New Jersey State Archives, the New York Public Library, the New York University Libraries, the Northwestern University Library and University Archives, the Pennsylvania State University Libraries, the Princeton University Library, the Rutgers University Libraries, the Saint Louis University Libraries, the Sandy Bay Historical Society, the Seton Hall University Libraries, the Siouxland Libraries, the South Dakota Historical Society, the South Dakota State Library, the State Historical Society of Missouri, the State University of New York at Buffalo Library, the Supreme Court Curator's Office, the Supreme Court Historical Society, the Syracuse University Library Special Collections Research Center, the University of California Berkeley Library, the University of Chicago Library, the University of Louisville Libraries, the University of Missouri-Kansas City Libraries, the University of Virginia Law Library, the University of Wisconsin-Madison Libraries, the Yale University Library Manuscripts and Archives, and the library at Patterson, Belknap, Webb and Tyler, LLP.

Among the many libraries I relied upon, none provided greater assistance than the Historical and Special Collections Department at the Harvard Law School Library, where the Holmes Papers are housed. Thanks especially to Margaret Peachy for her outstanding work organizing the collection and to Lesley Schoenfeld for walking me step-by-step through the process of using the collection and for then answering countless follow-up requests, all with exceptional speed, competence, and courtesy.

Although nearly all of the research for *The Great Dissent* was archival in nature, I was fortunate to come into contact with a few people who provided a more personal perspective on the events I describe.

One of these was Joe Kirby, who shared with me useful information about his great-grandfather. The other two were Tom and Mary Grant, the current owners of Holmes's house in Beverly Farms. They graciously gave me a tour of their home, answered my questions, and helped me envision what the place might have looked like a century ago.

During the course of writing this book, I have been blessed with a series of extraordinary research assistants and one terrific secretary. For their dedication and hard work, I thank Tenica Peterfreund, Shannon Stevens, Mariel Belanger, Maria Mihaylova, Kaja Stamnes, Jason Curreri, and Paola Guido, and for her meticulousness and organizational skills, I thank Silvia Cardoso. I have also been blessed with terrific colleagues, friends, and mentors who have given liberally of their time and wisdom. For reading the manuscript and offering thoughtful feedback, I thank Michelle Adams, Vincent Blasi, Kathleen Boozang, Carl Coleman, Tristin Green, and Rachel Godsil. For providing much-needed support and encouragement, I thank Mark Alexander, Baher Azmy, Jake Barnes, Robert Beatty, Gaia Bernstein, Kristen Boon, Jenny Carroll, Kip Cornwell, Michael Granne, Eddie Hartnett, Andrea McDowell, Michael Risinger, Brian Sheppard, and Charles Sullivan. I owe an especially large debt to Thomas Hackett, who not only read the entire manuscript but also served as a sounding board, grammarian, design consultant, and all-around editorial adviser. Everyone should be so fortunate to have such a talented and generous friend.

I am grateful to Seton Hall Law School for providing summer research stipends and a yearlong sabbatical to support this project and to the participants at faculty workshops at Seton Hall, Cardozo Law School, and Pace Law School, where I presented early chapters.

Thanks to Ryan Harbage for believing in the potential of this book and to Sara Bershtel and Grigory Tovbis for helping to turn that potential into reality. Their knowledge and commitment to excellence are truly remarkable, and it has been a pleasure to work with such fine editors.

Finally, I am indebted most of all to Arlene Chow for support in ways too numerous to count. Everyone else on this list was able to take a break from me and my book from time to time. Arlene was not. She lived with it and me from the start, and her affection, humor, and reassurance gave me the strength I needed to reach the end.

INDEX

ABOUT THE AUTHOR

THOMAS HEALY is a professor of law at Seton Hall Law School. A graduate of Columbia Law School, he clerked on the U.S. Court of Appeals for the Ninth Circuit and was a Supreme Court correspondent for the *Baltimore Sun*. Healy has written extensively about free speech, the Constitution, and the federal courts. *The Great Dissent* is his first book.